SLIPS OF THE MIND

THINKING LITERATURE
A series edited by Nan Z. Da and Andrea Gadberry

Slips of the Mind

POETRY AS FORGETTING

Jennifer Soong

The University of Chicago Press
Chicago and London

The University of Chicago Press, Chicago 60637
The University of Chicago Press, Ltd., London
© 2025 by The University of Chicago
All rights reserved. No part of this book may be used or reproduced
in any manner whatsoever without written permission, except
in the case of brief quotations in critical articles and reviews. For
more information, contact the University of Chicago Press,
1427 East 60th Street, Chicago, IL 60637.
Published 2025
Printed in the United States of America

34 33 32 31 30 29 28 27 26 25   1 2 3 4 5

ISBN-13: 978-0-226-83989-9 (cloth)
ISBN-13: 978-0-226-83990-5 (paper)
ISBN-13: 978-0-226-83991-2 (e-book)
DOI: https://doi.org/10.7208/chicago/9780226839912.001.0001

Library of Congress Cataloging-in-Publication Data

Names: Soong, Jennifer (College teacher), author.
Title: Slips of the mind : poetry as forgetting / Jennifer Soong.
Description: Chicago : The University of Chicago Press, 2025. |
    Series: Thinking literature | Includes bibliographical references
    and index.
Identifiers: LCCN 2024044680 | ISBN 9780226839899 (cloth)
    | ISBN 9780226839905 (paperback) | ISBN 9780226839912
    (ebook)
Subjects: LCSH: Poetry—History and criticism—Theory, etc. |
    Poetry—20th century—History and criticism. | Memory.
Classification: LCC PN1031 .S72765 2025 | DDC 808.1—
    dc23/eng/20241008
LC record available at https://lccn.loc.gov/2024044680

♾ This paper meets the requirements of ANSI/NISO Z39.48-1992
(Permanence of Paper).

Contents

LIST OF FIGURES vii

INTRODUCTION · Poetic Forgetting 1

CHAPTER 1 · And Action: Toward a New
Knowledge 21

CHAPTER 2 · Forget It! Poetry Makes
Nothing Happen 44

CHAPTER 3 · "Obvious Oblivion" and
Lyn Hejinian's Comic Affirmation 73

CHAPTER 4 · Origins and (Un)originality 96

CHAPTER 5 · Ambient Forgettability 121

CODA · A Reading Affair 147

ACKNOWLEDGMENTS 153

NOTES 157

REFERENCES 185

INDEX 201

Figures

2.1. Ted Berrigan, "Things to do today" (ca. 1970) 45
2.2. Joe Brainard, "Things to Do Before I Move" (1971) 46
5.1. Tan Lin, "This work is licensed . . ." (2012) 131
5.2. Tan Lin, ". . . called 'Chandos Classics'" (2012) 132
5.3. Tan Lin, ". . . like a descriptive catalog . . ." (2012) 133
5.4. Tan Lin, "Heath Ledger and Jackie Chan" (2012) 138

Poetic Forgetting

[INTRODUCTION]

Languages, generally speaking, are not made by forgetting but unmade by it. Yet for certain poets in the last 150 years, forgetting has come to mean something other than attrition. It has come to constitute a creative principle. The present work explores this principle, not as the mere rejection of a literary past or as a form of negative, apophatic poetics, but as a way for poets to generate and affirm their own unique languages. It puts to the test forgetting's very aesthetic meaning, or meanings, as I ask: What is forgetting's poetic allure? What new structures, forms of desires, styles, and ways of experiencing time does it allow? How does failing to recover the past counterintuitively work against the loss or dissolution of voice and language? And what is oblivion's relationship to writing?

Together, these queries constitute the object of my study, what I am calling in this introduction "poetic forgetting." Poetry, above all other linguistic arts, stresses the temporal nature of its musical grammars and the nondiscursive nature of the imagination, making it especially receptive to mental states that stress lapses in time. Forgetting, that enigmatic, seemingly irrational process by which things escape the mind and will, not only underscores poetry's own transgression of authorly intention but also illuminates the various time signatures and degrees of vividness with which poetic ideas are sensibly felt and thought. Slips of the mind, for better or for worse, share more with poetry than any other genre the power of making us see things anew. At its best, this newness is a radical inconsistency with how the world has been and how we have been in the world.

In the phrase under consideration, "forgetting" is already relational: it structures a poet's relationship with time, not just the past but also, as we will see, the present and the future. It shapes the relationships between a poet and certain temporally inflected affects, one's experiences of long or short feelings—yearning, contentment, and boredom being examples of long feelings, and passion, distractedness, and surprise being instances of short ones. When considered poetically, losing track of time engenders new experiences by disrupting selfhood and identity (the one who experiences) as well as objects of prior recognition (the thing being experienced). As a limit case for representation or a shaper of tense, poetic forgetting is a site to think about repetition and rhyme not merely as formal techniques, but also as the insistence or suspension of meaning. Being both voluntary and involuntary, it invites us to contemplate writing as a state of consciousness, engaged in matters of volition—and by extension, action and passivity. It mediates an individual's relationship with language, as a set of signifiers that recall their referents, as well as found material which either can or can't be traced back to an original source.

Beyond these distinct yet overlapping functions, poetic forgetting distinguishes between thinking and writing *about* forgetting and thinking and writing *through* and *with* it. While "about" approaches oblivion as a thematic matter—capable of lending itself to narrativization, theorizing, and the familiar metaphors of darkness, erosion, erasure, concealment, deserts, rivers, death, sleep, and inebriation—"through" and "with" approach forgetting as a kind of aid to composition, a medium that conditions and interacts with language itself. From this second category, one can glean a smattering of potential historical allusions: while the Chinese Tang dynasty poets sought in oblivion a poetry that could drown their sorrows, Friedrich Nietzsche argued that the origins of Western art were Dionysiac, that the poet's "self-forgetting" and "narcotic drink"[1] paradoxically brought humankind closer to, rather than further away from, our divine origins in nature and God. For the poet-aesthete of Søren Kierkegaard's *Either/Or* (1843), forgetting was a form of inner cultivation that, if perfected, assimilated experience into the balanced self. "To forget is an art that must be practiced in advance," we learn. "The more poetically one remembers, the more easily one forgets, for to remember poetically is actually only an expression for forgetting."[2] In Fernando Pessoa's opus *The Book of Disquiet* (1982), the fictional bookkeeper Bernardo Soares extended this process into an even more rigorous aesthetic discipline: repeatedly evoking the idea that "to write is to forget,"[3] he blurred the line between the life of art and the world of dreams. With this rich tradition behind it, *Slips of the Mind* grows out of the idea that there is a long kinship between poetry and forgetting beyond the latter's thematic appearance in or across literary history.[4] At the same time, it offers a more specific and unorthodox story closer to the present. Through a series of chapters revolving around individual authors (Gertrude Stein, Lyn Hejinian, Tan Lin) as well as topics that shed light on group poetics (futurity for the New York School and originality for certain inheritors of New American poetry), it speaks to how forgetting has left material traces, as methodology, on modern and contemporary verse.

In the English language alone, we forget in different, often poetic ways. When we say "he 'lost' his train of thought" or "something 'slipped' her mind," we reassign the respective agents of forgetting: in the first sentence, the subject performs the "losing," while in the second, the missing object is what commits the relevant act. In contrast to such ascription of human qualities to objects and events, a sentence like "the story fell into oblivion" is used to emphasize the *absence* of human presence. It stresses the depersonalized nature of forgetting as operating and exercising power outside the individual body. Oblivion is represented as a kind of a place, time, or condition, while it is also rendered an inaccessible non-place, non-time. When a person or story falls into oblivion, we do not suggest that the person or story is not remembering but that they have been lost to obscurity.

It might be said that we have termed "forgetting" what in fact entails a number of ambiguities. Aside from problems of agency, it is not clear, for instance, that when one is remembering, one is not forgetting, or that when one is forgetting, one is not remembering. This may be as simple as recognizing a person's face while failing to recall where it was one first came across it. Or, it could be as complex as nostalgia, which has been described as both "an affective yearning for a community with a collective memory"[5] *and* something that has "the status of the forgotten."[6] Even the very existence of the word "forget" begs the question whether "to forget" is always synonymous with "not to remember." Grammatically and logically speaking, "not to remember" is a negation of "to remember," but forgetting—while it may sometimes have the same meaning as "not to remember"—is itself a third term. The very fact that we have a word for it in our language suggests that forgetting possesses some kind of independence. It significantly reminds us that when we conceive of forgetting, we often consider it an actual process, not just the absence of another process.

In its various linguistic forms, failed recall tends to move away from abstraction toward physical, spatial metaphors. When something "*falls* into oblivion," it also does not "*enter* one's mind" or "*come into* consciousness." The example of "losing" is a stranger instance. To lose something—such as one's glasses—is physical enough, but what does it really look like? As with many of the other examples I offer here, the image of losing one's glasses, or forgetting where one has placed them, can actually be two images: one of having glasses and one of not having glasses. Even that, however, does not fully encapsulate the accidental misplacement of the object, thus distinguishing "lose" from a more forceful verb like "abandon."

4 **Introduction**

The language of forgetting thus opens up the realm of spatial analogy at the same time that it exceeds representation; such metaphors call attention to the crises of misrecollection at the same time that they offer methods of coping with, grasping, and *thinking* forgetting—by way of images, or not.

As for the word itself, "forgetting" is already, etymologically speaking, suggestive of its history as negation. Composed of the Old English prefix *for-*, meaning "away from, far," and *gitan*, meaning "to get, take, seize, or grasp," the word "forget" is defined by the *OED* as "to lose remembrance of." Scholars of forgetting have frequently tried to dismantle this opposition. Though outnumbered by the number of works on remembering (a few formidable ones include those by Francis Yates, Pierre Nora, Maurice Halbwachs, Mary Carruthers),[7] they tend to view forgetting and remembering as part of one dialectical movement, different levers driving a single mechanism. For instance, Maurice Blanchot, in describing the poet's inspiration, insisted that a memory with no recollection of its start has forgetting as its very essence: "The muse is not Memory, it is Forgetful Memory. Forgetting is the sun: memory gleams through reflection."[8] Less an oxymoron than a refined description, "forgetful memory" suggests that the more one forgets, the closer one is to remembering again, and the more one remembers and brings the past into the present, the more one must face the origin that represents an impossible memory. More recently, in his short book *Oblivion* (2004), Marc Augé not only equates oblivion with a natural influence, but also suggests that it works as a writer or sculptor might work: "Memories are *crafted* by oblivion as the outlines of the shore are created by the sea," he writes, later pointing out that "oblivion is the life force of memory and remembrance is its product."[9] Renaissance scholars Christopher Ivic and Grant Williams similarly urge their readers to see that "forgetting can no longer remain the negative space of an obsolete model of memory."[10] Nonetheless, the definitional step from "losing remembrance" to "opposing remembrance" remains a powerful and tempting move. What it points to is not necessarily the surface opposition between forgetting and remembering, but rather how forgetting tends to derive its definition or status from what it opposes.

Through the course of my study, I have been struck by just how well suited forgetting is to opposition. To return to the *OED*, early examples of "forget" often present it in a negative form, either in service of an emphatic ("ne forgeat" [never forgot], "neforgyte" [not to forget], "Nabbeð hie no þing forȝieten" [they have not forgotten anything]) or an antithesis, as in the liturgical text *Hours of the Blessed Virgin* (1540), "They shall Be registered so, they shall not be forgotten."[11] Ironically, these negative forms of oblivion, connoting either a person's resolve to never forget or the unforgettability of a person or an event, tend to presume and highlight the natural power of forgetting: so great is this person's resolution or the impression of this event, that it counteracts even the natural and seemingly inevitable force of erosion. When Thomas Wyatt repeats "Forget not yet" and "forget not this" in his lyric "Forget Not Yet the Tried Intent" (1557), poetry itself draws upon the negative strength of oblivion to convey a sense of steadfastness.

Other examples in the *OED* point to forgetting's long history against self-constraint and religious virtue. A passage from the early Middle English *Poema Morale* (ca. 1175), "Þe þe him selfe forȝiet for wive oðer for childe / He sal cumen on evel stede bute him God be milde,"[12] is suggestive of neglect, distraction, sin, and inadvertence. Elsewhere, forgetting's oppositional nature appears in a highly rhetorical context. Take the following three sentences: "Farewel, thou canst not teach me to forget" (1599), "Have you forgot that every man is now born in as good a state as Adam was made at first?" (1757), and "Men forgot how to fight for their country when they forgot to govern it" (1874). The first example, from *Romeo and Juliet*, employs the metaphorical power of erasure to signal the symbolic nature of memory as devotion, desire, and eternal love; the latter instances—from the founder of Methodism, John Wesley, and English historian J. R. Green—use forgetfulness as a point of critique and provocation. In the first, "Have you forgot" reminds the reader exactly of what should never be forgotten, alerting us to the paradoxical games one might play with forgetting. In the second, the inverse relationship between forgetting and governance implies forgetting's opposition to strength and national loyalty, even its kinship with absent-mindedness and forgiveness—making peace with, rather than fighting, an enemy.

The surface dichotomy of remembering and unremembering has functioned as a kind of proxy for other antagonisms, such as those between forgetting and truth, forgetting and justice, and life and death. Even in Mary Carruthers's claim that "the great vice of *memoria* is not forgetting but disorder,"[13] forgetting's traditional association with negation, loss, opposition, and "vice" casts a critical shadow. The opposition between oblivion and truth is another prime example. The Greek word for forgetfulness, *lethe*—denoting concealment and darkness—has the privative form *a-lethe* or *aletheia*, which is translated as "truth" or disclosure. Though one could contend it is *alethe* that acts as the negation, the dual etymologies reflect a line of thought stemming back to the complementary dialogues of *Meno* and *Phaedo*, where Plato posits a theory of anamnesis. Virtue, the philosopher argued, is a kind of knowledge that cannot be taught but exists eternally in human souls. Upon birth we lose such eternal truths and, in turn, must engage in recollection to access them again. Learning is not

6 Introduction

the acquisition of new knowledge but the return to former knowledge of innate ideas. Forgetting is at once the obstacle to this knowledge and the passage that makes return possible. It is a temporary phase, in contrast with truth's eternal nature.

In Plato's theory of anamnesis, forgetting's delinquency is akin to that of art's, in that both are said to distance us from the truth. Unlike those after him, Plato curiously does not characterize memory in terms of "mimesis" but rather positions truth-bound recollection against forgetting *and* art's imitative qualities. By the time one arrives at Aristotle, memory is no longer opposed to, but directly configured by images and likenesses. Depicting remembering as an extension of one's primary perceptive faculties, Aristotle nevertheless preserves the intellectual nature of memory by distinguishing between "mere" remembering and a more profound process of recollection. The latter is not just the recovery of memories but the repossession of knowledge or perception by way of an investigative search. Recollection is not relearning in the Platonic sense but a kind of kinetic reasoning. Forgetting, unmentioned in Aristotle's treatise on memory, thus remains telling even in its absence: it assumes an inactive and passive role within a tradition concerned with yoking truth and acts of recall.

I mention the classical example of forgetting's negative relationship to truth to stress just how easily the concept can become privative. Not only will questions of knowledge play a vital role in this book's first chapter, but a larger point of negotiation in *Slips of the Mind* is also whether, and to what extent, poetry can explore forgetting on grounds not simply dictated by remembering. Can poetic forgetting exist without necessarily suggesting loss, without constituting a technical, rhetorical,[14] or biological "error," without being the mere negation or opposite of another? The writers I examine tend to answer yes, though admittedly opposition cannot always be done away with. For some poets, forgetting continues to indicate opposition, including the opposition to remembering. In these cases, rejecting the past is oppositional without connoting lesser importance. For other poets, forgetting creates its own constellation of terms in and outside of memory altogether.[15]

*   *   *

Despite forgetting's association with neglect, disloyalty, mishap, and lethargy, the turn of the twentieth century troubled this long-standing account by ushering in an exceptional moment in the concept's history. In 1874 Nietzsche published *On the Advantage and Disadvantage of History for Life*, recasting oblivion as a willful and creative "art." Forgetting was not so much a part of the human predicament as it was something that allowed individuals to step outside of their own histories. An antidote to an imbalance in historical excess and to the crystallization of the past into inert knowledge, it was to serve as the foundation for cultural health, individual happiness, and action. Such a deliberate turn away from the past opposed three specific academic methods of historicism that the philosopher felt were divorced from everyday life and action: the monumental (the idealization of great past deeds into the imitable and beautiful), the antiquarian (the identification of the present with previous times and the use of history as justification), and the overly critical (the dragging of the past before a condemning court of justice). Along with his colleague Jacob Burckhardt at the University of Basel, Nietzsche held antipathetic views toward historiography's move toward science. He wrote against a pervasive bourgeois culture, in which the "expulsion of the instincts by history," a ready-made culture, and the ruling of "historical education and the universal frock of the citizen"[16] produced spectators rather than generators of life, abstractions rather than actions. The emphasis on forgetting, which extended into Nietzsche's work on genealogy, would come to have an impact on poststructuralist writers concerned with questions of origination.[17]

Taking the art of forgetting seriously, the Futurists soon adopted a Nietzschean attitude as a key pillar of the avant-garde. In 1913 Gino Severini pronounced, "We must forget exterior reality and our everyday knowledge of it in order to create new dimensions,"[18] echoing Umberto Boccioni's claim that "we deny the past because we want to forget, and in art to forget means to renew."[19] In 1915 Filippo Tommaso Marinetti wrote that Futurist theater would not "dwell on the historical theatre, a sickening genre already abandoned by the passéist public," but be able to exalt its audience, "that is make it forget the monotony of daily life."[20] "He who does not forget his first love," the Hylaea group had declared, "will not recognize his last."[21] Numerous invectives against the past abounded. By the time Marcel Duchamp claimed in 1954 that "Francis [Picaba] had the gift of total forgetting which enable[d] him to launch into new paintings without being influenced by the memory of preceding ones,"[22] forgetting had been officially secured as part of modernism's agonist legacy.

Visiting England in 1910, 1912, 1913, and 1915, Marinetti came to influence the literary sphere to which writers such as Ezra Pound belonged. The former brought with him his aggression toward an inert past, which Pound fully exercised in *Guide to Kulchur* (1938). "It does not matter a twopenny damn whether you load up your memory with the chronological sequence of what has happened, or the names of protagonists, or authors of books, or generals and leading political spouters," Pound exclaimed. "The domain of culture begins when one HAS 'forgotten-what-book.'"[23]

8 Introduction

Objecting to rote memory and schoolroom pedagogy, the modernist titan and provocateur affirmed forgetting as an authentic "test" for civilizations that had no need to recall what its members had already internalized and possessed presently and naturally.[24] According to Pound's presentation, forgetting eliminated the trivial; it was proof of a culture's fitness and vitality.

The Pound-Marinetti model is by now an old story. It represents a standard way of thinking about modernism's relationship with the past: forgetting as a reactionary ideological stance and ultimately forgetting as failure. Keeping pace with such developments, however, were burgeoning philosophies of time and mind that supplied forgetting with a separate conceptual momentum. As Victorian preoccupations with ancestry, descent, and deep time were in retreat, new disciplinary paradigms were themselves examples of cultural molting.[25] In a 1917 address, Alfred North Whitehead declared, "A science that hesitates to forget its founders is lost." For Whitehead, a disregard for earlier models would act in service of what he called modern logic, not meant to "shackle thought" or cause hesitation, but "give freedom and, above all, boldness."[26] His invitation to do away with the past stemmed from the idea that breakthroughs require us to give up some of what we know; forgetting is akin to an overcoming of intellectual hurdles. Those who answered this call—and who extended the lexicon of memory to include action, consciousness, pain, attention, desire, and identity—included Henri Bergson, Sigmund Freud, and the American pragmatists. While they shared with Pound and the Futurists a concern with forgetting's presentism and its definitional shift from folly to force, there were also a number of key differences.

To begin, take Bergson, who radically proposed that the meaning of forgetting could not lie in failed recovery, since the past, with its independent ontology, could not be lost or recovered to begin with. Incorporating forms of oblivion into a new theory of durée, he stressed the world as a space of and for action. He argued that objects and their images acted upon our bodies, and that through our bodies, we produced consequent actions, either reflexive or voluntary, in the world. Within this chain of action, forgetting played a crucial role. It was what distilled and linked pure memory with present perception, the latter of which entailed "our dawning action, in so far as it [was] prefigured in those images" in the world. Because perception was everywhere—literally "out there" in the realm of external objects and images—Bergson argued that "what you have to explain, then, is not how perception arises, but how it is limited, since it should be the image of the whole, and is in fact reduced to the image of that which interests you."[27] In other words, how did the whole of pure perception particularize and adopt our individual bodies as their center? His answer was forgetting: as a selective tool, it identified which parts of pure memory should slip into perception, thereby prolonging the moment into a durational space where movement could dispose the body toward action. Forgetting constituted a process that would allow the independent and otherwise inactive past a certain utility and materialization, an actualization in the present. For Bergson, it rose to the level of a necessary condition of action and shifted the problem of memory from conservation to selection.[28] Forgetting was not a loss of the past but rather a distillation of it according to use and salience.

Equally, if not more influential, were Freud's writings on the topic. Like Bergson, Freud thought the past was ever-present and that forgetting could be unconscious but intentional, motivated, in Freud's case, by the avoidance of pain. Where Bergson's theory of forgetting and action sought to foreground human "vitalism" over "mechanism," Freud's theory incorporated action by suggesting that improper forgetting would lead to the "acting out" of an emotional past, as in the case of repressed trauma. Unconscious compulsive repetition transpired when and where remembrance did not, with some forms of repression working to resist psychoanalytic cooperation. Freud thus invested forgetting with meaning even while observing how it could appear accidental. (The psychoanalyst Thomas Ogden expressed it cogently when he said that something that one can't recall is *important enough* to be forgotten.) By introducing an economy of individual memory and desire, while drawing upon older metaphors of memory such as the wax tablet and storehouse, Freud recanvased the relationship between language and various forms of misremembering.

Most famously, the talking cure encoded in the language of association the basis for self-narrative. Narrative, if constructed successfully, would have explanatory and connective power, analyzing the present self in light of its past and inspiring acts of recognition. A natural corollary was that dreams and free association might provide "detours by which repression can be evaded," recovering the lost memories for which symptoms had become substitutes. Freud argued that in distinction to the narrative faculty, a patient's "inability to give an ordered history of their life" was characteristic of neurosis, where "there are invariably true amnesias—gaps in the memory into which not only old recollections but even quite recent ones have fallen—and paramnesias."[29] But where the patient's remembrance began, the analyst's was cut short. Freud observed that his task was merely to construct material via induction—an idea that evolved into an imperative to forget in the work of English psychoanalyst Wilfred Bion. Believing that "the analyst should avoid mental activity, memory and desire,"[30] Bion wrote to his peers: "Do not remember past sessions."[31] At stake were the dangers of overdetermination. A session should give the impression of having "no history and no future"; the analyst should feel as though "he has not seen the patient before."[32] Because memory was contaminated by time and desire, Bion felt that tarrying with the past would interfere with and distract from a disciplined attention to present interaction.

In "Screen Memories" (1899), Freud further realized the implications of forgetting by describing amnesia as the default state of infantile and childhood memory. Most people, he observed, live a few years before retaining continuous memories, capable of recall in the long term. Where an adult is able to access a seemingly random childhood memory with little import, the question of how and why is necessarily raised.[33] Freud argued that in these cases, the unassuming memory is in fact related to a more significant trauma: we recall one event only because of its relation to another event that would prefer to resist consciousness. The event we remember is the result of a kind of compromise, a screen memory that seems to stem from childhood but in fact has been altered, worked over, and constructed to conceal an unpleasant experience.

Such a theory of substitution would be applied to the forgetting of proper names, foreign words, impressions, and resolutions in Freud's *The Psychopathology of Everyday Life* (1901). Misrecollection, when transferred onto the wrong object, produced a trace in language. Even words sharing the same sound or etymology could lead to the mental omission of both if one referred to a painful object. The relationship between the word of unwilled forgetting and the word of willed repression was thus metonymic, related by contiguity. A Freudian slip was the outcome of a kind of amnesia in the form of mishearing, misspeaking, misreading, or miswriting. Consequently, drawing a blank could be a kind of mistake, but never a form of total absence. Nor would its mistake be an innocent one. As Harald Weinrich notes, "[W]ith Freud, forgetting loses its innocence"; the more one is convinced "that his forgetting requires no justification," the more the question of "why" arises.[34] In the case of misremembering resolutions, Freud suggested that the act might even involve a kind of skill or counter-will. By proposing that one could avoid undesirable tasks by way of deliberate tactics, he paved the way for a number of more recent studies interested in "strategies" for everyday forgetting, including Daniel Wegner's "white bear" cases.[35] Following Fyodor Dostoyevsky's famous claim that when one tries not to think of a polar bear, one inevitably keeps thinking about it, Wegner and his colleagues termed this paradox "ironic rebound." To get around the problem, Wegner consequently proposed several strategies for avoiding unwanted thoughts. They included absorption, distraction, postponement, decreased multitasking, exposure, and meditation.

A third, final example of how memory and forgetting were being reinvented as key discursive terms can be identified in the works of pragmatists such as William James, John Dewey, and George Herbert Mead. Drawing on certain principles heralded by Henry David Thoreau and Ralph Waldo Emerson, American pragmatism cast a light on forgetting's history as an American specialty and even anti-intellectual tendency. While Thoreau had stated that the "Atlantic is a Lethean Stream, in our passage over which we have had an opportunity to forget the Old World and its institutions,"[36] Emerson felt that memory could detract from present living. "Man postpones or remembers; he does not live in the present," he lamented in "Self-Reliance" (1841). "Why drag about this corpse of your memory [. . .]. It seems to be a rule of wisdom never to rely on your memory alone, scarcely even in acts of pure memory."[37] The idea of vitality, presence, and spontaneity as particularly American would remain influential for James, as well as for many of the poets under discussion in this book.

On the one hand, forgetting for the pragmatists was what Louis Menand calls "an argument, in philosophy, for discarding obsolete verbal ritual and rejecting the authority of prior use."[38] On the other hand, its status extended beyond a mere cultural stance or license for present authority. It informed how thinkers theorized the processes of habituation, change, and action. For James, Dewey, and Mead, habituation involved the forgetting of original meanings, the recession of an activity from attention. It marked a certain threshold of consciousness. This did not mean that all habits were antithetical to willful action. Rather, Dewey averred that habits "are demands for certain kind of activities," organizing the way we behave and mediating between desires and objective conditions.[39] To break one habit and form another moreover required additional, active forgetting, an effortful discarding and act of replacement. Such questions of consciousness and will participated more broadly in the pragmatist call for a vitalist, action-oriented philosophy, one that would struggle against the past as a force of overdetermination. According to James, people think they "grasp" ideas, but what they grasp is never pure thinking, only "some substitute for it which previous human thinking has peptonized and cooked for our consumption."[40] The philosophical problem opened up a provocative site for poetic intervention. The question of how to create a language that would not reference the past but instead capture the presence of thinking would find an answer in Stein's epistemological poetics.

Forgetting, for the associationist that was James, was inseparable from the empirical enterprise of lived experience, related to a constellation of related concepts such as attention and stream of consciousness. Though his work on primary and secondary memory outweighed his

12 Introduction

work on forgetting proper, many of James's insights into the topic strike us today as commonplace. As an instance of our mind's selective activity, forgetting participated in what he and Théodule Ribot called the "foreshortening" of time—the ability to traverse the past in an amount of time shorter than the original time elapsed. Gaps in one's memory also introduced a kind of irregularity or uncertainty into experience: one could forget a thing one day and recall it the next. Amnesia could frustrate the most strenuous efforts at recollection but ease up the minute one relinquishes one's attempts. In the process of articulating these now-familiar phenomena, James individualized memory, arguing that memory could not just be a revival of any image in the present, but rather had to evoke our "time-perception" of pastness. Because such time-perception could only exist for a few seconds, in our retention of the recent past, the philosopher-psychologist argued that we use "contiguous associates" such as dates, names, and facts to help situate memories in the past. The sense of pastness, however, could not be general: memory had to "be dated in *my* past"; it had to produce feelings of "warmth and intimacy" and coincide with the belief that one had in fact directly experienced and lived through the past event.[41]

While an intellectual history of forgetting in major critical fields would take this project too far afield, the works of Bergson, Freud, and James represent a flourishing moment for the topic at hand. Their moment in history therefore uncoincidentally marks the start of this book's inquiry. In each of their works are frameworks that perplex forgetting as a mere stance, positioned against the past for the mere sake of newness. Such an impact is felt by the poets I study: the modern and contemporary writers who fill the coming chapters are invested in what forgetting can generate and open up—not just reject and shut down—in writing. For them, forgetting cannot simply be reduced to a total rejection of the past or be described in terms of what Paul de Man once called the "stripping down" of the self to "insidious forms of inauthenticity,"[42] even, as we'll see in chapter 4, when misremembrance is a form of deconstructive play.

*   *   *

With the exception of Pound's various cultural battles and the pragmatists' interest in public education, modernist theories of forgetting tended to share a common blind spot: the treatment of forgetting as an overwhelmingly individualized notion. Few could thus predict the crisis of memory that would ensue in the twentieth century. With the advent of both World War I and II, society witnessed forgetting's new emergence as a phenomenon at once collective, sociopolitical, and negative. By the second half of the century, the political legacies of fascism, genocide, suppression, totalitarianism, and censorship powerfully secured misremembrance's antagonistic position within history. Forgetting not only played a villainous role in the events that actually transpired, but it also became a villain to the project of political witnessing and historical writing itself. For this reason, Paul Ricoeur called it a "disturbing threat that lurks in the background of the phenomenology of memory and of the epistemology of history" and an "emblem of the vulnerability of this condition."[43] Such statements remind us that amnesia can be catastrophic and ethically wrong. At the same time, what Ricoeur calls forgetting does not actually refer to the *inability* to remember but rather, the *unwillingness* or refusal to engage with the past at all. Forgetting, in this sense, is a form of violence, of denial.

Though *Slips of the Mind* primarily focuses on systems of poetic valuing, it would be irresponsible to talk about forgetting in any manner without acknowledging its particular politics. In 1993 Carolyn Forché published her anthology *Against Forgetting*, which was concerned with poetry's relationship to political witnessing. Inspired by Anna Akhmatova, Forché's work was a gesture against political erasure. Counteracting forgetting's hand in complacency, Forché argued that poems had a duty to preserve firsthand accounts of extreme experiences such as war; remembering was an act of resistance against the normalization of trauma and its effects. In his famous winter conversations with Mark Halliday, the scholar and poet Allen Grossman reiterated this humanist impulse to witness. Declaring that "poetry is the historical enemy of human forgetfulness, the historical agent of the names of man against the obliterative powers of the world,"[44] Grossman defined poetry's primary goal as one of preserving the human image. On this point, Pound—who was included in Forché's anthology—would have agreed.

For many of us today, Forché's argument is familiar. The duty to remember is a non-question. The obligation to remember refers less to procedural memory (memory-"how") or propositional memory (memory-"that") than to recollective memory and witnessing (memory-"when"). It has less to do with individual psychology, or psychology at all, than with collective identity. "Remembering is a function of being a certain kind of people, of disposing ourselves toward certain ideals over time,"[45] Richard Miller writes, invoking Benedict Anderson's notion that imaginative political communities rely not only upon memory but also upon the passing down of memory into future generations. This is not to say that there is one large collective mind that recalls, but rather that memories from individuals become collective when those individuals define themselves as *members* of a group, when memories represent not only common or shared experiences but also community values.

14 Introduction

To think of memory in the context of collectivity usually means acknowledging its function as a kind of social glue. Conservative and conservationist in nature, remembering provides communities with a shared ground for the present by appealing to the past. For some, like David Rieff, this is not memory at all but something else that operates under its name: "Quite simply, the world does not have memories; nor do nations; nor do groups of people. Individuals remember, full stop."[46] James would likely concur. Ernest Renan likely wouldn't. Best known for his claim that "the essence of a nation is that all individuals have many things in common, and also that they have forgotten many things," Renan thought forgetting could constitute, rather than undermine, national identity.[47] Nicolas Russell, in his reading of Maurice Halbwachs, goes even further to suggest that in the latter's work, memory has "a certain independence from the vicissitudes of human existence."[48] Memory, in other words, belongs to the unspecified entity that is "humanity" (which includes even books) rather than any particular set of individuals.

Because various communities have been subjected to injustice and continue to have to fight to preserve their identity, memory is an important aspect of solidarity and survival. A collective "duty to remember," however, implies a further, more specific pairing of memory and justice—what William James Booth calls "the moral imperative of memory-justice." The idea, according to Booth, goes something like this: "To do justice is to remember, to preserve and guard in memory the injury, the victim, and the perpetrator."[49] But what does it mean to consider remembering a form of justice itself, implied to counteract injustices inflicted on members of a specific group? Is remembering really a form of justice, or is it what happens when justice fails? Is remembering always something that happens too late? Has an abstract sense of justice had to default to memory because it has no other ground, as linked to individual, personal lives, on which to work?

These questions might represent a skepticism, but there is an urgency and care that motivates this attitude. For one, it stems from an impulse to acknowledge and protect memory as something unique and fluid that begins on the personal level, as something that does in fact exist prior to institutional, ideological, and, yes, group use. While those who inflict injustices may use forgetting as a weapon, individual victims of those very traumas may experience a simultaneous desire to remember *and* forget. Even in everyday life, the problem isn't so much that oblivion itself is bad but rather that we are so often recalling the thing we'd like to forget, and forgetting the thing we'd like to recall. Furthermore, forgetting, though it can at times be escapist, asks us to consider the actual differences between disengagement and respite, prolonged withdrawal and temporary refuge. What can be harmful in some instances can function as relief from pain in others. And such a claim says nothing of the more complex psychological cases in which holding on to damage is felt as necessary or preferable to the possibility of ego formation around something *other* than loss or injury. This does not mean that one should return to modernism's blind spots regarding the potential exploitation of amnesia in the political and public sphere. Rather, more than a century's worth of lessons about the political abuses of forgetting should also warn us of the political abuses of remembering. My skepticism stems from a desire to distinguish between justice and the conservation of the past *without* devaluing either. The philosopher Charles Mills has written compellingly about why any conceptual approaches to memory need to be thought alongside actual social conditions. In light of that: What use is memorializing, archiving, or utilizing annual holidays, for that matter, when present injustices aren't addressed as present? How can remembering be an excuse for relegating the present into the past? Does the question of whether recollection is a form of strong justice eclipse the larger question at stake, which is simply, What makes for strong justice?

According to Avishai Margalit in *The Ethics of Memory* (2004), remembering is something that operates within our "thick" or ethical relations (relationships with people close to or like us) rather than our "thin" or moral relations (relationships with strangers). There is, he argues, an ethics of memory but not so much a morality of memory, since humanity as a whole is not yet really a community of memory. If this is true, how can remembering be a strong ground for justice, which arguably should be more extensive than the realm of our kin? Or, alternatively, should we not "remember" events that happen across the world, or events that happened in the deep past? Margalit steps outside of memory to answer these questions, appealing, for instance, to the need for reason in justice systems. And yet, the relationship between mnemonic and non-mnemonic grounds for justice needs to be clarified. There is, for instance, the issue of how courts use recollection in the form of eyewitness memory—an issue that is fraught with its own advantages and imperfections—and then another issue of how remembering comes to substitute for court justice when the court fails to set a certain precedent.

For Margalit, as well as for Ricoeur and Booth, the "duty to remember" generally operates by two arguments: first, that memory is our way of paying our intergenerational debt (what is owed to the dead), and second, that we must remember great evils in the past so that we never repeat or allow them to occur again. In Christianity, the two have historically converged in the notion that by remembering Christ and his sacrificial death on the cross, one remembers his commandments to live a life in virtue.

The idea is less about preserving or memorializing the past *as* past than it is about bringing the past into one's present state of mind and dedicating one's present life to God. Elsewhere, the idea of intergenerational debt appears to revolve around various affective motivations: guilt and shame as negative forms of motivation, and thankfulness and admiration as positive forms. In concerning itself with the dead, our obligation to remember inevitably deals with memory's powerful interaction with grief. By contrast, the prevention of future evils stems from the notion that the past is useful for contextualizing present struggles. There is no way to understand the race problem in America, for instance, without knowing the history of slavery, Jim Crow, civil rights, and the war on drugs. Part of understanding this history involves an internal critique of history itself, as something that potentially suppresses or replaces living memory. Pierre Nora argued that "memory is always suspect in the eyes of history, whose true mission is to demolish it, to repress it. [. . .] A generalized critical history would no doubt preserve some museums, medallions, and monuments as materials necessary for its own work but would drain them of what makes them, for us, *lieux de memoire*." Memory is vital, subject to a dialectic of remembering and forgetting, belonging to individuals and certain immediate groups. History, on the other hand, "is a criticism destructive of spontaneous memory."[50] To such a distinction, one can add the further difference between what is *actually* past and therefore can be remembered and what isn't in fact over and may require an alternative mode of engagement.

Finally, arguments about the "duty to remember" tend to presuppose an optimistic relationship between knowing and doing, a relationship whose weaknesses inform Rieff's study of continuous genocide and international conflict. Following Tzvetan Todorov in his argument that memory is more often than not self-serving, selective, and capable of being abused, Rieff claims that remembering has often led to more rancor, war, and resentment, rather than to peace and forgiveness. By contrast, the work of philosopher Sue Campbell is in favor of a more positive outlook on memory. Campbell states that "how we do and should value memory is tied to what we do as rememberers." "Good remembering" is not only a concept we need to grasp in memory discourse, but one that ought to be related to ethical action.[51] If we can understand what "good remembering" constitutes (for instance, remembering the significance of events and their emotional accuracy rather than mere factual details), we can extract and clarify the values that inform our practical life.[52] Here, the "duty to remember" presupposes that memory might be mastered and put to use, that memory can be trained to inform our moral choices.

I have raised, in the last few pages, a number of questions that *Slips of the Mind* does not purport to answer. Yet I include them to show how the duty to remember is the dominant discourse of memory in our culture and how this book speaks of its apparent opposite, forgetting, precisely in nondominant terms. Much has been done to categorize memory as procedural, semantic, episodic, collective, popular, folk, institutional, artificial, or prosthetic.[53] However, such distinctions have not carried over as easily to forgetting, which is often handled as a monolithic term. As cultural and political critics have been trying to understand forgetting as something other than antagonistic to postwar, post-Holocaust life, others have attempted broader schematizations of oblivion and its various forms.[54] *Slips of the Mind* continues this work of finding alternative meanings for forgetting, meanings that might shift within the replenishing frames of poetry. Thinking outside normative notions of oblivion, modern and contemporary poets have opened up forgetting as a diverse category representing a set of aesthetic potentials. Such diversity requires shifts in attention, and my own method of engaging with an assortment of literary and philosophical aspects—consciousness, poetics, genre, style, oeuvre, culture—is in part a testament to that. The writers I look at continuously turn away from certain aspects of forgetting, while working through new significances without having this process resemble some "development" or "revision." As such, I argue that forgetting inherently produces difference—difference in style, in poetics, in generic interest. It is not just a symptom of some anxiety of influence. It retains separate, even contradictory, meanings for each poet. If there is one takeaway from this section, it is that rather than fearing forgetting, we ought to acknowledge that it is capable of being utilized. As religious studies scholar Björn Krondorfer reminds us, embellishment, sentimentalization, adornment, spiritualization, sanitization, tabooing, and trivialization all underscore remembrance and misremembrance as human endeavors.[55] How we leverage forgetting—toward freedom or suppression, against overdetermination or progress—matters.

*   *   *

Broadly speaking, *Slips of the Mind* unfolds through a series of cases—three single-author chapters interspersed with two studies of forgetting's impact on collective phenomena—which are unified by various arguments about what kinds of poetry forgetting produces. Chief among these is forgetting's appeal to non-narrative writing—narrativization being the ordering of past events into a legible sequence—and its disruption of rational argumentation and causality. If metaphor works by association, forgetting de-associates, opening up space for new juxtapositions and meanings. If epic poetry memorializes the past by organizing great actions into forms easily memorized and transmitted in oral culture, this book suggests that other poetic forms are opened up by blankness. Without committing to the crude poles of forgetting/poetry and remembering/prose in the twentieth century (there are numerous counterexamples), I am nevertheless drawn to how absenting memory appeals to *certain kinds* of poetry, often experimental, and to how forgetting illuminates certain writers' ability to accommodate surprise or nonsense. Paradoxically, such experiments often push my discussions to include examples that live on the edges of poetry and prose, poetry proper and poetics, canonical and noncanonical work. (Note that I do not use "experimental" here to claim or signify an outsider position for my case studies but to denote, rather, a set of counter-traditions that might be bestowed and inherited over time—indeed, codified and re-exploded as a set of debates rather than stances.) At times, my examples also push my method toward one of collaging, where intra- and interrelations between texts take priority over a single paradigm of forgetting imposed "top down."

Arguments about misremembrance, however, are not the sole binding force at work. A number of other concepts—including authorial intention, genre, and the present—will come to stick. Moreover, my initial curiosity about Stein's capacious and provocative oeuvre compelled me to trace her legacy in consequent writers' works. It is not merely that John Ashbery, Bernadette Mayer, Lyn Hejinian, Charles Bernstein, Harryette Mullen, Tan Lin, and others all read and wrote about their predecessor, representing and reviving her legacy in a "school of Stein." Rather, I also propose that forgetting is one of the odd heirlooms the modernist confers onto later poets. A pursuit of difficulty, of syntactical innovation, and of a philosophical framework all allowed *un*remembering to do certain kinds of poetic work in Stein's writing. Together, the possible unearthing of forgetting's forms and definitions, its origins and limits, its universal yet personal nature, draws the writer and her inheritors to an audacious mode of literary invention. Readers of this book will therefore find that frequent return is made to the book's inaugural figure.

Additionally, *Slips of the Mind* takes as its main subject American poetry. With one exemption to this national throughline,[56] the book is bookended by emigration (the move to Paris by Stein) and immigration (the move from China by Lin's parents). It thus responds to W. H. Auden's claim that "if one compares Americans with Europeans [. . .] one might say, crudely and too tidily, that the mediocre American is possessed by the Present and the mediocre European is possessed by the Past."[57] This is not to say that poetic forgetting isn't a transnational phenomenon (it is), but to make a clarification about the book's scope, selection of evidence, and practical guardrails of nation, style, form, and lineage. Where exceptions to these guardrails best illustrate the book's claims, I make them.

For Stein, it is *The Making of Americans*, not the making of the British or French, that gives voice to modernity. English literature—having "lasted for some five hundred years or more"—had been defined by the homogeneity, habits, and stability of insular daily life. But American poetry, with its lack of history to overcome, was, in her words, "disconnected";[58] its modernity stemmed from moving in a way that wasn't moving against any prior backdrop or context. Decades later, the New York School would place its own premium on the American themes of optimism, futurity, freedom, and dreams. For those writing during the postwar boom, forgetting became a way of navigating these domains and negotiating change. To turn away from one's past and become someone new—or anonymous—was not only American but, moreover, urban and queer. More subtly in Hejinian's work, which was shaped by Russian formalism, we glimpse the influence of a counter-impulse in American poetry that nevertheless tries to situate its "Americanness" in an international context defined by the Vietnam War and global Marxism.[59] A return to domestic soil appears more evidently in the work of her environs: Mullen's forgetting deconstructs racial identity and cultural memory in the United States while critiquing the process of stereotyping as a signifying practice. Writers like Alice Notley, Robert Duncan, and Lissa Wolsak who either partook or inherited the legacies of "New American poetry" and what Ron Silliman called "the American tree" found ways of using forgetting to illuminate American poetry's relationship to origins and originality, firstness and novelty. For Lin, national themes of assimilation and immigration are shot through with forgetting—as is the question of consumerism, where commodities quickly grow obsolete even while vying for one's attention and a place in one's short-term memory. As we will see, Lin and Stein share an interest not only in leaving things behind, but also in a "Ford America" of assembly-line production, at once modern and ambient.

*   *   *

Depicting forgetting as a site of possibility rather than closure, this book takes seriously forgetting's "active and positive character"[60] as well as the idea that "one could *hope* thus to think forgetting."[61] It responds and seeks to overturn Umberto Eco's 1998 allegation that "it is not possible to construct an *ars oblivionalis* on the model of an art of memory."[62] While Eco had based his conclusion about forgetting on the art of remembering—claiming that within the chains of signification, everything was a sign for something else, and that no sign could actually negate or help us "forget" its own content—the present work says otherwise. To say there is no art of forgetting, after all, differs from saying there is no art of forgetting that can be constructed upon a theory of memory and semiotics. And in the chapters that follow, I believe that an *ars oblivionalis* is in fact at work for various poets. It is not that words suddenly produce absences (which Eco needs to conflate with forgetting in order to advance his claim), but rather that the *way* in which words are used might constitute an art of forgetting. Note the difference between Eco's assertion that language cannot help *us* forget and my claim that forms of misremembrance can help generate a certain poetic language. In what follows, I will consider how drawing blanks can foster an art of repetition, as well as how the decontextualization of words disrupts the link between one set of signs and another set of signs. I will consider how forgetting produces words and what happens between them, too. In response to Eco, I will also consider the reverse: how the undoing of memory is not just a motivating force but also a kind of aesthetic effect generated by a poem.

Without the aid of memory, poets are compelled to accept and use forgetting's agencies, linguistic range, movement across contexts, paradoxes, and ambiguities. Less a series of ideological pulleys than a kind of individualized process and movement, forms of misremembrance here remain poetically purposeful and liberating. It is forgetting's very shape-shifting nature that prohibits us from assigning it any stable meaning, while also permitting us to define it in terms of that malleability. At once latent, because it is mediating what has yet to emerge, and too soon, because it can enact a sudden interruption for which we are unprepared, it promises not the disbandment of meaning but varied means of making poetic language.

And Action: Toward a New Knowledge

[CHAPTER ONE]

Intuition teaches us that before one can remember, one has to experience. What it doesn't teach us is that before one can experience, one might have to forget. In 1910 Gertrude Stein wrote the lines, "She is forgetting anything. This is not a disturbing thing, this is not a distressing thing, this is not an important thing. She is forgetting anything and she is remembering that thing, she is remembering that she is forgetting anything."[1] The piece was "Many Many Women" (1933), a genre-bending work featuring a series of paragraphs all describing unidentified women referred to by the pronoun "she." Hallmarking Stein's development of her trademark abstraction and repetition, the idiosyncratic sentences generate a heightened experience of language by enacting the amnesia they describe. Inviting us to search both anaphorically and cataphorically for the proper referents to her elusive pronouns, Stein makes tangible the slippery feeling of forgetting itself. With the repetitive use of the present progressive, she stalls the forward movement of narrative time and action, refusing the finality of thought. Forgetting, in this grammatical form, is suspenseful and dramatic. The present, rather than being relegated to the past by the flow of time, is extended and experienced in its full strangeness. When the remembered thing turns out to be forgetting itself—"she is remembering that she is forgetting anything"—forgetting assumes the status of a positive word that resists the conquest of memory. It refuses us its referent (Stein never retrieves the object of the forgotten "anything") and remains a limit case for referential language, which at once becomes free-floating and excessive. The possibility of forgetting "anything" opens up the possibility of losing "everything," a leap permitted by the indefinite nature of oblivion's grammatical forms.

Such linguistic play is only one of many instances exemplifying the modernist's lifelong interest in a radical project of forgetfulness. But

22 **Chapter One**

such a project came to the writer neither immediately nor expectedly.[2] In 1902, Stein did not set out to create a work about the present but rather its opposite: a history. Taking her immediate family and cousins as models for the Herslands and the Dehnings, Stein began working on *The Making of Americans: Being a History of a Family's Progress*. Halfway through the composition Stein still believed in the force of memory: "I am knowing those I am remembering,"[3] she wrote, presenting the project as "a record of a decent family's progress respectably lived by us and our fathers and our mothers, and our grand-fathers, and grand-mothers."[4] The very act of reiterating the past, however, would come to mutate the meaning of repetition for its maker. Rather than recalling and replicating the past, repetition began to signify accruing information only to simplify that information by getting rid of its particulars. This shift refashioned a practice of remembering as a practice of forgetting. As the latter, saying something over and over again could be a kind of insistence of who or what someone was. Thus, by 1909 Stein had moved away from writing "a history of one family" to a "history of every one." The turn from family history to individual history was itself notable, marking Stein's forgetting of context, her separation of the subject from genealogy. By the time she published *Everybody's Autobiography* (1937), Stein said: "I have told all about her [my mother] in The Making of Americans but that is a story and after all what is the use of its being a story. If it is real enough what is the use of it being a story, and anyway The Making of Americans is not really a story it is a description [. . .] what is the use of remembering anything. There is none. And now really really remembering is very little done."[5] In short, between 1902 and 1911, a logic of forgetting had been born: the more the writer was recalling an earlier time, the more she was repeating it. The more she was repeating, the less she really needed the past and was able to forget it. The more she was repeating and forgetting, the more that repetition became insistence. The more she was insisting, the more she was creating emphasis. The more one was emphasizing, the more one was underscoring a thing's significance in being and discovering various ways and degrees of marking that significance.[6]

Having isolated the individual from the family, forgetting would soon account for a number of developments: Stein's refocus from histories to portraitures,[7] her critique of identity, and her idiosyncratic theory of genius. Yet, while the topic runs a wide gamut in Stein's work, this chapter focuses on one of forgetting's most peculiar and striking uses, namely, the integration of two divergent traditions in modernism: writing as knowledge and writing as action. On the surface, the two traditions of writing as knowledge and writing as action represent an unhappy marriage. Modernist action,[8] for one, is typically conceived of as "aggressive and spontaneous,"[9] unfettered, and "provisory and transitional."[10] Critics have attributed these characteristics to a range of causes, from the desire to liberate society from increasing regularity to the desire to collapse the distinction between art and life, the attempt to be "knowledge destroyers,"[11] and even the influence of extreme velocities in modern physics.[12] An emphasis on writing's nature *as* action—as opposed to as text, object, reflection, or representation—does not posit that writing is always literally an action but, rather, stresses what change writing can effect. Writing as action underscores what particular dynamic experiences writing alone can generate, referring to the temporal potential out of which writing arises. It emphasizes doing as a facet of aesthetic experience. Alternatively, writing that is committed to being knowledge has a much longer tradition of assuming a knowledge that is either accumulative or reflective, recalling and aggregating information over time. It presumes a return to prior places and times and a traversal of the past, from which one reconstructs a body of knowledge.

The diverging nature of the two traditions is prone to mutual critique. If writing is action, not prior to or subsequent to it, it is often said to lack the critical or historical distance to understand itself. The attack is a long-standing one, a descendant from the enduring tension between action and judgment, mind and body, *vita activa* and *vita contemplativa*.[13] In the context of modernist literature, the tension acquires an emphasized temporal dimension. Given that action belongs to the realm of the present, the attack on presentism is usually upheld on the grounds that "if life in the present [is] spontaneous, unpredictable, inexplicable, life in the past [is] a life of explanations, a chain of causes and reasons."[14] Modernism's attempt to self-pronounce—which persists in the question "What is the present?"—has been made to confront its very epistemological validity ever since.[15] The argument is that trying to understand what is happening as it is occurring may conflict with the nature of knowing itself.

By contrast, writing that is committed to knowing may be cumulative and passed down, but is said to be separate from, or even antithetical to, true doing, hence Friedrich Nietzsche's vitalist attack against historicist excess and William Carlos Williams's blunt pronouncement, "Bla! Bla! Bla! Heavy talk is talk that waits upon deed."[16] Writing that knows may refer to, study, or recall external actions but is not spontaneous or generative of action. It can represent but does not express. Its status is that of experience after the fact, not experience itself. Articulating this as one of modernity's paradoxes, Paul de Man noted: "The spontaneity of being modern conflicts with the claim to think and write about modernity."[17] Indeed, in his own account of the militaristic magazine *BLAST*, Ezra Pound had observed that upon being published, it "was regarded as manifesto, as an action, which it was," but that "an excessive preoccupation with that particular part of its function obscured the more durable elements, the level criticism."[18] The assumed split between performative language and "level criticism" is telling. As Charles Bernstein puts it, a certain kind of writing can "make its own particular marks on language, allowing for greater levels of abstraction and reflection, which has often resulted in diminishing the amount of action and 'doing.'"[19] The impossible cohabitation of literary consciousness and literary action runs parallel to the apparent impossibility of representing the present as it is happening. The representation need not be creative; the implication is that any theory or model of the present that takes fleeting action as its content is both lagging in time and fossilizing of action's ephemerality.

Against the modernist dichotomy of action and knowledge, Stein's work nevertheless marshals forth the idea that the two traditions need not be antagonistic or mutually exclusive. They can in fact be wedded to constitute writing's very duality with the help of a third term: forgetting. As an aesthetic and compositional tool, forgetting initiates new forms of present knowledge that are non-accumulative and non-progressive, while defining aesthetic action as something that does not take the past as reference but is in constant, ongoing formation. In this way, Stein's project distinguishes itself from the poetics of nothingness by French Symbolists[20] and the deliberate destruction of the Futurists, who identified forgetting as a way to self-appoint cultural authority and accelerate society into what Sascha Bru, following François Hartog, has called a new "presentist regime."[21] For Stein, forgetting is an ontological and epistemological issue. Rather than being an obstacle or error in cognition, it marks an epistemological shift from memory's usual kinship with knowledge and becomes an alternative mode of knowing. Moreover, leaving behind the past is not just about the prioritization of the present per se. It concerns itself with *presence* and the possibility of knowing what is vitally before one's self. However elusive and slippery a term, "presence" denotes the ability to create a sense of immediacy and contact. This is significant because Stein's knowledge is not brought about through critical or historical distance, but rather its precise opposite: proximity. "To understand a thing means to be in contact with that thing and the human mind can be in contact with anything," she writes in *The Geographical History of America* (1936).[22] Forgetting the past brings one closer to the "exceeding struggle of knowing really knowing what a thing [is] really knowing it knowing anything."[23] When Stein argues that "knowledge is not succession but an immediate existing," she suggests it has a presence that is active, emphatic, and living—"immediate" rather than successive.[24]

For Stein, to forget is thus both a negative response to the nineteenth century and a positive catalyst for an active life of writing. On the one hand, forgetting answers to a growing skepticism toward the epistemological accuracy of memory and, by extension, history. Just as the refusal of the present as a mere extension of the past arises from a backlash against progressive time, so too does Stein replace the narrative impulse that drives historical representation with anti-narratives that foreground atelic actions (activities and states) over telic ones (accomplishments or achievements). On the other hand, forgetting gives Stein the means to attend to what is before her—to shift from memory to attention, learning to unlearning/genius.[25] As forgetting allows Stein to grasp the presence of the present, it also gives knowledge the temporal advantage of action. The coexistence of knowledge and action in the ongoing present lies at the heart of writing's dual nature: writing as knowing must know itself as it is being performed or acted out. In contrast to more masculine notions of modernist action as a heroic deed or historical accomplishment, Stein's sense of action often defies easy memorization; it is ongoing, incomplete, and mental—related to modes of feeling and knowing. While the first half of this chapter will flesh out forgetting's contribution to writing as knowing, the second half will rethink writing and knowing as forms of atelic action—specifically as states and activities. For Stein, a writing that knows must also exercise itself as a practical knowledge rooted in doing, and a writing that makes something happen must also be knowing of itself in the act.

* * *

Readers of Stein are no strangers to the epistemological stakes of her experimental writing. Natalia Cecire notes that Stein's retroactive canonization as "experimental" is completely bound up with the performance of epistemic virtues "containing ethical as well as epistemological valences."[26] Where Linda Voris has shown how "knowledge is an embodied process for the radical empiricist,"[27] Johanna Winant and Jennifer Ashton have also offered successful accounts of Stein's respective investments in the "possibility and the problems of explaining based on inductive reasoning"[28] and categorization: how to "know the whole of the person" and consequently "turn from a phenomenological model of wholes to a logical one."[29] Critics have also been attentive to Stein's temporal poetics, how she viewed individuals and their personalities as "fundamentally rhythmic,"[30] how habit formation was at once a protection against the shocks of history (Liesl Olson) *and* an adaptive process of assimilation

(Omri Moses).[31] As I build off these accounts, as well as two other noteworthy pieces of scholarship—Sharon Kirsch's chapter on forgetting's relationship to rhetoric in Stein's work[32] and Elizabeth Freeman's work on Stein's revision of pathologized and atelic concepts, where the pathological includes amnesia and aphasia—I underscore forgetting's two-pronged approach to knowledge. It functions as an exposé of the limitations of memory, as well as a compositional method aimed at attuning the author to a new kind of knowledge based on inference, clarity of distinction, observation, and presence.

In *Wars I Have Seen* (1945), Stein's work about life during the Second World War, the author begins by locating the question of knowledge within the project of writing one's memories: "I do not know whether to put in the things I do not remember as well as the things I do remember."[33] Here, the things that Stein does not remember are not necessarily forgotten; rather, like one's birth, they enter a category of facts that are historically true but not verified by one's memory. She writes, "To begin with I was born, that I do not remember but I was told about it quite often [. . .]. The next thing I heard about myself was that I was eight months old."[34] In the following pages, the author accumulates a variety of mental experiences that invite us to question the project of memoir: the speaker can recall the place of an event but not the actual event; the speaker describes the specific stage in her life when she "really did begin to remember," implying an earlier period of lesser or false remembrance; and the speaker notes how there were things she "could be helped to remember by hearing them told again and again," emphasizing the role of external aids in strengthening one's mnemonic faculty.[35]

Repeatedly acknowledging while using memory's fallibility as the basis for writing, Stein does not make her primary concern memory per se, but rather how knowledge can be acquired outside of remembering. Writing becomes a means of knowing the limits of recollection while also trying to bypass them. The attempt to circumvent memory is partially motivated by the belief that remembrance is subject to the problems and risks to which imagination is similarly subject in classical philosophy: that of trying to represent what is absent by creating semblance or "false" likenesses. Unlike the conventional understanding of imagination, however, the stakes of memory are such that it lays claims to knowledge. The traditional Western model of thought attests to the positive collaboration of memory and learning.[36] In the Aristotelian model of recollection, for instance, recollection is an investigative, logical, and effortful recovery of prior knowledge necessarily conditioned by the lapse of time. Though based in images, Aristotelean recollection extends beyond the mere sake of remembering past episodes or events. It passes into and reinforces scientific knowledge, even when the beholder of knowledge may not necessarily recall the learning process or moment of acquisition.

For Stein and many at the turn of the twentieth century, this precise yoking of knowledge and memory no longer holds.[37] Memory does not enable but rather precludes comprehension. After all, who can tell on the basis of reflection whether one's memory is true? In Stein's 1937 account of why flying in a plane instills little fear when compared to climbing a mountain, she notes that even though one is certainly higher up in a plane, "everybody knows that somebody has fallen from any cliff and not been killed so anybody can remember that but anybody falling from the air is killed so no one can remember that."[38] In her playful and arguably facetious account, Stein differentiates between subjective experience and objective knowledge, what is episodic (time-stamped and related to personally experienced events) and what is semantic (factually and more generally known through concepts and ideas). The latter, which is marked by its unchangingness, is best achieved by sidestepping acts of recall altogether. In the above example, Stein's point is that relying on memory can lead to absurd conclusions. Memory's epistemic validity is called into question; recollection no longer bears the "scientific" logic implicit in an Aristotelian framework and is associated with a kind of logical fallacy.

The admittance of forgetting in Stein's work follows the general reprioritization of discovery over recovery during modernism. It coincides with the rise of a knowledge that is paradigmatic or revolutionary in nature rather than developmental or "progressive." Ironically, though, the epistemological limitations of memory constitute its intellectual value. The problem of remembering accurately produces objective statements about subjective fallibility. Regarding Stein's epistemology, Winant has shown how Stein reasons inductively while encountering the conundrum that for all the empirical facts one acquires over time, one can never be sure that one has all or enough of the facts, or that individual facts are generalizable. One might add to this by observing how Stein's work reinscribes this very problem of insufficient evidence as a self-evident truth capable of producing more claims. A short, characteristic example of what kinds of statements are possible when one is forgetting occurs in *Stanzas in Meditation*, completed in 1932 and published in 1956: "Could I have been bright before or not. / I wonder if I could have been bright before or not. [. . .] I could not nor can I remember."[39] Memory is not a method but the *very object* under question; it is not synonymous with poetic logic but what poetic logic scrutinizes. Another, more complex case can be found in *Everybody's Autobiography* (1937). Writing about time and genre, Stein observes: "Really the trouble with an autobiography you do not of course you do not really believe yourself why should you, you know so well so

28 **Chapter One**

very well that it is not yourself, it could not be yourself because you cannot remember right and *if you do remember right it does not sound right and of course it does not sound right because it is not right*" (emphasis mine).[40] Here, remembering right and being right ("it is not right") are mutually exclusive, precisely because Stein wants to detach epistemology from the past. Being right is associated with sound, not only as an aural presence but also as soundness, common sense—it is a matter of what Cecire calls objectivity's virtue, its critique of everything else as "'bad science' or even 'not science.'"[41] Being right is rooted in and justified by the presence of the present, or as Stein writes: "That is what makes today today that there is very little remembering done."[42] The retroactive project of autobiography, by contrast, is a mode of written remembrance incompatible with a good epistemology. To "remember right" is not to remember things accurately, but to merely remember in the true nature of remembrance, which inevitability entails fallibility.

Stating the problem of memory does not exempt Stein from her own work as autobiography. It does, however, demonstrate that given memory's diminishing authority, Stein turns to what she *can* explain from a position of apparent disinterest, where she is able to generate literary authority. In differentiating between remembering and being, the poet discovers the grounds on which she can prioritize the presence of the present (insistence, concentration) over the presence of the past (memory) or the presence of the future (expectation). The upshot of the presence of the present is twofold: first, writing achieves clarity when it is completely focused on the here and now. When Stein says "if you do not remember while you are writing, it may seem confused to others but actually it is clear,"[43] clarity has nothing to do with being able to understand something because it is familiar or recognizable by others. Rather, it is closer to the notion of distinction, based on eighteenth-century ideas that were being revisited by Charles Sanders Peirce and other contemporaries, and which I temporarily bracket and return to later in this chapter.[44] Second, a writing of the present is one that makes something happen, as opposed to reflecting on something that has already transpired.

Consider the experimental prose piece *A Long Gay Book*, written in the period from 1909 to 1912. Throughout it, Stein depicts what it is like to be someone who is doing anything: loving, arranging, resenting, mentioning, forgetting, et cetera. She repeatedly concludes that in presently being a person, one had to *come to be* that person. It is not necessary that one remember who one was, merely that one infer it from the present. Similarly, beginning an action is not the same as completely doing or finishing it. One knows this not because one remembers the action's origin, but rather because one is doing something, not beginning to do it:

If in having been one one was one then that one the one that one was was one having come to be that one. In having been one one who was one was one and in having been that one that one was one having come to be that one. In having come to be that one one having come to be that one was one coming to be that one.[45]

Regardless of whether events and processes are linked by causation, the *facts* of the events are significantly linked not by writing by memory, but by writing as explanation. The explanatory logic works backward and forward: the state of "having been one" leads to the prior state of "having come to be that one" to "coming to be that one." The progress of Stein's description as a way of knowing "one" is both elaborative and regressive, but in a way that excludes memory.

Writing without recollection, however, does more than open up, as Kirsch says, "a space to address failures of memory."[46] It also actively generates knowledge and partakes in its elaboration, becoming an alternative to knowing. To ask why Stein is so invested in forgetting as a topic and tool—that is, what it allows Stein to achieve, argue, and criticize in her creative vision—is inseparable from how forgetting appears in the composition itself. In her authoritative study of Stein's notebooks, Ulla Dydo notes that the writer intentionally crossed out the original names or nouns of persons and places, replacing them with more neutral pronouns. This act of erasing "in order to prevent attention from shifting to the references"[47] is one manifestation of deliberate forgetting as a way toward new forms of epistemological questions. As evident in *A Long Gay Book*, Stein's works from 1909 to 1912 often play with generic pronouns, causing the author to move between the mutually constitutive yet distinct questions of "Who?" and "What?" On the one hand, *Who* "everybody," "anything," or "she" is depends on specific sources and references. On the other hand, *What* "anybody," "anything," or "she" is depends on viewing these terms as general categories. An oscillation from one question to the other depends on the abstraction that forgetting facilitates. Letting go of the specificity of referentiality permits one to generalize from within language itself.

Similarly, Stein's unique method of counting via "one one one"—which appears in *Everybody's Autobiography*, "Poetry and Grammar" (1935), and "An Instant Answer; or, A Hundred Prominent Men" (1928)—has often been read as a model of total knowledge that isn't based on accretion.[48] In *Stanzas in Meditation*, Stein writes:

One which they won.
One two.
I often think one two as one and one.

30 **Chapter One**

One one she counted one one and this made
Economy not only which but of which
They will not kneel of which they do.[49]

Here, the basis of Stein's "economy"—her mode of arrangement and organization—is counting by deliberate forgetting. Thinking "one two as
one and one" approaches each entity through discrimination without preassigning the grounds or context of difference. While accumulative counting results in the problem of diminishing difference as one enters higher
terms[50]—and also requires an increased vigilance toward miscounting
and misremembrance—counting by ones implies forgetting precedence
and controlling the precision and scale of one's attention. Enumeration
occurs but no succession or addition. Where two differs from one because
two is greater than and contains one, "one one one" does not define each
subsequent term by its relation to the first. It merely suggests, on a more
fundamental level, that there are specific features that belong to a thing
and other features that belong to some other thing, hence making them
appear as separate entities. As a common denominator, "one" becomes
the yardstick by which all things can be measured while remaining distinct. "One two" begins to sound much more like "one too."

The art of forgetting thus supplies Stein with a way of knowing that
is rooted in difference and distinction rather than similarity, which is
the traditional basis of remembrance and knowledge.[51] In "An Acquaintance with Description" (1926), difference becomes the basis of definition
as a way of knowing a thing. Opening with the one-sentence paragraph
"Mouths and Wood" while repeating the ungrammatical sentence "What
is the difference between not what is the difference between," the piece
asks its audience to locate the difference between various items like "a
hedge and a tree," "forests and the cultivation of cattle," "a small pair and
that color and outside," and "she is very happy and a farm." Stein writes:

> What is the difference between not what is the difference between. What
> is the difference between not what is the difference between. An acquain
> tance with description or what is the difference between not what is the
> difference between not an acquaintance in description. An acquaintance
> in description.[52]

And later:

> What is the difference between three and two in furniture. Three is the
> third of three and two is the second of two. This makes it as true as a de
> scription. And not satisfied. And what is the difference between being on

the road and waiting very likely being very likely waiting, a road is connecting and as it is connecting it is intended to be keeping going and waiting everybody can understand puzzling.[53]

Stein's diction is an everyday vocabulary. Most readers know that three is not two, that being on the road implies movement and waiting, stasis, and that "What is the difference between" seems like the complete opposite of "[What is] Not what is the difference between." The power of such moments, however, is that the instant the writer asks her audience to uncover a difference between such disparate things, we are inclined to think there are infinite differences and turn instead to search for a similarity in order to discover some grounds for meaningful comparison. Perceiving difference, which is based on the idea of seeing difference against the terms of difference *and* similarity, forces the reader to forget or divest themself of the usual chains of signification. To hold on to familiar associations would render such juxtapositions nonsensical. The question is not whether there is difference but how to meaningfully express difference in order to know something. Or, as "what is *the difference between*" (emphasis mine) suggests, how to meaningfully measure difference, how to "subtract" or divest from cultural associations until "the difference"—what makes two things distinct—is the essential remainder.

In Stein's example of "a hedge and a tree," the difference may reside in arrangement or time. While a dictionary might state that hedges consist of rows of trees or woody shrubs, Stein raises the possibility of defining a hedge or a tree through form and scale. Stand close enough to a hedge, and a single tree may be what fills one's vision. Stand afar, and the same tree may blend into and be obscured by the hedge-at-large. Study a hedge, and it will emerge that a hedge bears no dynamic temporality, only maintenance and homogeneity, whereas a tree's change is captured in its growth and unique formation.

I offer such potential interpretations only to show that Stein is not after "dictionary definition" but rather *how* definition or distinction occurs in the first place, prior to any recollection and association. The answer lies in forgetting. As Thornton Wilder reminds us, "words were no longer precise" for Stein. "They were full of extraneous matter. They were full of 'remembering'—and describing a thing in front of us, an 'objective thing,' is no time for remembering."[54] In other words, if memory produced a kind of imprecision in both words and the knowledge they conveyed, definition and clarity needed to emerge from its absence instead. The force of this epistemological assumption is implicit even in Stein's prioritization of syntax over diction. If the definition of words usually resides in diction—where usage is historically conditioned, transformed, and transmitted—

32   Chapter One

Stein defines words through grammatical relation. Rather than appearing nonsensical, Stein's sentences are often adjustments of expected meaning. In the case of "What is the difference between not what is the difference between," Stein makes us read "between" not as preposition but as a kind of modifier for difference. She withholds the expected comparison of "between X and Y," thereby giving the phrase "the difference between" a different semiotic function and allowing its semantic meaning to be known in another way. Instead of asking what the difference between two items is, Stein asks what difference is in the first place. By making this shift in meaning possible through the positioning and emphasis of words in her sentence, Stein reveals a poetics that runs counter to remembrance and reference. Meaning emerges from forgetting certain chains of association, from emphasizing the logic of grammar over semantics. How things are defined is shaped by the way grammatical subjects relate to objects, or how prepositions relate to clauses.

The epistemological weight of forgetting opens up a plethora of critical possibilities beyond the scope of this chapter. Yet even in this space, we have observed the following: memory muddles and interferes with Stein's knowledge of what the world *is* by using what the world *was* as an index. Forgetfulness not only exposes the limits of memory but also affords knowledge of present existence through non-mnemonic means such as direct observation, induction/inference, and distinction. This idea of having present existence, or presence, is worth pondering for a little longer. Consider Stein when she writes, "[T]he human mind knows that it is what it is. It even knows that human nature is what it is therefore it need not remember or forget no the human mind does not remember because how can you remember when anything is what it is. Or how can you forget when anything is what it is."[55] Here, forgetfulness points to a discrepancy not between past and present, but rather between what something is and is not. While much of identity in Stein's work is centered on temporal (dis)continuities, the lines here indicate something else: one cannot remember the present because there is nothing to remember in the present. This is what distinguishes the human mind for Stein from human nature. The human mind "does not remember because how can you remember when anything is what it is. Or how can you forget when anything is what it is."[56] In other words, forgetting occurs when something is absent, but if the present is present, what is there to forget?

This is not simply linguistic theatrics. Knowing by attending to the present means concentrating on listening and seeing, *not* listening or seeing *as*. The move away from listening/seeing *as* toward listening/seeing *proper* is as much a move away from knowing as remembrance as it is a shift away from writing by metaphor, since seeing *as* entails recognition, similitude, and matching up objects with preexisting schema. As metaphor first suppresses difference on a logical plane in order to draw connections on a higher, figurative plane, it ultimately prioritizes a victory of similitude over difference, predicate over subject, genus over species. Metaphor, like memory, results in a recognition where a thing is not perceived directly, but perceived as or in terms of something else. This pivot away from metaphor by Stein follows a much earlier argument in literary history: that metaphors, unlike similes, confuse distinct entities, indicating how a writer's emotional state and involvement has colored the accuracy of perception.[57] Stein, however, revises this claim by asserting that one can know and perceive something correctly precisely *because* of present feeling, as opposed to in spite of it. A direct feeling into objects and into herself is a method of paying attention that brings Stein closer to, not further from, things as they are.

For instance, when Stein describes the category of men who are "being living" in *A Long Gay Book*, she says: "He has in him his being certain that he is being one seeing what he is looking at just then, he has in him the kind of certain feeling of seeing what he is looking at just then."[58] The author associates concentrated perception with epistemological certainty— "being certain" of oneself and one's object of attention. What is perceived by the senses is not—as Yves Bonnefoy would later say—appearance or likeness, but presence. Later on in the text, Stein goes on to write with even more feeling and certainty:

> In all men in their daily living, in every moment they are living, in all of them, in all the time they are being living, in the times they are doing, in the times they are not doing something, in all of them there is always something in them of being certain of seeing the thing at which they are looking.[59]

Stein's increasing sense of knowledge is matched by an intensity of scale: "all men," "every moment," "all the time," "there is always something." Attentiveness by Stein not only penetrates through perception to feeling, but also attempts to reach a level of conviction. Certainty arises from a kind of passionate feeling: passion neglects the past because as an affective presence, it engrosses on the scale of totality, being monarchial and isolationist. The present object of concentration and feeling supplants all others. Stein therefore overturns earlier somatic conceptions of forgetting as being a symptom of lethargy, suggesting that forgetting is no longer the deterioration of willed activity but how the subject wills *excitation*, the opposite of a defunct relaxation. It is one of the ways in which

34 **Chapter One**

arousal, hence poetic intensity and pleasure, becomes possible and conducive to knowing.

* * *

For Stein, forgetting marks a temporal shift in how to know: writing through direct observation, contact, and feeling reverses the hegemony of memory in the world of cognition. By turning away from recollection and reflection toward immediacy, the writer reverses knowledge's reliance on the past and places it in the same realm as action: the present. Yet it remains to be seen how forgetting actually shapes Stein's poetics of action, making it compatible with knowledge. When the poet says in *Stanzas in Meditation*, "How do you do how do you do / And now how do you do now / This which I think now is this," she not only seems to repeat her question out of a kind of forgetfulness but also literalizes the colloquial greeting by asking what means and methods produce action in a constantly shifting deictic present.[60] The question "How do you do?" leads us to investigate the nature of poetic experience as doing: if writing is knowing and writing is action, what is the precise relationship of the two? And if knowing *is* a kind of action when writing is involved, what does knowing exactly *do*?

Even a preliminary answer to such questions requires the initial step of observing Stein's conception of writing *as* action in her writing *about* it. As a subject, action appears most explicitly in Stein's "historical" works. Given that historical writing takes the recollection of great past events as its basis, the genre provided an apt opportunity for Stein to position aesthetic action and forgetting as both distinct and prior to remembering and its narrative concerns. In *Everybody's Autobiography*, Stein writes specifically about and against historical action by the military, beginning with how the war had "nothing to do" with her and Picasso's evolving friendship:

> The war had nothing to do with that of course not. Wars never do, they only make anybody know what has already happened it has happened already the war only makes it public makes those who like illustrations of anything see that it has been happening. [. . .] Everything has been done before the war and then the war makes everybody know it and then everybody acts as if they were doing something but really they are only carried on by momentum [. . .].[61]

Right away, Stein introduces the idea that wars are irrelevant to everyday living because they do not enact any real change. Despite war's fixation with accomplishment and deeds, Stein views it as having no connection to what is happening because "everything has been done before the war." In other words, war is not synchronous with, or constituted by, action, but rather serves as action's aftermath. Wars have no causal authority; they are merely effects. When Stein says "wars never do," she also plays on a dual meaning of the phrase: wars not only do not constitute true action but they are also bad, in the sense that "they won't do." Wars offer illustrations of true changes that have already occurred elsewhere—often inside certain individuals. Though Stein does not explicitly mention forgetting, the problem of knowledge, tense, and memory are implicit: wars seem to produce knowledge, but one that is problematically out of sync with actual doing. By the time knowing is publicized, it becomes representational and is already on the path toward boredom or dullness.

The critique is similar to Stein's attack on newspaper writing, which cannot resolve the predicament of seemingly combining knowledge and action but in "false time." In a lecture, Stein says, "Newspapers want to do something, they want to tell what is happening as if it were just then happening [. . .] as if the writing were being written as it is read."[62] What Stein is suggesting is that newspapers operate by deceiving the reader into feeling that yesterday is today. Newspapers rely on a false sense of presence and immediacy, but in fact are both too late for real life and too early for writing—they write what has already happened and what they recall from memory, hence destroying all possibility of not only discovery but also writing as action. In their implicitness of "something always happening,"[63] daily newspapers feign a synchronicity with something like Stein's continuous present, but unlike Stein's work, which *makes something happen*, newspapers describe a thing that has concluded, depriving writing of the intensity or feeling that constitutes a creative force. In contradistinction to a writing that still relies on memory, Stein's definition of modernity entails a kind of action that runs counter to remembrance, representation, and reflection: "We in this period have not lived in remembering, we have living in moving being necessarily so intense that existing is indeed something, is indeed that thing that we are doing."[64] Locating action in something as ongoing and inconclusive as existing, Stein describes everyday life as an activity and state that bears the intensity or excitement that winning or losing a war, or reporting on a huge story, usually claims. Though counterintuitive, wars and newspapers have the commonality of not starting anything. For Stein, writing can "make history" only if it replaces linear narrative with a self-referential "movement so great that it has not to be seen against something else to be known."[65] This movement is so great it forgets what precedes and follows it, disconnecting itself so as to make something happen. Such an aesthetic understanding of action explains why a writer who is so invested in forgetting can also be

36 Chapter One

preoccupied with history; as the past lost its didactic potential as magistrate vitae at the turn of the century, history became something that was made up of singular, individual, unprecedented events. History was not something that could determine or guide present and future action, but something that was itself the product of human deeds and constructions. The best writing would "make" it.[66]

Stein's sense of action thus shifts from those that depend on memory—for example, the actions depicted by newspapers and historical accounts—to those that encourage a kind of forgetting: activities and states. Activities and states are homogeneous in their content and atelic in their form, replacing and replenishing themselves without requiring the past for contrast or comparison. Their repetitive nature moreover emerges out of a kind of forgetfulness.[67] As early as pieces like *A Long Gay Book*, "Many Many Women," and *G.M.P.* (1933), Stein indicates an interest in how forgetting can contribute to the formal presentation of atelic action, as well as how atelic actions can incentivize forgetting on the part of the reader and writer. By having activities and states feature prominently in portraiture[68]—which usually focuses on a person as the primary holder of agency—Stein demonstrates that she is less interested in recounting what her subjects have done (this would be the work of reportage, biographical history, or remembrance) than in how actions are integral to the intelligibility of those subjects. Take, for instance, the full version of this chapter's opening example. In "Many Many Women," Stein writes:

> She is forgetting anything. This is not a disturbing thing, this is not a distressing thing, this is not an important thing. She is forgetting anything and she is remembering that thing, she is remembering that she is forgetting anything.
>
> She is one being one remembering that she is forgetting anything. She is one not objecting to being one remembering that thing, remembering that she is forgetting anything. She is one objecting to there being some objecting to being ones forgetting anything. She is one objecting to any one being one remembering that they are not forgetting anything. She is one objecting to any one objecting to her being one forgetting anything. She is not one remembering being one objecting to any one objecting to her being one forgetting anything. She is one remembering that she is one objecting to being one remembering that they are not forgetting anything. She is one remembering something of being one objecting to some being one objecting to forgetting anything.[69]

Stein's work is hardly a traditional recounting of a person's life accomplishments. There is nothing here that one can summarize. There is also very little that one can "remember" in the sense of creating mental short-cuts to recall information. There is even less in the passage to turn into retroactive narrative, since the paratactic order of what's happening resists "reordering." Rather, Stein's focus on activities and states encourages forgetting at every moment, as if to clear mental room for the next long sentence, which is bound to draw upon a set of key words that keep changing their meaning depending on their context. The writer puts aside traditional aspects of history or memoir: identification of "she" is less important in the normative sense (naming and identifying her) than putting into motion the subject's activities and states. Action is not simply a thing "she" does. It is synonymous with who she is. Whereas a woman who forgets now and then remembers later suggests a change in state, a woman who "is forgetting anything" is more like a sun that is shining: the description of forgetting is an essential quality that manifests itself experientially. Characteristic of Stein's work, quality here is not adjectival. Stein, who does not write "she is forgetful," uses the aspectual function of "forgetting" as a happening, an action that entails and consumes time, starting, restarting, and continuing in a habitual manner. Forgetting, objecting, and remembering are as much repeated "stages"[70] as they are constitutive elements of the subject's existence.

The "buildup" effect of Stein's lengthening sentences is itself an active process based in the creative power of forgetting. As early as the sixteenth century, it was noted that "a man forgets many things, or at least some things, when forced to read continuously."[71] In the case of Stein's continuous present, the reader is at first tempted to memorize what is happening and in what order. Intense observation, however, soon draws the reader into an absorptive state located in the present. They are soon welcome to relinquish and forget the individual placement and meaning of words for the sake of Stein's "gist." The insistence of certain phrases promises reoccurrence, thereby rending retention superfluous, while the whole of the portraiture is to give way to the feeling of present existence, not to remember what happened first, second, or last in a given paragraph. Words easily pass out of memory, and the usual problems of narrative—remembering names of characters, their background, and so on—become irrelevant because writing is generative rather than reproductive, and reading is staying in time with Stein's sentences rather than remembering previous facts. In fact, because the sentence is the main compositional block for Stein—the question is always how to generate enough movement and activity within a single one—I would contend that the length of each present moment follows the duration of each sentence. Where the drama of a paragraph is in its having a beginning, middle, and end, the drama of a sentence lies in the tensions within its inherent unity. Held together by grammatical rather than narrative logic, Stein's sentences often toe the line between coherent meaning and nonsense: a sentence's tentative significance appears to be simultaneously threatened *and* closer to fulfillment with each outward extension of Stein's predicate. Things come together just when they seem to unravel.

The way in which certain actions grounded by forgetting's presentism come to replace memory-based identity is also significant: actions play a role in making the world intelligible not only because physical events are part of the collective and visible sphere but also because mental events give rise to subjects themselves. In Stanza VI of *Stanzas in Meditation*, the act of "liking" is an inherent link between deed and doer:

> This one will be just as long
> As let it be no mistake to know
> That in any case they like what they do
> If I do what I do I do too
> . . . .
> Do you change about mutton and onions or not.
> This is why they sleep with a ball in the mouth
> If not what is there to doubt.
> I have forgotten what I meant to have said ahead.
> Not at all forgotten not what.
> It is not whatever not is said
> Which they may presume to like
> If at no time they take any pains
> Not to like it.[72]

Stein's tone of self-evidence—"no mistake to know," "what is there to doubt"—hinges on the idea that if you "do what you do," then you must do it because you like doing it, and if you don't "take any pains / [n]ot to like it," then you must be liking it. The present always excludes alternative realities; could-haves, would-haves, meant-to-haves are irrelevant—you either "change about mutton and onions or not." The double negatives aren't litotic understatements. They really *do* end up canceling out each other, along with all forms of hesitation. For all of Stein's difficulty, then, we see how she simplifies actions so that they are first order. Actions are linked to subjects not because subjects perform them through a complex and potentially ambivalent process of reasoning and feeling. Rather, they are linked because subjects are defined by the very actions they are performing. For what reason could a person do what they do other than the fact that they *want* to do it? Subjecthood for Stein relies on a unity between outer and inner. There is a kind of Jamesian behaviorism here, but one that doesn't exclude the will so much as it collapses the distance between intention and expression. "Liking"—the basis of every individual's distinct taste or preference—is a form of strong volition that is simultaneous with doing and being. Who or what one is, is made transparent by present action, not narrative reconstruction of the past.

Beyond the ways in which forgetting permits certain activities and states to give rise to subjecthood, it also affects the act of writing itself. Reflecting on her past work in one of her lectures, Stein writes: "I began to wonder if it was possible to describe the way every possible kind of human being acted [. . .] and I thought if this could be done it would make A Long Gay Book."[73] Here, the actions of "every possible kind of human being" correspond with her own compositional process, where Stein renders people in terms of activities and states while also rendering activities and states in terms of subjects:

> Coming to be anything is something. Not coming to be anything is something. Loving is something. Not loving is something. Loving is loving. Something is something. Anything is something.
>
> [. . .]
>
> Being loving is happening. Being a dead one is happening. Completely loving is something that is happening. Being a dead one is something that is happening. Some are knowing all that thing, are quite knowing all that thing.[74]

In both passages, Stein makes her conceptual and grammatical subject action itself. The selected actions are those that range from emphasizing process over culmination ("coming to be") to actions of refrainment ("not loving," "not coming") and states ("being a dead one," "being loving," "knowing"). But if the implicit question underlying each of the examples is "What is action?" the answer remains elusive, or the act of answering itself has no terminal point or conclusion. More often than not, the action at hand equals more action, as in the case of "[b]eing a dead one is happening," or it equals the word "something," which plays on the ongoing "-ing" of the verbs. Less definitional than it is to emphatic, "is something" in these passages presents a paradoxical effect. On the one hand, the indefiniteness of the pronoun creates a certain sense of deferral, which is prolonged by its repetition. On the other hand, to be something is to have a certain integrity and to possess some sort of form or definition. It is this tension between the unknown or deferred and the known and asserted that comes to constitute the nature of writing as an expressive action that

40 **Chapter One**

also represents *the fact* of the action. In other words, the nature of Stein's content gets reinterpreted on the level of composition. Action in Stein's portraits is not only located in the semantic content of "what happens" but also in the very temporal and formal tension of happening as the kind of activity and state that writing can be. It is this tension that contributes to a new kind of excitement. Whereas memory and succession tradition-ally create suspense through elements like anticipation, epiphany, plot-ting, determination, execution of intentions, and the challenge of stabiliz-ing the self, Stein's forgetting presents the alternative problem of how to ever create drama from the present alone.

It can therefore be said that action not only manifests itself on the level of semantic content, but also constitutes language's nature as a medium.[75] While writing about action, Stein generates a process of writing that per-forms and mirrors such active qualities. One way of moving between these two levels in a text like *A Long Gay Book* is through the grammatical choice of the present progressive, which merges the infinitive (being) with a cho-sen verb (doing). As linguists have noted, progressive verbs are somewhat paradoxical in that they are at once indicative of temporariness *and* on-goingness, representing the present neither as instantaneous nor sub-ordinate to the infinite regress of the past or infinite advance of the future. They possess an internal structure that is durational, and implicit in this duration is an expectation for change. Present progressives in particular build upon forgetting and its recursive temporal nature. The tense is one that resists recourse to deep history.

According to linguists, however, the present progressive can also be about more than just duration or temporality per se. John Goldsmith and Erich Woisetschlaeger have significantly shown that the progressive and simple present tense in English denote different *knowledge-types*.[76] The simple present tense states the structure of things (which may change) and is propositional. The progressive, on the other hand, is phenomenologi-cal and descriptive. The sentence "The engine doesn't smoke anymore" entails a structural claim of change (we infer that something like repair or a changing of the engine's parts has occurred), whereas "the engine isn't smoking anymore" is observational and conditioned by some sort of physical proximity.

Using Goldsmith and Woisetschlaeger's study, we can return to a set of Stein's sentences like "Being a dead one is happening. Completely loving is something that is happening. Being a dead one is something that is hap-pening." On the one hand, the phrase "Being a dead one is something" makes writing seem propositional. Stein "tells" us it, and like other sen-tences that follow a similar structure, it has a stately posture and a sense of finality, denoting a particular ontological status. On the other hand, "is something that is happening" bears a phenomenal structure. Writing that appears to be ontologically stable becomes processual and unfolding. The progressive invites the reader to interpret the depicted actions as contemporaneous with the time of speaking. Ironically, the confluence of what "is happening"—which often refers to what is perceived in the present—and something interior like "loving," which is not literally perceivable, creates the peculiar sense that Stein is both observing and inducting at the same time. This is possible because Stein replaces the reflective quality of remembrance with the observation of her own thoughts. The thoughts may rely on memory, but the important thing is that the observation doesn't. In other words, the movement between semantically knowing something and experientially knowing something reflects the way in which writing works. By observing itself as it is describing a given subject's actions, writing produces a second knowledge, which is not merely knowledge of its content, but of its own nature as an activity and state.

For Stein, then, writing itself is like an activity in the progressive tense and a state of being. The event of writing and discovering what is being written is as much as something that happens *to* Stein, a state she finds herself in, as it is a thing that happens *by* her, an activity she generates. The significance of this self-referentiality and mixed agency is not unlike the ambivalent nature of forgetting. Forgetting, both voluntary and involuntary, can be linguistically rendered as internal or external to the self. This duality is key to understanding Stein's writing as a way of both doing and knowing. In "Poetry and Grammar," Stein describes her passionate relationship with active present verbs in the following terms:

> I have told you that I recognize verbs and adverbs aided by prepositions and conjunctions with pronouns as possessing the whole of the active life of writing. [. . .] A long complicated sentence should force itself upon you, make you know yourself knowing it and the comma, well at the most a comma is a poor period that it lets you stop and take a breath but if you want to take a breath you ought to know yourself that you want to take a breath.[77]

Here, the "the active life of writing" and the life of knowledge are not antagonistic. In fact, knowing a subject's actions is not enough—what is important is to be in this state *consciously* and to be in it consciously means putting knowledge into present action itself: "make you know yourself knowing it." The implication of this is not simply that objects of knowledge have to be animated into mental processes in order to be thought. Rather, it suggests that language "makes" something happen: it "makes you know yourself knowing it." The writer who organizes language as an exercise of

42 Chapter One

her own will experiences, in turn, the imperative of writing: whether it is the use of a "long complicated sentence" or a comma, the activity of writing demands an exercise of consciousness, an ushering forth of otherwise unconscious states such as breathing. What might seem involuntary—the sentence "forces" itself on you—is in fact mixed in agency. Even non-observational knowledge has to become quasi-observational since the key to writing as action and writing as knowing is to pay attention to yourself *as you are knowing something*. The elevation of what you know into knowing what you know is precisely the activity that writing does and the state it espouses. Knowing what one knows might seem like a mere tautology, but what it really refers to is the experience of performing knowing as a phenomenon one is aware of having. This means that it is different from experiences of coercion or hypnosis, where one has the feeling of someone else performing the action for him or her.

Writing, for Stein, is not only a physical activity one does with one's hand, but also the act of raising the occurring action to the foreground of consciousness, which is always existing and happening in the present. The critic E. L. McCallum has even extended this to the modernist's impact on readers, stating that Stein's work "returns us to the experience of the text, reflecting on the reading as we are reading."[78] Indeed, in Stein's works, a human subject may be in a state of excitement or may be performing the activity of "loving completely." By themselves, these may remain unconscious, but if and when they are rendered in art, writing makes recognizable or conscious *that* "one is feeling anxious," or *that* "one is being one loving completely." When Stein writes, "I was creating in my writing by simply looking,"[79] she suggests that unlike mere seeing, looking at—or paying attention to what one sees—makes conscious of the fact *that* one sees, and also makes recognizable to oneself *what* one sees. Perception comes in contact with perception-that, and present phenomena once again leads to propositional knowledge, which is actualized or experienced through the activity of knowing. The ever-present propositional nature of writing is why writing for Stein can never be automatic.[80] To know how to write is to exercise a practical knowledge of it.[81] Yes, it is to be one writing, but it is also to know *how*, *that*, and *what* it is one is writing.

Following forgetting through to its Steinian end opens up a number of avenues that far exceeds the boundaries of its traditional sense. To think of the poet's radical use of unremembering is, among other things, to think of knowledge as something other than the afterlife of action and action as more than a spontaneous occurrence of instinct, indifferent to knowing. Through forgetting, Stein surprises readers by documenting the interactions between the two, revising knowledge's nature as cumulative and action's definition as being sudden. The states and activities featured in her work are by definition ongoing, but what *is* immediate is the knowing of these states and activities, a knowing that relies on a constant forgetting of what otherwise disrupt one's concentration.

On the level of style and technique, Stein's use of erasure, her emphasis on syntax over diction, her choice of juxtaposing language over associative language, and her employment of the present progressive have all come to feature as ways of forgetting. But these compositional tools also add to forgetting's conceptual weight, serving as licenses for particular critiques or endorsements of different aesthetic ideas, including the argument here that writing can be knowing and doing at the same time. To have a writing that is both knowing and doing is to understand the duality of Stein's writing itself, as something that both *exists*, like a fact, persisting through time so as to seemingly exist outside temporality, as well as something that *happens* or *occurs*, like an event, temporal by nature. Stein's knowledge is to a degree semantic, marked by its unchangingness and independence from memory, but experiential observation *of oneself* in the process of knowing is also key to Stein's writing as action. Writing as knowledge must not only refer to its content as it is being written but also be a practical knowledge of itself, a practical knowledge that is at all possible because it is rooted in doing. Aided by forgetting, writing ascertains the nature of external objects while linking these objects with a secondary knowledge, in reference to the knower. Writing presents the semantic fact of its occurrence. For Stein, it is this raising of composition's own experience to consciousness that signals writing's action as intentional rather than automatic. For the poets who will follow in chapter 2, intention remains equally significant, not because it leads to a poetics of doing but because it raises the possibility of a poetics of not-doing, of forgetting to do.

Forget It! Poetry Makes Nothing Happen

[CHAPTER TWO]

In his treatise on memory, Aristotle had claimed that "there is no such thing as memory of the present while present, for the present is object only of perception, and the future, of expectation, but the object of memory is the past."[1] With memory limited to things prior, one might think that forgetting ought to follow suit. Yet, less than twenty years after Stein's death, poets of the New York School took exception to this rule. Rather than turning their attention to retroactive memory, they began to employ what memory theorists now call "prospective memory." Defined as the ability "to carry out intended actions at an appropriate point in the future" or the capacity "to remember to remember," prospective memory presumes a temporal outlook conditioned by the framework of reminding.[2] Although recollection and reminding both involve calling something to mind, recollection evokes a unique singular occurrence in the past, while reminders can call to mind the future, pointing to things located outside one's present or past realm of perception.

Taken seriously in the past several decades, prospective memory initially stemmed from earlier research in directed forgetting, a paradigm that emerged in the sixties with psychologists such as W. S. Muther and Bernard Weiner. Aimed at determining how certain commands and cues could influence the recognition, retrieval, and recollection of disparate items, their experiments involved commands and directions, thereby finding equivalents in the world of art. In a description of architecture, Lawrence Halprin claimed that "even a grocery list or a calendar [...] is a score."[3] For Halprin, "planning for a future event"[4] was the fundamental purpose of a scoring mechanism, but the path from score to execution was more indeterminate than what a direct and economical approach might dictate. With analogous forms in visual and audible media, such as those by Lee Lozano, Sol LeWitt, John Cage, and Nam June Paik, artists in the postwar decades joined Halprin in converging upon an "alternate poetics, of deeply prosaic everyday statements, composed of short, simple vernacular words, presented in the form of lists and instructions."[5]

What kind of poem, then, might "instruct" forgetting? This chapter begins to craft a response by looking at the genre of the to-do list poem—what Mark Hillringhouse, in a 1985 interview with James Schuyler, once called a "truly representative of a brand of 'New York School' writing."[6] A spin-off of one of Frank O' Hara's "'I do this I do that' / poems,"[7] the to-do list poem replaced the present with the future as its scene of action, thereby introducing a degree of indeterminacy into a seemingly straightforward form.

Brought to the foreground of American poetry with the help of writers like Schuyler and Ted Berrigan (fig. 2.1), the to-do list poem tapped into a number of literary and cultural traditions. It referenced the economical method of making lists in Benjamin Franklin's *Autobiography* (1791) and Henry David Thoreau's *Walden* (1854),[8] as well as the genre of travel literature/the travelogue—as in Joe Brainard's 1971 list-drawing "Things to Do Before I Move" (fig. 2.2); Gary Snyder's 1966 "Things to Do" poems "... Around Seattle," "... Around Portland," "... Around a Lookout," "... Around San Francisco," "... Around Kyoto"; and Berrigan's "Things to Do in Providence" (1970) and "Things to Do in New York" (1969). It referenced the use of "procedures of mechanical and indexical recording"[9] under John Cage's influence and the rise of self-help culture. Seen

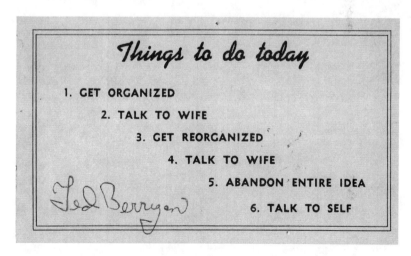

Figure 2.1. Ted Berrigan, "Things to do today." Postcard sent (ca. 1970) to Pat Nolan. By permission of the Estate of Ted Berrigan. Photograph: Pat Nolan (https://thenewblackbartpoetrysociety.wordpress.com/).

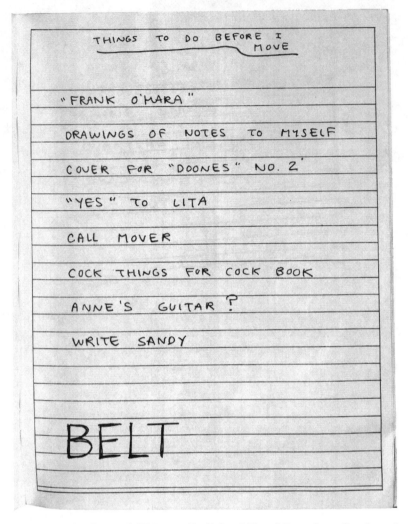

Figure 2.2. Joe Brainard, "Things to Do Before I Move." From *Some Drawings of Some Notes to Myself* (New York: Siamese Banana Press, 1971). By permission of the Estate of Joe Brainard.

by critics, including Terence Diggory and David Lehman, as a categorizing aid and aesthetic technique, the "to-do" poem also figured prominently in creative writing programs,[10] leaving critics to wonder whether a poem *about* what to do could instruct a writer what to do in a similar fashion. As Larry Fagin's guide to catalog verse suggests, the "to-do" poem is a flexible poetic form. It appeals to beginners of poetry as well as the most sophisticated writers.[11]

Reversing the typical temporal direction of memory by making the future its unspoken horizon, the "to-do" poem also revises a typical notion regarding New York School poetry. Whether it's Libbie Rifkin's claim that Berrigan's work "mounts an assault on its scholarly future," Richard Howard's assertion that "[John] Ashbery *wants* us to elude the notion of project," or Michael Clune's reading of Frank O'Hara as "shopping without a list," there exists a critical assumption that a poetics of spontaneity has to coincide with having no plan.[12] No plan? No future.[13] François Hartog went so far as to describe the "Swinging Sixties" as a period that sported "forget the future" as its quintessential slogan, the "clearest sign of the radical exclusion of anything but the present."[14] As a form of prospective memory that documents desires, promises, and tasks, however, the "to-do" list poem complicates this lack of planning. The genre records the future as a set of actions that bear an indexical relationship to present intention.[15] This index nevertheless signifies distance rather than proximity. The very aesthetic form that seems to prioritize the recollection of future tasks and actions paradoxically espouses a kind of forgetting that is essential to the poem as a site of possibility rather than actualization, wishful thinking rather than resolution, changing one's mind rather than seeing things through.

In one kind of "to-do" poem, what seems like an attempt to remember in is in fact an attempt to forget. Here, it isn't that New York School poets don't make promises or plans, as most critics argue; rather, they *merely* make them, only to forget, ignore, discard, or later recover them without reinstituting them. The shift, while appearing subtle, accounts for the genre's adept navigation of time, tense, and sentiment. As Frank O'Hara writes in "Muy Bien" (1961): "I like to make changes in plans / as long as the cook / doesn't get upset."[16] In a second variant version of the "to-do" list poem, the power of the genre derives from a future or vision that is in fact unachievable through practical instruction. Unlike the nature of self-help books during the postwar era, such as those championed by Norman Vincent Peale and Dale Carnegie, the power of "positive" or future-oriented thinking in this poetry is never meant to generate genuine belief that one can control one's happiness or one's tomorrow. Where "to-do" poems turn on themselves as practical imperatives or instructions yielding concrete results, they can nevertheless be read as "to-feel" poems. A "to-feel" poem builds upon forgetting to guide both a speaker and reader toward certain attitudes about oncoming events.

The paradoxical nature of the "to-do" list poem calls into question the very assumptions behind future-oriented intentions. In most cases, one makes plans to later recall and follow through on them. Coherence with one's prospective memory means an affirmation of identity over

48   **Chapter Two**

time, since "making good" on one's promises and contracts presupposes someone who is calculable and trustworthy. As one's own self-proclaimed guarantor, the individual who makes a promise ordains the future in advance. In Nietzschean terms, the individual gains mastery over themself as well as the circumstances of the future—so much so that their words seem to withstand and defy accident and fate. Moreover, the one who makes a promise evokes a set of assumptions or "rules" that are necessary for the promise to qualify as an adequate speech act. According to John Searle, these rules include some propositional content that predicates a future act, as well as content that is exceptional and surprising: one promises what one isn't already presumed to do. Underwritten with sincerity, a promise "intends that the utterance of T [some sentence] will place him [the promiser] under an obligation to [. . .] perform a certain act."[17] However, as linguist Leslie K. Arnovick contends, Searle too easily assumes the face value of promissory words. Arguing that the traditional verbal indicators of intention "will" and "shall" have in fact weakened over the centuries in their power to inextricably bind words and deeds, Arnovick observes that "will" and "shall" have shifted to a more neutralized indication of the future at large. The replacement of the stronger option ("shall") with the weaker nature of "will" in various cases is indicative of the very fact.

The tension between present projection and actualization, the intention to remember and actual recollection, is part of the "to-do" poem's affective power. Accordingly, the genre rethinks what poetic responsibility or "sincerity" can mean. Take Schuyler's "Things to Do" (1977). The poem *does* paint a kind of future, but the work speaks less to resolutions than it does to the malleable nature of promises and plans as potentially forgettable. Though it begins with practical chores, it eventually takes on the garb of wishful thinking, of bucket-list making. Even as the speaker of "Things to Do" envisions a future, we never know if he intends to remain faithful to its realization. The poem whimsically starts:

> Balance checkbook.
> Rid lawn of onion grass.
> "this patented device"
> "this herbicide"
> "Sir, We find none of these
> killers truly satisfactory. Hand weed
> for onion grass."[18]

The very writing down of a to-do list occurs precisely because forgetting exists (i.e., "in case I forget") and is meant to serve as a form of resistance. However, rather than counteracting obliviousness, Schuyler welcomes it.

With his very first line, "Balance checkbook," Schuyler pokes fun at the whole checklist's reliability, since part of his "to-do" list is remembering to be the economically responsible person whose fiscal credibility would in turn give the poem's goals good standing. Someone who had already balanced his checkbook would not have to set personal reminders to accomplish the deed. Balancing a budget means constraining future spending by reviewing past expenditures, but Schuyler ignores such frugality. Ridding the lawn of onion grass becomes a predicament of going to the store and searching for the right product. Rather than being an efficient plan, the opening lines represent only a delay in the process of riddance, returning the speaker to the possibility of hand weeding. Whether or not one completes a task is less important than moving on to the next reminder. Each goal becomes forgettable once the poet has rendered it in language, and the poem is quick to liberate its speaker from any one specific topic:

> Give
> old clothes away, "such as you
> yourself would willingly wear."
> Impasse. Walk three miles
> a day beginning tomorrow.
> Alphabetize.

Unlike the word "will," which attaches the contents of the future to one's actual belief, the modality of "would" speaks to hypothetical situations that attach the future to what is imaginable but never actual, forgettable rather than set in stone. It introduces to the orbit of imperative action a dimension of passivity that is even weaker than one's usual experience of uncontrollable motives and wants. The reminder to organize past clothes for some future donation or discard does not lead to execution but to "impasse." When Schuyler includes, "Walk three miles / a day beginning tomorrow," the line is humorous because the resolution to walk is, on second thought, pushed off to a tomorrow that is always tomorrow's tomorrow. Intentional forgetting takes the form of procrastination. "Alphabetize," which might refer to the speaker's books, has a tongue-in-cheek character given that it names another index that the "to-do" list poet might or might not eventually adopt for his work. Forgetting one index for another is always a possibility.

As Schuyler's to-do list grows, the shifts from item to item grow increasingly drastic. The self-reminders, "Answer letters / Elicit others / write Maxine," are followed by "Move to Maine. / Give up NoCal." Such musings do not refer to immediately practicable tasks so much as they do to dreams or wishful thinking. As opposed to wanting or willing, fantasies

and wishful thinking are at once more lackadaisical *and* more weighty because they point to something desired but thought to be unachievable.
In the context of what Adam Philips calls the "unlived life," what *doesn't*
happen to Schuyler's speaker—or what is merely wished by him—is as significant as what does happen. The poem resonates with Kenneth Koch's
Wishes, Lies, and Dreams (1970), in which readers are asked to write poems
"about how things might be but really aren't."[19]

By the time Schuyler's poem reaches more abstract resolutions—"Send.
Keep. Give. Destroy."—the work has picked up pace, moving through verbs
as if what's relevant is not accomplishing one's goals, but making one's intentions partake in the writing of the poem. Speed espouses both urgency
and forgetting. The act of jotting down intentions sanctions the needless-
ness of remembering them:

> Brush rub polish burn
> mend scratch foil evert
> emulate surpass. Remember
> "to write three-act play"
> and lead "a full and active life."

"Remember" here is not retroactive but prospective. Placed at the end of
the line, the weight of the enjambment immediately tips into lightness, as
Schuyler alleviates the preceding pause. It's not that the speaker will not
go on to write a play or live a full, active life. Rather, as Schuyler qualifies
his own aspirations in quotations, using the clichéd language of cultural
self-improvement, the tone is one of an earnestness that doesn't take itself
seriously. The poet directly evokes the future as prospective memory—the
poem in fact depends on such evocations—but such "memories" represent alternatives and sites of potentiality, not facts set in stone. The imperative "remember" belies the forgetfulness that implicitly operates as a
second option. The emphasis is not on a single future, but rather futurity
as a set of options, capable of being forgotten or replaced by the next task
that comes to mind. Memory, when it is prospective, does not necessarily
need to be recalled.

For Berrigan, the to-do list poem can encompass even more explicit, not
just indirectly welcomed, forms of oblivion. Where Schuyler's "to-do"
lists are often tender, domestic, and familiar,[20] Berrigan's are cool and detached before they turn devastating, driving the genre to its limits as prospective memory. "Things to Do in Providence," for instance, is a poem
that moves in and out of the "to-do" form to become a meditation on how
the familial span of three generations realizes itself in the quotidian.[21]

Rather than asking whether one can forget specific intentions, the poem questions whether there are any worthy intentions to make and maintain in the first place. Thus, the motivations behind Berrigan's "to-do" list are not to be assumed but only potentially discovered (and potentially lost) through living itself. This kind of recurring existential force permeates the poet's work, manifesting itself in an ability to fast-forward through an entire life to death, so that the future-oriented nature of the genre collapses into a kind of self-elegy. The self-elegy does not memorialize or monumentalize. It instead attempts to master time by imagining, confronting, and determining the tone, value, placement, and emphasis (or lack thereof) of one's end. In poems like the aforementioned "Things to Do in New York," *Red Wagon*'s "Things to Do on Speed" and "10 Things I Do Everyday" (1976), "Memorial Day" (composed with Anne Waldman [1971]),[22] and "Things to Do in Anne's Room" (1970), Berrigan's unorthodox way of envisioning the future renders dying the ultimate prospective memory. Dying is our very last thing "to do." And yet, as the horizon of the future, one's death in the "to-do" poem can *only* be envisioned and not actually experienced. The poet evokes it, not to fulfill it, but to experience it as a kind of impossibility, as the very tension between what a poem projects and what it must ultimately leave unactualized.[23]

In "Things to Do in Providence," Berrigan turns the "to-do" poem on its head by questioning whether one can in fact advise or instruct anyone on how to live. Characteristic of New York School poetry, value in the poem is personal, with the mundane and the profound standing as equals. There is no one way "to do" one's life, besides being ready for its very passage and end. Faced with his grandmother's death, the speaker of the poem returns home in search of what to do, as well as *how* to do any given thing within the constraints of his hometown and past. Forgetting and personal history work in tandem, as the "to-do" poem becomes a force field where the poet can affectively contemplate the ephemerality of his circumstances. The speaker evokes prospective memory as what could potentially fill his time *and* as all the displaced futures that never came into fruition. In "Things to Do in Providence,"[24] Berrigan deliberately welcomes the potential hazard of forgetting that comes with this form of future-oriented remembrance:

Crash

Take valium   Sleep

Dream &

forget it.

52   **Chapter Two**

*

Wake up new & strange

displaced

at home.

Read the Providence Evening Bulletin

No one you knew

got married
had children
got divorced
died

got born

tho many familiar names flicker &
disappear

Berrigan's forgetting is transgressive and comically macabre. Playing off the trope of the pre-travel "to-do" list—most prominently, for instance, Henri Bergson gives the example of Labiche's M. Perrichon, who "makes certain of not forgetting any of his parcels: 'Four, five, six, my wife seven, my daughter eight, and myself nine' "[25]—Berrigan uses forgetting to save his speaker from the tedium of being in Providence. He induces self-oblivion with the help of Valium and later "give[s himself] the needle." Drugs lead to dreams, which denote the literal sense of thoughts one has during sleep, as well as personal aspirations or cherished goals. In the former case, they represent a point of antecedence for the forgetting self. In the latter, they refer to a prospective memory, a future that is nevertheless not worth bothering with. When Berrigan says "forget it" (a phrase that Schuyler also uses in "Things to Do When You Get a Bad Review" [1969]), he suggests that one should forget the happenings of sleep *and* abandon the whole plan of knocking oneself out. The immediate asterisk break and juxtaposition provides further evidence for the speaker's discarding of initial intentions. By waking up to a state of tabula rasa, Berrigan is able to forget and say "never mind," exchanging his first set of plans for a new compositional position ("Wake up new / & strange") in the poem. The force of Berrigan's phrasing is such that the instructions project futures that are then quickly eclipsed. Each task represents a quick remedy to the mind that is searching for something more substantial than the daily evening bulletin.

When the speaker places his own banal tasks alongside the cliché milestones of bourgeois life, one wonders about the place of possibility and fulfillment in the poet's future. One hears the monotony of a nonvarying foot in Berrigan's "& strange / displaced / at home" as well as his trisyllabic breakdown of "got married / had children / got divorced." The touchstones of middle-class life are rendered as casually and as forgettable as various interchangeable, daily activities:

> Sit
>
>   watch tv
>
>   draw blanks
>
> swallow
>   pepsi
>   meatballs
>   * * *
>   give yourself the needle:
>
>   "Shit! There's gotta be something
>   to do
>   here!"

When Berrigan exclaims, "There's gotta be something / to do / here!" the poem becomes not only a question of what one does in a place but, furthermore, what one does with one's life. Over the course of the poem, the poet seeks an answer in the commonplace, putting aside the grand plans of youth for smaller, more mundane acts like doing the laundry, reading, and taking walks. Where "draw blanks" is a form of prospective memory, it also makes unnecessary the urgency of a "to-do" list. The phrase "give yourself the needle" is likewise a future-oriented imperative, but one that weakens the rigid aims of another program, namely, the twelve-step or self-help plan. The poet foreshortens the future, replacing the long-term goal of "getting clean" with transitory remedies to occupy one's time, even aid the forgetting of time's passage.

In one of the poem's most poignant moments, the reader overhears the speaker on the phone with his mother and learns for the first time that both

54 Chapter Two

were conceived before their parents' weddings. The "unplanned" futures that the two births emblematize issue in a moment that binds mother and son. Forgetting to plan for the future represents not only the literal precondition of life but also a point of disclosure. Present discovery, in turn, does not exclude or dilute the significance of the future but simply revolves around a future that was unforeseen. As the speaker's grandmother approaches the end of her life, Berrigan writes:

> Alice Clifford waits me. Soon she'll die
> at the Greenwood Nursing Home; my mother's
> mother, 79 years & 7 months old.
>> But first, a nap, til my mother comes home
>> from work, with the car.

The moment is reminiscent of Berrigan's anaphoric poem "Wishes," written in 1971 and published in 1976, when the speaker says, "I wish death, but just not now," and the nature of wishful thinking suddenly merges with a strong willfulness to control the terms of one's death, and therefore one's life. In both cases, the very form that evokes futurity places a hold on the mentioned event. What is left for Alice Clifford to do can in fact wait. In Berrigan's contemplation of mortality, what emerges is not the falling away of futurity but a desire to continue living with the future in mind: "Living's a pleasure: / I'd like to take the whole trip / despite the possible indignities of growing old, / moving, to die in poverty, among strangers: / that can't be helped."

Through forgetting, the prospective nature of the "to-do" poem at once evokes and resists the future, not to weaken the significance of futurity, but to emphasize a shifting attitude toward it. On the one hand, deliberately forgetting past intentions could theoretically attest to "false and faulty," "insincere and broken" promises, forms of deception where there is a "practical (if not moral) dilemma."[26] On the other hand, poems by Schuyler present a more positive alternative: to make a "to-do" list only to say "Forget it!" is to offer glimpses of human connectivity, happiness, and delight in the mere imagining of a future rather than its actualization. In his breezy poem "A Picnic Cantata" (1977), the poet writes: "Oh dear, look here, / we forgot all about the radishes / and the relish." The speaker, already cleaning up and ready to leave his picnic, suggests that there *was* a plan to eat the identified goods but that he and his friends have no intention to revive it. Forgetting is a small misfortune that turns out not to be a misfortune at all. A refusal of post facto recollection, the moment represents a state of lyric pleasure. As the pun indicates, there is a "relishing" in what remains untouched and unconsumed. Both speaker and reader take satisfaction in what was overlooked and never put to use. Forgetting, rather than being coercive, evolves as a form of acceptance because the speaker refuses to pursue regret.

Both Schuyler's "December" (1969) and "The Morning of the Poem" (1980) trouble the reputed problems of forgetting by stressing its claim to either happiness or tenderness. In "December," a man falls in love with the holiday season despite his cynicism toward its overcommercialized nature. The capitalist spectacle is a perfect opportunity for protest, but the speaker comes to adore the mere sensual and decorative qualities of New York's festive accoutrements. Along the way, the poet conveys the notion that promises and prospective memories open up futures without determining or demanding their materialization:

> It's like what George and I were talking about, the East West
> Coast divide: Californians need to do a thing to enjoy it.
> A smile in the street may be loads! you don't have to undress everybody.
>   "You didn't *visit* the Alps?"
>   "No, but I saw from the train they were black
>   and streaked with snow."
> Having and giving but also catching glimpses
> hints that are revelations: to have been so happy is a promise
> and if it isn't kept that doesn't matter.[27]

As humor passes into revelation, the phrase "to have been so happy is a promise" stands out as characteristic of Schuyler and his environs. Already, the idea of forgetting one's grand plans is implicit: although Californians "need to do a thing to enjoy it," New Yorkers don't need to climb the Alps if they've seen them. They don't need to act on all acknowledgments of attraction by enticing everybody to bed. In the last two lines, the idea of future feeling emerges fully, although the speaker withholds full clarity about what is or was promised to take place in the future. Is "to have been so happy" supposed to be a promise for some unmentioned thing? Or is the speaker promising "to have been so happy"? The ambiguity arises from the confluence of tenses, of the infinitive's evocation of futurity with the pastness of the present perfect. If the speaker is promising "to have been so happy," the tense suggests that the speaker is or will be *beyond* the state of happiness (otherwise, one might promise "to be so happy"), though this state of "having been" remains relevant, as some sort of intention and wisdom. On the other hand, if the state of having been happy is meant to fulfill something in the future, it might be the case that the speaker is alluding to the possibility of future memories, the accruement

56 **Chapter Two**

of meaningful experiences one can later salvage. In either case, the next line's addendum is significant. Followed by a break, the line "and if it isn't kept that doesn't matter" rejects the conditions of promising, which include a genuine belief in a future occurrence and an obligation to "make good" on one's word. Nothing is guaranteed. To not keep a promise is to emphasize the insignificance of remembering to keep it. It is enough to have made it.

The same mode of prospective memory infuses Schuyler's opus "The Morning of the Poem." In one particularly salient passage, the speaker imagines writing an elegy for the painter Fairfield Porter, but his inability to commit to the task becomes a part of his own grieving process, his own acceptance that one cannot control fate. The recollective function of elegy thus converges with the incompleteness and rejection of closure that forgetting permits. The potential futures that were unfulfilled by the dead coincide with the speaker's own.[28] Schuyler writes:

> [...] were
> You buried in your sneakers? Of course not,
>   though in a tender joke you were:
> A nosegay tossed on the coffin: but this is not
>   your poem, your poem I may
> Never write, too much, though it is there and
>   needs only to be written down
> And one day will and if it isn't it doesn't matter:
>   the truth, the absolute
> Of feeling, of knowing what you know, that is
>   the poem[29]

The present poem allows the poet to dream up another poem without having to deal with the materialization of the latter, which, for the tender present, is still "too much": too much memory, too much pain, too much responsibility. The nonexistent elegy *is* prospective, that is, cast as a poetic possibility, but it is precisely its virtual nature, its ability to be only imagined, that serves as a contrast for Schuyler's subsequent definition of poetry and poetic sincerity: "the absolute / Of feeling, of knowing what you know." To be able to forget the future act of writing is to emphasize how writing can be a redundancy, even a superfluity, to present intention, feeling, and knowledge. The experience of the future poem is already accessible in this instance, in the sense that it is available *as* absence—as both the missed friend and the missing elegy, wedged between what is already gone and what has yet to transpire.

To know "what you know" and to sense "the absolute / Of feeling" becomes the ultimate task or responsibility of the forgetful New York School poet, even if such a task conflicts with the literal items in a "to-do" list. The tension between intentionality and realization—and the forgetting that threatens their link—is a way of thinking through the future while organizing the structure of poems. As recent as Ron Padgett's "Inaction of Shoes" (2011), the poet begins by writing, "There are many things to be done today / and it's a lovely day to do them in / Each thing a joy to do / and a joy to have done." The lines feign completion when in fact the speaker can only experience joy "because of the calm I feel / when I think about doing them." To "almost hear them say to me / Thank you for doing us" is to bring intentionality closer to realization only to slip right by it. Like shoes that travel nowhere, one ends up "Not doing anything."[30] Transforming itself into a space for desire, the poem evokes a future that stands in for possibility rather than actualization.

In Berrigan's "Things to Do in Anne's Room,"[31] a lack of realization or future recollection does not vitiate the power of intentions, plans, or prospective memories but, rather, stresses that power and willfulness of intention itself. In a series of imperatives, Berrigan paints a future that is made tangible by the power of desire itself. The speaker begins by telling himself:

> Walk right in
> > sit right down
> > > baby, let your hair hang down
> > It's on my face that hair

In contrast to this chapter's earlier examples, "Things to Do in Anne's Room" depicts its speaker as actually carrying through with the declared instructions. Soon the speaker is "on my knees," performing both speech acts and physical deeds:

> > unlace Li'l Abner
> shoes
> > place them under the bed
> > > light cigarette
> > study out the dusty bookshelves,
> > > > sweat

This "to-do" poem takes on the meticulousness of instruction, which needs to be precise if it is to be followed or reproduced by another subject. Yet the tasks also anticipate their unknown end, leaving the reader unsure of what Berrigan's commands amount to. To unlace one's shoes and place

58　Chapter Two

them beneath the bed is to evoke, figuratively or by association, the resting of poetic feet, the end of a writer's day at work. But what seems so real and realized, moment by moment, in the poem is in fact the power of intention, not execution:

>   Now I'm going to do it
>   SELF RELIANCE
>   THE ARMED CRITIC
>   MOBY DICK
>   THE WORLD OF SEX
>   THE PLANET OF THE APES
>   Now I'm going to do it
>   deliberately
>   take off clothes
>   shirt goes on the chair
>   pants go on the shirt
>   socks next to shoes next to bed
>
>   the chair goes next to the bed
>   get into bed
>   be alone
>   suffocate
>   don't die
>
>   & it's that easy.

It is the power of willing in this last section—"Now I'm going to do it" and "Now I'm going to do it / deliberately"—that in fact does what is otherwise impossible, which is to blur the future and the present, to realize the future in the present. What is forgotten is not intentionality but the very temporal distance that separates intention from execution. Intentionality appears to fulfill itself, leading the poem's speaker to somehow "suffocate" yet not die. The sense that such (im)possibilities could suddenly become actual and even "easy" becomes symbolic of the "to-do" genre's work, which is not to fulfill (and thus negate) possibility through its actualization, but to actualize possibility itself.

∗　　∗　　∗

So far, the "to-do" poem has presented forgetting the future as an inducement to poetic freedom. What happens, however, when this neglect is no longer possible, when a past intention demands to be fulfilled, and the poet is reinscribed in a system of causality? It is one thing, after all, to repress the past and another to deny that the past has imminent consequences. One could even argue that an imperative like "Forget it!" is counterproductive, making it nearly impossible to actually draw a blank. To evoke the command is to have already said too much. Rather than retreating into inconspicuousness, the phrase draws attention to what one hopes to obliviate.

Such questions, in raising notions of difficulty and will, harken back to Stein's own influence on the New York School. In a letter to Anne Waldman, the artist and writer Joe Brainard wrote: "I am still reading [Stein] on the toilet and I still find her very *difficult* and I was thinking how great it would be to hear Gertrude Stein out loud. . . . I am way, way up these days over a piece I am still writing called *I Remember*" (emphasis mine).[32] Though waves of memory would occasionally flood out of Brainard during the composition of his 1970 work—which uses the anaphora "I remember" at the start of each new paragraph—he told the poet Tom Clark that he had "practically no memory and so remembering is like pulling teeth."[33] Around the same time, in 1971, Bernadette Mayer, who was working on an extensive photography and diary project called *Memory*, said, "One of the reasons I did it [*Memory*] was to be nasty to Gertrude Stein who always said you can't write remembering, so I wanted to say that maybe you could. [. . .] But in a spirit of fun, I was doing it *with* Gertrude Stein."[34]

In the above statements, Stein serves as an impetus for not only Brainard's and Mayer's "emotional science"[35] experiments but also their exploration of memory as an index for psychological effort, for either "pulling teeth" or having "fun." Georges Perec, who admired Brainard and admitted to being "afraid of forgetting," once noted that "nothing seems easier than to draw up a list, in actual fact it's far more complicated than it appears; you always forget something."[36] The apparent simplicity of writing a list belied, for Perec, the effort involved in remembering and the "ease" of omission. Yet, it could be argued that this was precisely why Brainard could go on to generate two more volumes of *I Remember*: there was always something he had forgotten in the last iteration, always something to return to. Despite the difficulty of voluntary recollection, waiting for things to "gush up" was something Brainard could be "happy about."[37] Padgett, in his afterword to the cult classic, notes that Brainard was a "hard worker" but that "the beauty of it all is that Joe made it [writing the book] look so easy. And in some ways it is."[38] The relative facility of Brainard's *I Remember* stands in contrast to Stein's work—which demanded from the reader what Ashbery called "almost physical pain"[39]—as well as Mayer's dense and maximal project. Brainard captures

60 **Chapter Two**

memory's discreteness, whereas Mayer registers the compulsiveness of the mind. *Memory*, eventually published in 1975, is not only about retrieving past memories but also *creating* them, about preserving the present with tomorrow in mind. For Brainard, forgetting was something that had already occurred. For Mayer, it was something anticipatory: one had to catch things before they slipped away.

The added aspect of recording to remembrance at times led Mayer to periods of overwhelming panic. Not only was the monthlong project of *Memory* responsible for the retention of a recent past and present; it was also responsible for everything the poet had forgotten, or might forget, to do: "Chance it's morning you forget to see blue you leave it out [...] a man & a woman went by you forget to see green you stare at green you wait to stare at green & in the country you see red." And later: "You leave it out you forget to see red [...] & so fatiguing you rest a specific area of the retina you see."[40] Such moments of concentration followed by fatigue are palpable as one senses the tremendous effort behind the work. Play is followed by exhaustion. In both *Memory* and its follow-up, *Studying Hunger*—which Mayer completed in 1972 and published in 1975—the exertion behind recording intentions at times renders the project a broken record. The sentences "I try to forget &— / I try to forget &" falter and are left incomplete.[41] Mayer records her desire to "oppose MEMORIES" and "to do this without remembering," but she cannot actually stop accumulating "data."[42] Sleep is often the speaker's only reprieve. In *Memory*, Mayer writes: "A process fills its old bed & then it makes a new bed: to you past structure is backwards, you forget, you remember the past backwards & forget."[43] In *Studying Hunger*: "This form is a list / of what I have to do / a long length / of short lines / I fell asleep," "forget any substance of meaning, forget substantives, their color, get it gradually paler, seeing sound vibrations in sleep-closed eyes."[44] The struggle to record is also the struggle to stay awake, to confront and write through the wish for cessation.

Mayer's projects thus push the work of documentation to a certain cognitive limit. Memory is not a recording device so much as it forms the subject of poetry's recording abilities. I mention her and Brainard not to deviate from my primary topic, but to suggest that there can be an account of forgetting by New York poets who famously wrote about remembering. Poetic projects can specifically intend to forget or to not forget. But these intentions do not always predict their own consequences, what surfaces within their constraints. As a catalyst for surprise, forgetting materializes even in books purportedly about memory, as they end up undoing their own premises. If, for Mayer, the impossible question is how to keep going, how to take in as much as possible, the question for someone like Ash-

Forget It! Poetry Makes Nothing Happen   61

bery is whether or not *forgetting* can be sustained. For the latter, "to leave all out" is always desired as a purer, truer way of being, but it is also unattainable for the historical subject. It is this impossibility that I want to tarry with for the remainder of the chapter. Shot through with amnesiac desire, Ashbery's poems ride up against the difficulties of willing ignorance rather than the facility of omission. In doing so, they underscore writing's thorny relationship to will and desire, the limits of poetry as it attempts liberation from compulsory commands.

Again and again in his early work, forgetting undergirds Ashbery's vocabulary and range of feeling: there is "that sound like the wind / Forgetting in the branches that means something"; the famous lacustrine cities that "grew out of loathing / Into something forgetful"; the "making ready to forget" and "wondering whether forgetting / the whole thing might not, in / the end be the only solution"; and the idea that "we are being called back / for having forgotten these names."[45] Intentionality, too, is omnipresent, but often located somewhere external to the poet. Manifesting itself as the intention of history or "'the system' of modern life,"[46] intention binds and dictates the future in a way that is far greater than any individual. The future is the project of the past, the time of realizing consequences. It confronts, however, a singular counterforce or what Ashbery calls a "private project": the poet and his desire for oblivion.[47] Forgetting operates as resistance, but a weak one in the face of larger powers.

One of Ashbery's own "to-do" poems marks the very shift from a rejection of plans, wishes, and fantasies to the impossible fantasy of forgetting itself. At first glance, his canonical "The Instruction Manual," composed in 1955, seamlessly embodies the genre's paradoxes. The task of writing an instruction manual is "to do" a "to-do book," a task that the speaker then turns away from in the name of alternative wishes, affective journeys, and daydreams. Where manuals tend to favor regularity, mechanical correctness, and rule-abiding structures, Ashbery's poem is excessive in its lush spiritedness. Composed while the poet was writing and editing college textbooks in the employment of McGraw-Hill, "The Instruction Manual" is in many ways an anti-"to-do" poem. The poet names his task not to achieve it, but to forget it in the name of another set of experiences. What begins as a work assignment transforms into a travel guide instructing us how to forget, escape, and feel. Ashbery begins:

As I sit looking out of a window of the building
I wish I did not have to write the instruction manual on the uses of a new
    metal.

62 **Chapter Two**

> I look down into the street and see people, each walking with an inner
>   peace,
> And envy them—they are so far away from me!
> Not one of them has to worry about getting out this manual on schedule.
> And, as my way is, I begin to dream, resting my elbows on the desk and
>   leaning out of the window a little,
> Of dim Guadalajara! City of rose-colored flowers!
> City I wanted most to see, and most did not see, in Mexico!
> But I fancy I see, under the press of having to write the instruction
>   manual,
> Your public square, city, with its elaborate little bandstand!

The instruction manual interrupts the speaker's state of reverie numerous times, heightening the tension between a given assignment and the poet's imaginative task. What the textbook employee *must* do is what creates the space for what he wishes he *could* do, which in turn reveals what the *poet* must do. Each step of the poem's efflorescence entails and depends on the speaker's own exclusion from his vision ("they are so far away from me!" "City I wanted most to see, and most did not see, in Mexico!"). The speaker's objective is not to recall one's immediate prospective memory, thereby affirming one's professional identity, but to neglect both aspects.

If the poem is the antithesis of an instruction manual, the feeling that is opened up by "forgetting to do" nevertheless becomes a valid alternative to completing one's job. Here, Ashbery's interests veer closest to Stein's atelic actions—knowing, being, and feeling. In his review of Stein's nonnarrative writing, which was fittingly entitled "The Impossible" (1957), Ashbery observed that "*Stanzas in Meditation* gives one the feeling of time passing, of things happening, of a 'plot,' though it would be difficult to say precisely what is going on. Sometimes the story has the logic of a dream."[48] His examples of this sensation included two lines by the modernist involving misremembrance: "he asked could I be taught to be allowed / And I said yes oh yes I had forgotten him." Drawing on Stein's influence in "The Instruction Manual," Ashbery replaces the straightforward narrative of the "to-do" plot with the forgetful logic of *day*dream. His speaker doesn't just observe; he admires, fantasizes, appreciates, connects, listens, and wonders throughout the poem. For the speaker to feel the excitement of Guadalajara in "The Instruction Manual" is for the speaker to become overwhelmed with sensations, to forget necessity, to be too distracted to get anything done. This is the privilege of the traveler, the man of leisure, but it is also, paradoxically, the "job" of the poet. Affiliated with travel literature, where traditionally "instructions issued by those who stay at home have not always been followed" and travelers have instead tended to "follow their instincts and opportunities, rather than directions from home,"[49] the liberties of the "to-do" genre include being able to neglect one's origins, to wander off, and to explore the future as a province for the unknown.

As the speaker loses track of his initial prospective memory, Ashbery's language increasingly trades in the language of instruction and rigidity for the delights of indiscriminate inquisitiveness:

> The couples are parading; everyone is in a holiday mood.
> First, leading the parade, is a dapper fellow
> Clothed in deep blue. On his head sits a white hat
> And he wears a mustache, which has been trimmed for the occasion.
> . . . .
> Let us take this opportunity to tiptoe into one of the side streets.
> Here you may see one of those white houses with green trim
> That are so popular here. Look—I told you!
> It is cool and dim inside, but the patio is sunny.

Rather than following "first" with "second" and "third," Ashbery produces decorative excess through his well-documented uses of digression and distraction. When the speaker employs directives like "Look" or elsewhere "Wait," he is not instructing us to actually look or wait, but, rather, telling us to navigate an affective terrain marked by curiosity, romance, and surprise. Such affects exist in the grammar itself, in the poet's use of exclamation marks (there are a total of ten) and parentheticals. To travel with feeling is to redirect initial wonder toward gradations of pain and pleasure. And yet, within this emotional range, the speaker also teaches the reader how to relax, how to *let go of* or even forget one's feelings, modifying them with varying temporal exposure, intensity, association, and resemblance. Feeling in Ashbery's travel guide involves maintaining a casualness without letting it tip into casualty. One feels wonder, fancy, and nostalgia without engaging the stronger and arguably more negative feelings of shock, jealousy, or despair. The relaxation one experiences in Guadalajara affirms the poem's suggestion that there is arguably nothing "to do" there. Things and people are busy only in the way nature is busy—busy being. "The breeze ruffles her long fine black hair against her olive cheek."

By the poem's end, "to do" nothing emerges precisely as the poet's task—with forgetting at once lubricating non-activity and constituting this poetic remit. Yet the speaker's freedom remains a short-lived fantasy. Par-

64 **Chapter Two**

ticularly salient to Ashbery's work is an impossibility that operates as the horizon of the poem:

> What more is there to do, except stay? And that we cannot do.
> And as a last breeze freshens the top of the weathered old tower, I turn
>   my gaze
> Back to the instruction manual which has made me dream of
>   Guadalajara.

Just as the traditional travel narrative concludes by bringing its protagonist home, Ashbery returns his speaker's gaze to the instruction manual. The poet reasserts the "to-do" poem as a constraint that is as real as the temporary transcendence of it. Rather than employing the genre to dismantle its hold on the future, the poet grasps that his speaker's fantasy remains a possibility only in the face of the actuality of his mundane project. The inextricability of one future from another is generative of the bittersweet pathos that pervades Ashbery's poetic world, a borderline realm in which one has to learn to live "between the lives we have and the lives we would like."[50] Futurity always remains on the far side of this "in-between" space. The poem is what offers a view of it, a feeling toward the future without necessarily collapsing the distance between it and the present.

Forgetting in Ashbery's world is thus twofold: on the one hand, it preserves the feeling that the poet had experienced while reading Stein, the sense that "it is still possible to accomplish the impossible."[51] On the other hand, it achieves this suspension effect by taking the form of procrastination. To forget that tomorrow will arrive is to pretend one can reverse the directionality of time itself, to transform the state of waiting from one of killing hours to buying more of them. It is to pretend that in the face of running out of time, one can simply lose track of it instead. Oblivion is thus motivated by the desire to relieve the present from looming deadlines at the very same time it emerges as a symptom of the knowledge that those consequences are real. This forgetting is always a desired attempt, followed by a painful eclipse. It brings the poet closer to a guaranteed failure while raising the question of whether a lost cause can still be meaningful. The poet who seeks to turn away from history looks forward only to find the fast approach of all that has transpired. Nevertheless, it is significant that Ashbery still exercises a desire and attempt to forget, since what is predetermined and imminent does not preclude the *sense* or *feeling* of being able to think and act freely in the present. Fate may be written in stone, but it also has to be lived, and living (at least in modernity) is never felt as if it is fated. This very condition of false feeling ends up exposing the tragic underside of the poet's desire for oblivion. Implicit in Ashbery's forgetting is a desire to uphold a presentist and phenomenological view of time against an eternalist framework that says the past, present, and future all already exist as set realities.

In "The Ecclesiast"—composed in 1962 and published three separate times in the sixties—the poet struggles to come to terms with the future's inevitable arrival. Such a grappling is characteristic of Ashbery's ubiquitous sense of cultural lateness and what Ann Keniston has described as that lateness's rhetorical strategy: the chronicling of "impossible and distorted chronologies," the refusal of closure or resolution, and the "insisting on repetition or prolepsis, the last of which creates artificial situations of remembering."[52] (By way of Ben Hutchinson's work, one might even conceive of Ashbery as "the last man," hence the poet's assertion "It is late to be late" in *Some Trees*.[53]) The poet's longing for obliviousness, however, differs from Edward Said's theory of late style, which posits an aggressive refusal to abdicate art's right in favor of life's finiteness. It is true, as Said says, that lateness is the dilemma of "being at the end, fully conscious, full of memory."[54] Amnesia, however, serves as a kind of deus ex machina to this denouement. Like sleep, it folds its own mimesis of death, but without pain, into an earlier stage of life: the innocent newborn who has no memories at all. Forgetting, in other words, is not a breach of life's cycle but a mode of illusory continuation—not from life to death, which consists of the making and accumulation of memory, but from death to life, which is its very reversal. It is significant that Ashbery's desire to divert his gaze from a future that is culminating is not enabled by an *actual* belief that forgetting can conquer temporality. Rather, what he seeks is a larger system that might accommodate and synthesize the very conflict between the freedom permitted by forgetting and the inevitability of its failure against time. This system is poetic language.

Giving expression to the vanity of life and all human agency, labor, and effort, "The Ecclesiast" veers between dream logic, detailed juxtapositions, and depictions of the apocalyptic alongside the nostalgic. Though it is initially easy to overlook the place of forgetting, the poet prepares the conditions for oblivion from the start:

"Worse than the sunflower," she had said.
But the new dimension of truth had only recently
Burst in on us. Now it was to be condemned.
And in vagrant shadow her mothball truth is eaten.
In cool, like-it-or-not shadow the humdrum is consumed.
Tired housewives begat it some decades ago,
A small piece of truth that if it was honey to the lips
Was also millions of miles from filling the place reserved for it.

Chapter Two

You see how honey crumbles your universe
Which seems like an institution—how many walls?

Then everything, in her belief, was to be submerged
And soon. There was no life you could live out to its end
And no attitude which, in the end, would save you.
The monkish and the frivolous alike were to be trapped
in death's capacious claw[55]

Characteristically Ashberyian, the poem's opening puts into motion a pattern of using the passive and future tense.[56] Both features work in tandem to construct the very conditions that eventually yield the desire to forget the future *and* dictate its impossibility. For one, the passive tense—"is eaten," "is consumed," and later "were made," "is ended"—withholds agency, creating a sense of predetermination. A greater force is at work without the poet explicitly mentioning what or who that force is. Things occur, but not by the will of the subject. The power of the future and the future past, alternatively, lies in their elicitation of prospective memory. In phrases like "was to be condemned," "was to be submerged," and later "you shall never have seen," "tomorrow you'll weep," and "that is to be your one reward," the speaker expresses intentions and plans that have yet to be, or were not, completed, leaving the temporal placement of the poem's present ambiguous.

These conditions are vital to the forgetting that transpires because they raise the question of forgetting's mixed voluntariness and involuntariness, the question of personal agency amidst larger societal plans. As the poet blurs the distant past with more recent occurrences and the impending future, the temporal position of the poem shifts along with its existential position. A sentence like "Then everything, in her belief, was to be submerged / And soon" makes uncertain whether the submergence has already been successful, whether it remains imminent, or whether such a belief was wrong in the first place. The possibility of this last situation—that what was to happen never did or will—reveals an indeterminacy within the poem. On the one hand, the future as told from the present establishes certainty from the speaker's point of view; on the other hand, this premonitory knowledge seems to offer a way out. Since the speaker knows what will happen, can't they use this information to stop or change what will occur? Knowing the future while the future has not yet occurred opens up the present as something distinct from that very destination. The present measures itself against the advent of the future.

As one moves deeper in the poem, the key, emergent question is whether one can acknowledge an end time that renders all things worthless while holding on to the "special meaning" of lived experience. Typically, conclusions impose judgments of meaning by making prominent closure and totality, but the opposite is true in "The Ecclesiast." Here, closure is the *start* of meaninglessness, weeping, and condemnation. Only does meaning exist prior to the poem; it is something that has been recalled and retold. One can't hold on to meaning without realizing the tragedy of its ill-timed nature and impurity:

> But listen while I tell you about the wallpaper—
> There was a key to everything in that oak forest
> But a sad one. Ever since childhood there
> Has been this special meaning to everything.
> You smile at your friend's joke, but only later, through tears.
>
> For the shoe pinches, even though it fits perfectly.
> Apples were made to be gathered, also the whole host of the
>   world's ailments and troubles.
> There is no time like the present for giving in to this temptation.
> Tomorrow you'll weep—what of it? There is time enough
> Once the harvest is in and the animals put away for the winter
> To stand at the uncomprehending window cultivating the desert
> With salt tears which will never do anyone any good.
> My dearest I am as a galleon on salt billows.
> Perfume my head with forgetting all around me.

Memory's misfortune has its belatedness to blame. Recollection creates a breach between living and the reflection of living by throwing into relief the latter. To "smile at your friend's joke, but only later, through tears" is to describe the bittersweet posterity of retrospection. Ashbery describes a shoe that fits perfectly except for the fact that it also pinches. He names a forest that has a melody, albeit a sad one, apples that can be gathered but only with "ailments and troubles." The predicament of desiring one kind of past without its inevitable fate and implications re-poses the question Maurice Blanchot once put forth: "Something has disappeared. How can I recover it, how can I turn around and look at what exists *before*, if all my power consists of making it into what exists *after*?"[57] Nostalgia is language's condition at the same time that language is future oriented in bringing poetic works into creation. The world that the poem and its maker exist in is no longer the world as it once stood; and who else but the poet is responsible for this? By ushering in the poem's newfound life, by

68 Chapter Two

letting poetic consciousness intrude, the writer cannot return to halcyon days. Looking forward is therefore an essential part of making, but because Ashbery's future is one that must really confront "death's capacious claw," there is a desire to forget this fact. If only the poem could both write and erase itself—if only the speaker could induce his own oblivion—then all complicit parties might be spared the consequences of their nature.

When Ashbery's speaker says, "There is no time like the present for giving in to this temptation," he acknowledges future consequences only to diminish consequentiality's significance, appealing to the sensibility of "to-do" list poems. Just as the rhetorical question "Tomorrow you'll weep—what of it?" dismisses what's forthcoming and the power of regret, so too does the futurity that renders tears futile ("which will never do anyone any good") turn into an expression of comfort by the speaker. And yet, consolation is a strictly human endeavor. It is not only different from help; it emerges and exists precisely because man *cannot* be helped. Consolation, as it has been said, "lets suffering remain but, so to speak, abolishes the suffering from suffering."[58] Forgetting the future, then, is a way of lessening pain as much as it is a way of realizing poetry's simultaneous capacity for comfort and inability to create change.

The request to enter a state of oblivion arrives most explicitly at the stanza's end: "Perfume my head with forgetting all around me." The line is grammatically an imperative but affectively a plea. To render forgetting as a kind of perfume is to render it as a kind of lingering in the present, an opiate that alleviates difficult sensations, diffusing through time and space. A perfume of forgetting breaks down the clear boundaries between past, present, and future while expanding the horizon of consequence. The phrase "all about me" evokes images of self-forgetfulness, the dissolution of one's own orientation in time and space. Significantly, the line also marks a turning point in the poem. Before, the "you" of "The Ecclesiast" had functioned as a kind of substitute for the speaker's own self. It had served as a device for monologuing. The line beginning with "Perfume my head," however, expresses a gesture toward a truly other addressee. Because one cannot command forgetting on one's own, one must invoke someone or something else. Forgetting can only come about through the gift or will of another.

For Ashbery, forgetting means both escape and relief from a painful fate. By the end of "The Ecclesiast," the poet mentions the projects of history a second time, suggesting that prospective memories have been recalled. But in this reiteration, Ashbery's dialogic other appears beyond his own life. Forgetting has made a kind of dying bearable, ironically survivable:

[...]
Perfume my head with forgetting all around me.

For some day these projects will return.
The funereal voyage over ice-strewn seas is ended.
You wake up forgetting. Already
Daylight shakes you in the yard.
The hands remain empty. They are constructing an osier basket
Just now, and across the sunlight darkness is taking root anew
In intense activity. You shall never have seen it just this way
And that is to be your one reward.

Fine vapors escape from whatever is doing the living.
The night is cold and delicate and full of angels
Pounding down the living. The factories are all lit up,
The chime goes unheard,
We are together at last, though far apart.

The poet has invoked a funereal voyage. He has described a busy "they," but one that is not perceived by the "you" who wakes up forgetting. The key sentence—"You shall never have seen it just this way / And that is to be your one reward"—suggests a perspective of being on the other side of a person's history or life, since it is being delivered by a speaker who has omniscience over what *isn't* in store for his dialogic other. Moreover, the latter's reward is the very *absence* of those memories that constitute Ashbery's images. Forgetting *is* achieved, but only for a self that is no longer the poet, a self that belongs to language alone. The irony of the poem therefore lies in the fact that the poet can neither be granted the perfume of forgetfulness nor self-induce a state of blankness. He can, however, give forgetfulness away.

When it takes the form of a trapped feedback loop, wanting to forget calls to mind the very thing one hopes to suppress in the act of suppression. The structures of Ashbery's poems often enact this: their nonlinear nature is not only due to the fact that the future is both before and behind the speaker as the past's, but also because the primary speaker is unable to forget or move on in the time of the poem. Tracing the temporal movement in "The Ecclesiast," one sees that it cycles through the past, present, and future numerous times—and in various orders—before the fourth stanza, at which point the speaker requests forgetting and the present becomes the dominant temporal mode. The recursive nature of the poem's situation

70 **Chapter Two**

manifests itself in the paradoxes of forgetting. The same conditions that produce the desire for oblivion also prohibit its actualization, thus causing forgetting to oscillate between being a personal exercise of will against the arrival of the future and being a result of it. If we recall Ricoeur's notion of memory and forgetting—he says recollection takes place when the past is truly distinct from the present, truly "other"—we see that Ashbery's past does not have enough of the "otherness" that would otherwise usher it into this category. Rather, the past is constantly assimilating the terms of the future, while the present behaves as both a mediation and a buffer to prevent complete integration and collapse.

The poetic present struggles to define itself as truly separate from the past and the future, that is, from causes and their effects, intentions and their realizations. It struggles to define itself as free—and to define that struggle as freedom itself. However, just as the poem's internal speaker exercises the desire to forget in order to finalize its separation from causality, so too does he confuse the *feeling* of present freedom with actual freedom. In other words, while the ability to remember an intention without acting upon it might indicate strong resistance or liberation in another poem by another poet, it is not so in "The Ecclesiast." Ashbery's speaker remembers the past and, by doing so, demonstrates knowledge of what will occur. Such knowledge of what will happen, of what is "already" (intended) and "not yet" (realized), is the very same knowledge that brings about a secondary knowledge of its own potential uselessness. When past plans are capable of being recalled but not yet acted out, the present cannot do anything with what it knows except try to *un*-know by forgetting. Tellingly, both of the poem's speakers end up outside the living present. The initial speaker asks for forgetfulness, potentially as a form of death, while the second speaker eventually ends up outside the very situation where projects return, speaking from an apparent point of omniscience or eternity. Such a commonality explains the first and only "We" in "The Ecclesiast," which appears "together" yet "far apart" at the end of the poem, positioned against and outside of a living world of "they."

While a considerable amount of time has been spent on "The Ecclesiast," it is not always the case that forgetting the future is, for Ashbery, bound up in a tragic attempt to escape closure, vanity, or regret. The protagonist in "The Thief in Poetry" (1977) says, "the future still makes plans"[59]—that is, plans to arrive and occur regardless of the individual—but one's attitude toward this need not be despairing. In *Flow Chart* (1991), Ashbery writes:

> who knows what may happen? In the meantime, look sharp, and sharply at
>   what is around you; there is

always the possibility something may come of something, and that is our fondest wish though it says here I'm not supposed to say so [...][60]

Here, the future's inevitability permits happy forgetting: why worry about what one can't control? The tone comes closer to the poetic register of Schuyler's work, as the speaker exchanges the problem of "what may happen" for a present that is simply "the meantime." There is optimism, but it takes the form of a wishful thinking. And though the speaker expresses his wish for a "fond" future, that wish is not impervious and remains qualified: "though it says here I'm not supposed to say so."

In his biographical note in the anthology *A Controversy of Poets* (1965), Ashbery states that he would like his work to be as convincing in form yet elusive in content as music, so that "what remains is the structure, the architecture of the argument, scene or story." He continues:

I would like to do this in poetry. I would also like to reproduce the power dreams have of persuading you that a certain event has a meaning not logically connected with it, or that there is a hidden relation among disparate objects. But actually this is only a part of what I want to do, and I am not even sure I want to do it. I often change my mind about poetry. [...] I would prefer not to think I had any special aims in mind.[61]

Often edited out by critics, Ashbery's last few sentences provide as much insight into his "goals" as his more straightforward comments on musicality and structure do. Ashbery reveals what he would like to do only to forget the necessary retrieval of his own intention: "I am not even sure I want to do it." The sentiment is a reminder of the poet's ever-present velleity, a weaker version of Berrigan's "Forget it!" It attends Ashbery's conceptualization of conditional desire as distinct from desire proper. The former is less assertive, more involved in a future that remains bound by unreal or imaginary circumstances. Conditional desire is contingent on certain external scenarios, anticipating an "if" or a "but." By contrast, to want is to will in a way that is more tightly bound to results; it binds and commits one to the object of desire. In the case of wanting, external factors and scenarios do not cause one's desires to be more flexible or forgettable but, instead, directly anticipate the victorious feeling of fulfillment or harrowing disappointment of one's wants.

When it comes to how forgetting the future manifests itself in the tone and character of individual poems, much depends on what is remembered or being planned as prospective memory. Yet, if there is anything to unite the poets in this chapter, it is that, first, memory is not simply isolated to the past and that, second, plans and promises *are* made, contrary to usual thought. Forgetting the future is a way of establishing or finding the proper attitude toward the conditions of these plans, and also a way of positioning oneself rhetorically or stylistically in a poem.[62] Forgetting's meaning ranges from the revision of intention to the rejection of someone else's proposals. It entails a degree of distraction or procrastination as a way to dream up future alternatives. Stylistically, the imperative, conditional, future, and future perfect tense all play a role in its conveyance. Whereas a heterogeneous list can be the result of digressing from one plan to another, it may also be the case that digression goes beyond embellishment to protest or belie the nothingness of vanity. In what follows, the sociality of New York School poetry and the question of genre continue to provide headway into forgetting by discovering a conversant in a radically different poet: Lyn Hejinian.

"Obvious Oblivion" and Lyn Hejinian's Comic Affirmation

[CHAPTER THREE]

Where fate may highlight the tragedy of our inability to repress or recall on command, comedy's various fortunes may be more welcoming of our attempts and failures to forget. In 2001, between the publication of her prose-poem autobiographical sequence *My Life* (1980) and its follow-up, *My Life in the Nineties* (2003), the Bay Area experimental poet Lyn Hejinian published her book-length poem *A Border Comedy*. Composed of fifteen digressive sections, each a continuous yet nonlinear meditation on topics as wide ranging as ghosts, laughter, and geese, the self-titled comedy arose from an idiosyncratic process of forgetful memory.[1] Because Hejinian, best known for her association with Language poetry, was "having trouble making the line unfamiliar to herself,"[2] she began to work on all fifteen books of *A Border Comedy* at the same time. The key to her composition was forgetting—not by *not* generating the work, but by *adding more* of it. "There was a gap of about a week between sessions of work on any one book, with the result that I was always slightly disoriented, always alighting in territory whose conditions I'd forgotten or had never had time to learn," Hejinian observed. "In order to keep writing fresh the memory of it has to fade. Unfamiliar, it is 'of the moment.'"[3] Like the Surrealist method of "exquisite corpse," forgetting here was a contraption for writing. A way of defamiliarizing yesterday's work, it was not about cutting out material but, rather, producing and accumulating it. It guaranteed that Hejinian would remain uncertain about the direction of her work; it put her in a perpetual border zone.[4]

The intentional enforcement of these compositional blind spots might be surprising given that Hejinian is typically known for the ways "a woman writer remembers."[5] Upon the success of *My Life* and its expanded versions in 1987 and 2003, critics began focusing on the author's experimentation with postmodern autobiography. The revision of recollection as forgetful

74 **Chapter Three**

thus begs the question of genre. Why, we might ask, would a writer best known for poetic autobiography turn to comedy? After all, as Sianne Ngai has noted in summarizing Agnes Heller's work, "no past oriented emotion seems [. . .] central to comic experience."[6] In this chapter, I want to propose that the question—in redrawing the traditional dichotomy between comedy and tragedy to interrogate the relationship between comedy and autobiography—does less to pose an opposition than to introduce a gradual transformation in Hejinian's work, whereby an earlier negative critique of "essentialist self-reflection"[7] is replaced by something positive: the assertion of a world outside oneself. Forgetting, I argue, tracks this process, finding a natural expression in comedy. In turn, comedy capsizes oblivion's usual associations with loss, error, suppression, and privation, replacing them with *worldliness, excess, affirmation, sociality*, and *surprise*.

* * *

A redrawing of generic categories along the lines of forgetting and memory might begin with *A Border Comedy*'s very title. A writer other than Hejinian may very well have chosen to express dislocations of time through "a border *tragedy*." In the last chapter, Ashbery's sense of oblivion was suffused with the melancholy of simultaneous desire and impossibility. In the Anglo-Scottish tradition of Border ballads, dialogue and brief narrative often come together to depict the pain of political violence, treachery, and bereavement. Yet borders, like those between forgetting and recalling, or forgetting and forgetting more, are comic, not tragic, in Hejinian's world. Following the ideas of Bergson, a border—what feigns clear delineation—actually marks the convergence of two situations, two possible sets of explanations, capable of coincidence and confusion. The result is what the philosopher calls a "reciprocal interference of series."[8] A single situation, in belonging to two series of events, produces more than one potential interpretation of meanings. Capable of mix-up, it gives rise to comic misunderstanding.

In the decade and a half leading up to *A Border Comedy*, Hejinian's obsession with borders allowed her to increasingly traffic in comedy. A loosening up of her language had led her to feel that "my poems are somewhat clumsy," but that she was also "finally doing in poetry what I have thought I should do—it's all exploration and inquisition at this point for me."[9] This feeling, which was arguably a comic one in line with forgetting's at times uncontrollable agency, became most apparent when, from 1983 to 1991, the poet visit the USSR seven times. Those visits included extended stays in Leningrad with the poet Arkadii Dragomoshchenko, whom Hejinian would eventually translate, and his wife, Lina. As a foreigner, Hejinian experienced the "dizziness"[10] of trying to recontextualize every word, thing, or person she encountered. The creative result of this vertigo was a hybrid work straddling generic borders, a novel-in-verse called *Oxota* (1991). "I had told Arkadii that I wanted to write a 'Russian novel'; he and our friends found the thought terrifically amusing. [. . .] I carried a notebook with me and wrote down everything that people told me to put into my novel," Hejinian recalled.[11] Already, the "terrifically amusing" work marked a shift away from *My Life*'s meditative nature toward a more gregarious work with a larger cast of real-life characters. The multiplicity of subjects was important for Hejinian, as she and her contemporaries rejected the binary positionality of the us/them, West/East division that had defined the Cold War. With the possibility of numbers came Hejinian's prospect of comedy. In *Oxota* she writes, "Women do have a sense of humor / And a sense of utensil," playing on the proximity of the domestic "utensil" to "utility"[12] and adding to this a number of jokes regarding cultural difference: "Our Russian workers like to dig holes, Arkadii said, while Americans prefer machines that scoop."[13] "A Soviet Faulkner, A Soviet Rilke / there are constant predicates and variable subjects."[14] "If there can be socialist realism then there can surely be / bourgeois lyricism."[15] Using the gimmick of a switcheroo, Hejinian was discovering a more abrupt rhythm: "I felt the proof of points but no continuum."[16]

Comedy, as Hejinian subscribes to it, is thus less about what makes something funny than how it relates to art-making and the world. Rather than being a method of clarifying and organizing things, it "admits the disorderly into the realm of art."[17] Such disorder, however, is less destructive than it is creative, less troubling than it is happy. In fact, in her 2001 review of Hejinian's work *Happily*, Marjorie Perloff offers an account of the etymological kinship of "happy" with the verb "happen"—*hap* being the Old English word for "chance or fortune," as seen in mis*haps* and *hap*hazard. Linking happiness with presence, she argues that a book like *Happily* "is less a memory piece than an ode to a happy contingency."[18] For anyone familiar with Hejinian's poetics, the critic's words call to mind the poet's chronic phrase "this is happening," which refers not only to deictic contextualization but also to a conscious experience of experience as it occurs. Happiness is thus only a short step away from comedy's perfectly timed surprises and forgetting's presentism. As Hejinian would soon discover, failures in recall could serve as opportunities for comedic interruptions, moments of déjà vu, and lucky accidents.

Such an awareness of what is presently happening refers to Hejinian's more general inheritance of Stein as a "comic writer," someone who once told Charlie Chaplin that she would like to see him turn street corners over and over again. The modernist's "funniness has something to do with the vibrational movement that she achieved," Hejinian once wrote. "She is often in mood amused."[19] Indeed, in the abbreviated title of *A Border Comedy* (ABC), there is a Steinian quality of simplicity and beginning again. And at one point in her book-length poem, Hejinian even writes, "I'll continue, to the left and to the left."[20] Yet, while Stein's vibrational poetics was meant to detach subjects from their backgrounds—the goal being "an intensity of movement so great that it has not to be seen against something else to be known"[21]—Hejinian's work does not mean to eliminate contexts but to shift between them. The result is that the writer's position is not one of single-mindedness, in which the author's mind seems to be cut off from any precedence, but relationality and multiplication. Stein's goal was to be like none other. Hejinian's, coming from a Marxist and feminist background, is to be *with* others and to be *othered*.

Such an emphasis on plurality over singularity is the passport with which the traditional differences between comedy and tragedy can be mapped onto the differences I am posing between comedy and autobiography. Critics have often noted that tragedy "requires a sense of individuality"[22] and that "the tragic stage is the inner one."[23] In a tragic world, all vices and traits are subsumed by the character themself, who in turn tends to universalize their situation through individualization (becoming a stand-in for all of humankind). In a comic world, characters are subject to the influence of vices and fortunes larger than the individuals. (For this reason, it has been argued that under the forces of late capitalism, we tend to view all tragedies as being at risk of being parodied.) As Robert Heilman writes, the scene of comedy is "an immediate world [. . .] where the conflicts are not between impulse and imperatives that are elements of the psyche but between individuals who are elements of society."[24] Moreover, the genre particularizes, calling attention to local, cultural, or national contexts. It is the variety of details implicit in comedy that puts it at the threshold of chaos and lawlessness—law, by contrast, being that which generalizes and unites. By transcending the borders of selfhood through forgetting, Hejinian resists the idea that all experiences can be subsumed or generalized under one orderly rule (or a person's life). By the same token, it is precisely the transgression of one experience, context, or set of characters to another that highlights the fact that no matter what, the poet is always bound *to* experience. This is a vitally human position, as opposed to a divine one. In tragedy, boundedness belongs to and within the self and represents the failure of the individual at its highest powers to defeat the limits of their own career. In comedy, boundedness to experience includes and highlights the external world.

To put it another way, the power of forgetting to structure genre is as follows: In its improperness and accidental qualities, its disruption of identity and temporal flow, forgetting indexes a shift from individuality (the core of autobiography) to sociality (the core of comedy), from what Bergson calls the "depths of [one's] own nature" and an effort at "inner observation" to something directed outward.[25] Whereas autobiography focuses on constructing—or, in Hejinian's case, deconstructing—a specific self through the curation of intentionally meaningful details, comedy relies on a sense of worldliness created by external mistakes and foibles, accidents and fortune, not one protagonist but various personalities. Comedy thus not only "helps us test or figure out what it means to say 'us,'"[26] thereby constituting a form of in-group solidarity, but is also inflected by forgetting as a social act of othering. Splitting and multiplying the self into various perspectives, forgetting turns "I" into "you" or even the more radical, plural other "they."[27] Hejinian's comedic world replaces self-discovery with the discovery of others, fragmentation with plenitude. It elevates amnesia's status from a negative and secondary aspect of memory to an essential turbine for poetic creation. As will become clear, the divergences between autobiography and comedy nevertheless find common ground in Hejinian's commitment to both as genres of realism.

*   *   *

As this chapter's main focus, *A Border Comedy* arguably represents a high point in Hejinian's harnessing of forgetting's energy, what Rae Armantrout once identified as the former's "freewheeling" style.[28] But the work was not entirely spontaneous, and it participates in a longer trajectory in the poet's development. To contextualize the 2001 book within a wider oeuvre, I have already mentioned the ways in which *Oxota* and *Happily* were natural stepping-stones to discovering the humor in dislocation and the comic presentism of what Hejinian called the "fence of forgetting."[29] But aspects of forgetful memory are also central to two other textual precursors. As early as her first collection, *Writing Is an Aid to Memory* (1978), there is an awareness that the phenomenon of time passing is itself a kind of oblivion. Consisting of jagged lines and often incomplete sentences or phrases, the work arose from the author's awareness of "the disquieting runs of life slipping by."[30] The various sections already bear out a growing investment in the genres of autobiography and comedy alongside memory and its faux pas. Hejinian writes, "now is hilarious," alluding to humor's deictic accentuations, and also: "many comedies emerge and in particular a group / of girls," "carried giddy by digression," "autobiography sees the world," "mind / with memory," "the rate of forgetting is greatest / storing that and these processes." Yet such ideas remain in topical form; they are reflectors of the sole poet's mind, quasi-propositional objects that enable Hejinian to

78 Chapter Three

work out what it means to think poetry in a "full and extensive solitude." And indeed, throughout the debut, thinking poetry means slowing down consciousness enough to actually register it in language. When Hejinian writes, "I remember a very good joke, something which everyone / can understand / as thoughts should be / slow better and if there were time enough," she suggests that writing is an aid to memory because it is a form of dilation, whereby time is made accessible to human cognition and experience. In this expansion, writing can paradoxically call attention to our impatience, as well as our habits of mind. We see that remembering is a way of being in time rather than any retroactive imposition of normative structures on the past. And yet, for the 1978 poet, forgetting is not yet a method of writing. It remains a limit of poetry rather than a primary source of it.

The second text worth mentioning is Hejinian's poem "Oblivion," which appears in her collection *The Cold of Poetry* (1994). The poem begins by signaling a change from earlier work: forgetting, rather than being defined as what causes things to "slip by," is what brings things into being. It is "oblivion to type / To undertake more,"[31] the poet observes. The absence of recall is not just an *assistance* or an *obstacle* to doing but the very agent of action itself:

> Night takes no note of time
> Time's part of some light
> Oblivion takes its agency in the responsibility of night
> Noise and oblivion neighboring
> Near, but not to objects seen—near to sights themselves
> Then of sounds not ears
> Near to the subjects which veer
> In swoon, that perfect balance of the head
>
> Memories are most easily made in memories
> The many densities are dependent on all other surrounding densities
> But only a woman could have thought it
> Womanhood expressing anger and sex, then dream and sleep
> Many times I began to write my memories, writing but not from memory
> A support, an other—across the floor from me is the . . .
> Overhead there is a noise[32]

What would it mean to write memories, but not from memory? Is it possible that one could write from forgetting instead, thereby writing toward "my memories"? These are the questions posed by Hejinian as she renders oblivion a source of autogenesis in the poem. Forgetting both precedes and gives way to temporal movement and proprioception. Here, it is not writing that is an "aid" to reminiscence but oblivion's alterity that operates as a "support" for composition. The power of this othering leads to multiplicity as well as border crossing. Hejinian goes on to write in the work, "Male merging into female—and providing memories / Male and female accumulate memories—of each other, of everything."[33] In its dismissal of strict borders, forgetting amasses time while depersonalizing it and thus making it strange:

> "Death is like the Sun," my friend said, "you can't look at it"
>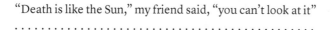
>
> A man and a woman are exceeding themselves by half again until there are three persons' hands
> A concave shadow casts
> The fingers close toward the sun
> I can imagine what might work to light the obvious oblivion
> A zone which is sleep where dream remains
> It fills with life just one side of it
> Only the sight of her front and own feet—because she has short memory
> Humans accumulate innumerable reminders to compensate for their short memories[34]

Already a harbinger to Hejinian's late work *Positions of the Sun* (2018), the lines here resonate with the metaphor first posed by Blanchot, whom the poet goes on to cite in the poem. In *The Infinite Conversation*, the philosopher had posited: "Forgetting is the sun: memory gleams through reflection."[35] Oblivion, like the sun, can't be looked at. Instead, our relationship to it is a kind of indirectness, detour, mediation. Rather than leading to total blindness, forgetting produces shadows and relationality, as when bodies intercept light to cast an image. It redirects; it yields odd numbers, concavity, and strange proportions, moving us in oblique directions. In contrast to our "short memories," oblivion encourages us to "exceed" ourselves. Alongside images of light and dark, front and back, the pairing of "obvious" with "oblivion"—with its contradictory play on the Latin root *ob*, meaning toward or in the way—becomes suggestive of a movement of forgetful memory: what is obvious must become oblivious, and what is oblivious must become obvious in the original sense that it must be re-encountered after being lost and re-encountered frequently. Poetry in turn works to illuminate this process.

In his study of *A Border Comedy*, Gerard Bruns contends that Hejinian elevates moments of absent recall to the status of a "creative principle,"

80 Chapter Three

writing that "forgetting, paradoxically rais[es] amnesia to the level of in-spiration and, therefore, to that of poetic experience as well."[36] This is ev-ident in the poet's rejection of sequential composition, which I have al-ready described and which Hejinian herself describes in the poem:

> [. . .] passage of time facilitates forgetting
> Then forgetting makes what's been written unfamiliar
> As if some other writer had been writing
> And each of my returns to each of the books is prompted
> To immediates in a sudden present
> Only pastness, which provides forgetting, can provide it
> And I who am so well-disposed toward you[37]

In the passage's domino effect of agency—time as it causes forgetting, forgetting as it causes defamiliarization, defamiliarization as it prompts return—and its use of the word "facilitate," there are echoes of Hejinian's earlier works that we can now perceive. But other than the project's overall design, what other forms of amnesia are operative?

For one, the use of ventriloquism and the anecdote stand out as two forms of poetic displacement. Ventriloquism, whose own etymology of *ventri* (belly) and *loqour* (to speak) evokes Stein's "Lifting Belly" (1915–17) and the vibrational qualities of laughter, entails the activity of forgetting one's own voice for another. As the animation of inert objects, it suggests that the external world is active as well as interactive. Alternatively, the anecdote involves the separation of a self-standing event from the suc-cessivity of other events. It is either a digression from the main narrative, something that can be left out, or a detail that typically needs to be fur-ther incorporated into a larger narrative by way of interpretation. Hejinian calls the anecdote a "span / Consisting of separate facts / Each tenuously connected to the next," something that provides "a view."[38] Together the two techniques animate Hejinian's verse as she moves from the high level of the philosophizing poet to a lower, theatrical level:

> We must begin
> What is your name?
> NAME: Dummie
> That's tempting
> DUMMIE: I'm wearing a red mask and you may squeeze its lips
> LIPS: Repeat repeat repeat repeat repeat repeat
> EXPLORER (*squeezing*): The principle of exploration does not entitle the
> explorer to ownership of what she handles
> HANDLED: Why Shriek?

HISTORIAN: Personification puts real problems back in the world they inhabit
PERSONIFICATION: We have to solve these problems—they are troubling the lives of real people
PEOPLE: Don't feel bad, Personification—you're doing all that you can
LIPS: Repeat repeat repeat repeat repeat repeat[39]

And elsewhere:

NAMES: Hardly
UNNAMED: There once was a muscular sandpiper who found a ruby of historic size amid the obscurities and glimmers of the rising tide, also there was a vegetarian bartender once, his shoes squeaked indoors and out, and there was a burly doctor too, and a man with a chirp in his ear which called him terrible names
But to those he answered: *No!*
Asking who
And casting suspicion
To fall as it may
On the one who will play
A misfit[40]

What are we to make of such moments that can only be categorized by their energetic bursts, their surges of feeling, their comically absurd staging of inexplicable life? For one, I want to claim that remembrance is antithetical to this kind of language. While recollection can construct interiority through psychological continuity, the comic action here depends on a self-forgetting, an "upset and recovery of the protagonist's equilibrium," as Susanne Langer puts it, "his contest with the world and his triumph by wit, luck, personal power, or even humorous, or ironical, or philosophical acceptance of mischance."[41] For another, the difficulty of recall coincides with a language whose syntax and meaning are both in states of discord. The chaos arises from voices that seem to be talking past one another or in non sequiturs. While speech acts have historically stressed regulation, what Searle called "rule-governed form[s] of behavior" and "constitutive rules,"[42] the performance of dialogue here relies on misreading the rules of literary meaning. Ventriloquizing is exponentialized, as each new "dummy" engineers the effect of an unintended effect.

The most conspicuous misunderstanding of literary etiquette in the passage is the reading of prosopopoeia as literal. Figuration, rather than upholding both a concrete and an abstract notion, involves actual metamorphosis from the symbolic to the real. Put another way, the interrup-

82   Chapter Three

tive nature of the passage works toward a comic effect by externalizing internal thought as speech and then ventriloquizing speech as its own character. The absence of memory throughout renders the language anti-immersive and non-durational. Introjections cause us to constantly displace interiority with externality, to temporarily lose track of where we are in the poem. Moreover, by literalizing metaphors, Hejinian draws attention to several long-standing poetic notions, including the Emersonian notion that the poet is a "Namer" and that words have wills. What happens, she asks, if we actually give things names as if they were living subjects? What if we actually talk back to our words? What kind of poetry would ensue if we enacted Stanley Cavell's claim that "the answer to the question 'What is art?' will in part be an answer which explains why it is we treat certain objects, or how we can treat certain objects, in ways normally reserved for treating persons"?[43] The comedy of the passage responds by suggesting that the question is one-sided. Words, as it turns out, can largely ignore us in order to produce discourse among themselves, occasionally turning us ("a vegetarian bartender," "a burly doctor," the man who chirps) into the objects or subjects of their own tales. It's not that the poet isn't causally responsible for the words in the sequence. She is. But the nature of the dialogue suggests that while words cannot have meaning without the author's intention to write, it does not follow that they must mean what the author intended—for this is to ignore how social and literary conventions, and the transgression of these conventions, constitute meaning.

In the passage under discussion, forgetting that words are words also leads them to acquire bodies. The "shrieks," "squeaks," and outbursts mark a deviance from the more contemplative, slow-building, perceptive language of *My Life*, exposing the body as being a physical operation that is performing in place of any higher "self." Poetic experience is not an out-of-body event but, rather, a very material, corporeally situated experience. At the same time, the appearance of multiple, unsynchronized entities creates a claustrophobic and crowded effect. Poetic voices get detached from any metaphysical being, joining a cacophony of other chattering entities. The result is, as Hejinian writes, a "falling" sensation, whereby words bump into one another. Sequentially is replaced by overlap. The comic effect works by creating rapid motion among seemingly stubborn non-persons. Forgetting, relying on speed here, involves the short-circuiting of memory such that there is no time to remember. A certain momentum is paradoxically created by the reader's tripping over the inertia of certain lines.

In place of one speaker, Hejinian adopts masks, one-time personas, a bird of chance and happenstance, "the one who will play / A misfit," and "PERSONFICATION," which ironically speaks of "real people." She replaces memories, chronologies, or personal histories with bits, digressions, and quick fires of dialogue. Presented like jokes, poetry here deals with what Freud had called bewilderment and illumination, sense in nonsense.[44] The passage above is only one example of the plethora of things *A Border Comedy* ultimately gives voice to: Nerve, Potato, Thinking Character, Flirt, Mexican poet, Horizon, Man, Man as Husserl, Guide, Crow, Utopian, Comic, Sound, Branch, and so on. The very fact that, in the ventriloquism above, "NAMES" belies itself—drawing a conflict between the supposed function of a name (i.e., to supply stable reference and identify) and its literal function of anonymity—exposes an inauthentic poetic voice, made even more absurd by the character of LIPS. LIPS is less a serious mouthpiece than it is an instrument of mimicking things. If the first sequence of "repeat" refers to the previous invitation to "squeeze its [the mask's] lips," we can imagine that only a sequence of stuttering blabber or silence might ensue.

Let us consider the mimetic nature of Hejinian's dialogue even further. In "Laughter" (1900), Bergson had suggested that imitation and repetition are part of the mechanical inelasticity that society finds humorous. The funniness lies in the transformation of organic, supple, and adaptive humans into mere uniform and absent-minded (self-forgetting) bodies— or, more extreme yet, things. "We begin, then, to become imitable," he writes, "only when we cease to be ourselves"[45]—when intentional, individualized actions are replaced by automatic and reproducible gestures. Though Bergson's primary project was to incorporate humor into his overall metaphysical project, "ceasing to be ourselves" seems like a good way of describing the power of forgetting in Hejinian's work, even if this selflessness does more than suggest a substitution of an authentic, organic self by mere simulacra. For while parody in a line like "Repeat repeat repeat repeat repeat repeat" draws attention to the material aspect of a comic language—and how language can be at once overly self-conscious and not conscious at all—a less abrasive, more affirmative humor also exists in the poem's implicit comic rhythm. Bergson describes this cadence when he writes, "actual life is comedy just so far as it [. . .] forgets itself," for if it were always alert, "there would be no coincidences, no conjunctures and no circular series."[46] For Bergson, the pleasure of these patterns, and our ability to laugh at them, is not exclusively aesthetic but stems from regular life itself.

The mechanical nature of Hejinian's ventriloquized exchange contains something equally real and human as it reflects lived experience. As language speaks of itself, we share in a metalingual pleasure. The language being used appears wittier than the characters who use it, but as the poet shows, the characters *are* the language being used. As the various

84 **Chapter Three**

"dummies" begin to discuss *us*, the "lives of real people," we experience the sense of being mirrored inside the very object of ridicule.[47] Entering into reciprocity with the poetic characters and their language, we discern that the question, to our amusement, is Which came first, the subject or the object? the reader/writer or the poem? The goal is not to settle the matter through theoretical means but to foster an ongoing disruption of causality and linearity. Comedy in these moments creates a sense of vitality distinct from rigid habit and closer to the expression of mental and physical energies.

The power of writing through forgetting derives from the divergence, addition, and arguably schizophrenic movement of voice, persons, and thoughts. Elements of comedy—such as interruption, repetition, plurality, sociality, and surprise—are its results. Forgetting, however, also creates a specificity to the text that makes it impossible to go back and re-create the logic that motivates certain divarications. An additional way in which forgetting manifests itself in comedy is therefore denarrativization. Hejinian writes: "Rather than retrace my steps I'll continue, to the left and to the left again as long as it takes, so that no one will know of my indecisiveness."[48] In Book Eight of *A Border Comedy*, she calls attention to this circular and amnesiac process of blurring one's start and end:

> Thus the apples are effortlessly disguised
> As objects of appetite
> That could never be traced back
> Their denarrativization having been achieved
> Through an excess of referential and symbolic detail
> As in a baroque sleep around a medieval dream[49]

It is not a lack of memory traces but rather a surplus of them that generates a style of forgetful writing. The idea harkens back to Umberto Eco, who, in denying the possibility that words can negate their own meaning, nevertheless suggested that "it is possible to forget on account not of defect but of excess, just as, though it is not possible to destroy the meaning of an assertion pronounced aloud, it is possible to pronounce *another* assertion *in the same moment*, so that the two assertions are superimposed."[50] This bombardment of detail is itself a kind of poetic trick that undermines readerly attention and writerly intention, ushering us into poetry's magic. The "objects of appetite" one might associate with a fixed subject can't be linked to some underlying will or set of desires. In being "disguised" as alluring, the Edenic temptations of the passage are instead presented as tantalizing decoys, forms of misdirection. It's not only that *they* can't be "traced back." It's also that their very manifestation—with "an excess of referential and symbolic detail"—is an obstacle to returning to some original meaning or purpose. Indicative of how the poem resists a model of scarcity, the surplus of details also participates in a kind of comic misvaluing: the part takes precedent over the whole, the thing becomes more important than the point of the thing's appearance.

The comic appeal of denarrativization explains why the juncture of dreams and amnesia is of interest in the above passage. Sleep, as an analogue to forgetful memory, permits an anachronism: the baroque appears alongside the medieval. We lose sight of things at the very same time that lost things reappear in dreams as unfamiliar. Representing a state of obvious oblivion, sleep constitutes a break in consciousness as well as a necessary component in the comic restoration and continuity of daily life. From it, a number of other forgetful things ensue, including anacoluthon, digression, and mixed-up chronologies:

> The question is, do I want to make something happen
> By waiting here
> Eye to hole
> Hole to view
> Increasing
> What if I had to change holes
> What if the hole disappeared
> As in a case of amnesia
> Leaving no distinction between the past and future
> Brought on by sleep which follows sex
> With its doubling and duplicitous effect
> A backward motion
> A sleep that restores the lapse
> As memory
> Viewing what one might have done[51]

In the quoted passage, forgetful memory works by first disturbing and then restoring the scene's equilibrium. The language of causality ("make something happen") yields to an unanticipated changing of holes and positions, which produces comic effects by varying their proportions. The sexual lines "Eye to hole / Hole to view / Increasing" are forms of metonymy that temporarily disturb one's point of view. As the speaker is led to a state of "amnesia," and the "hole disappear[s]," the speaker is forced to give up not only agency but also their position as a voyeur. Rather than remaining at a safe distance where comedy can remain a "comment on life from outside, an observation on human nature,"[52] the speaker gets reinscribed in the scene. The relative security of the initial viewing hole becomes a time

86   **Chapter Three**

trap, a wormhole. Within this poetics of forgetting, linearity is replaced by circularity: "Eye to hole / Hole to view" takes on the quality of being sequential *and* chiasmic. The word "follows" (which reappears in the title of Hejinian's *The Unfollowing* [2016]) evokes both the sense of coming after and coming behind. The word order in the passage—"amnesia," then "sleep" and "sex"—reverses the actual causal nature of events. Inducing the "backward motion" of falling sleep, oblivion here is the necessary medium through which the unsettling and restoration of balance occurs. The voyeuristic gaze that derives its sense of freedom from remove is replaced by comedy's liberatory capacity for replenishment and change.[53]

While the short-circuiting of memory often manifests itself in boisterous eruptions or moments of vertigo in Hejinian's work, comedy's illumination of forgetting's social and additive nature is legible even in quieter moments. At one point in *A Border Comedy*, Hejinian uses forgetting to remind us of Mark Twain's formula that "tragedy + time = comedy." Rather than subtracting from memory, the process of losing track of things mediates the relationship between a poetic subject and an expected event, allowing the subject to experience temporality as mistiming, latency, and delay:

> Provoking, perhaps, a psychological turnaround and emotional reversal much
>
> > like the one that so often occurs in response to a sound one has too long been anticipating and begun to forget—the sound, for example, of invited guests arriving way after the time appointed and talking noisily as they approach the door, which one perceives not as a pleasant fulfillment of expectation but rather, now, as a sudden, startling interruption[54]

The passage is not necessarily funny. But there are other reasons why it participates in Hejinian's notion of comedy. Revising Kant's argument that humor is expectation followed by nothing, anticipation here in fact does lead to *some*thing. The event that is supposed to take place at a certain time becomes the same event at a different present moment. This event is moreover a gathering, a moment of sociality. Hejinian, who elsewhere writes about the host/guest relation as a metaphor for the mutual estrangement of a writer/reader,[55] suggests that forgetting constitutes the condition of encounter. Momentary absent-mindedness also transforms the nature of this meeting from being the object of fulfillment to the very thing that intrudes. Like the described door, the speaker's consciousness is a threshold or "border"—one that ushers in a number of existing possibilities. Through forgetting, one arrives not at the end of a social event but at the start of one.

When the absence of recollection again appears in the context of being a guest or a foreigner, Hejinian's focus is on how continuity, in addition to disconnection, can form a comic rhythm. The suggestion is that forgetful memory can itself be habitual, a "constancy." Harkening back to the themes in *Oxota*, she writes:

> For a foreigner
> I have to check my pocket to make sure I have the key and I wonder if I'm
>   doing this *again*
> Perhaps, in my absent-mindedness—my being foreign—I'm not
>   constantly losing the key but (in my absent-mindedness) constantly
>   finding it
> Producing the repetition of relief[56]

If absolute forgetting—a forgetting that would have to entail even forgetting forgetting—involves the total erasure of memory traces, then the key in the above passage is not forever lost but merely part of a temporary lapse. Forgetful memory forms a powerful, incessant rhythm that extracts and brings the absent-minded subject back into the world. This rhythm is a comic one. Continuity in experience, rather than total disjuncture, participates in what Hejinian calls "return / for which forgetting is the precondition / and memory the condition."[57] This process not only provides variation but also "relief," the basis for comic release.

In a series of notes, the eighteenth-century philosopher Gotthold Ephraim Lessing once argued that "an absent-minded person is said to be no *motif* for a comedy. And why not? To be absent, it is said, is a malady, a misfortune, and no vice [. . . and] comedy must only concern itself with such faults, as can be remedied."[58] The history of comedy has since proved otherwise, with scatterbrained and inattentive characters being liable to blunder as well as charm. Yet Lessing is right when he goes on to note that absent-minded characters do in fact think; they simply don't think "in accordance with [their] present sensuous impressions."[59] The irony of forgetting here, then, is that it is a forgetting *of the present* that makes the situation comic. Getting lost in one's thoughts or memories renders Hejinian's speaker oblivious in other terms, namely that she might literally have gotten lost in a foreign country. And yet, when the speaker returns from her negligent state, there is comfort that the physical world (and her key) still exist. The fact that both of course do—that they don't just disappear because the speaker stops thinking about them—is what makes the situation comedic rather than tragic, worldly in its magic rather

88 Chapter Three

than completely fantastical. The implication is that the poet's state of mind is not the same as the state of the world. That forgetting returns us to the latter is significant.

To pursue this significance, let us quickly summarize our findings thus far: we have seen how forms of amnesia disrupt solipsism in forgetting's embrace of comedy, foregrounding the multiplicity of things and their contexts. But beyond this embrace, there is also a direct link between self-forgetting and a rejection of idealism. As I have just mentioned, Hejinian's work posits that things don't just exist in our heads. They call attention to reality, not as inner life, but as exteriority. If negative theology and transcendentalism offer ways of pointing to another world, comedy accepts and embraces *this* world, *this* life. One must then ask whether comedy achieves something that autobiography likewise claims to do, which is an appeal to some sort of realism. The answer is yes, but whereas autobiography matches personal experience to impersonal things, comedy can call attention to their discrepancy.

The notion of realism is not incidental but key to Hejinian's oeuvre. She once noted that "more even than film, and certainly more than music, dance, or painting, of all the arts we burden literature most with the task of answering to reality."[60] In her essay "Who Is Speaking?" (2000), the social corrective that is normally assigned to comedy drives it down to earth, as it were: "to improve the world, one must be situated in it [...] one must be worldly."[61] The argument is that poetry should be a form of participation in reality, and it must create sociality by generating knowledge of our surroundings and not just knowledge of the self. When the poet writes in *A Border Comedy*, "It is outer, not inner, knowing that allows for empathy,"[62] the distinction attests to a real border, one that importantly resists a reading of any environment as a simple projection of the ego. But if comedy acts as one way of getting at the real "outside" world, it does so *not* because it is rooted in verifiable facts the way autobiography is. Nor is it simply what Cicero calls *imitatio vitae*, "a copy of life." Instead, the genre presents the autonomous nature of reality by distorting rather than reflecting our experience of it. Consider these two passages from *A Border Comedy*, situated a few pages apart:

> The image of the mirror is especially popular for comedy
> That early representative of literary realism
> Mortifying "I" in my experience, desire, striving
> From the mirror another drop of hot wax falls
> The image a nipple on the nose
> Two eyes, the mouth, and cheeks
> Upon me

Checks
But I'm (laughably) an earnest "I" and I long to improve
My comedy . . .[63]

[. . .]

But I'm much less interested in self-scrutinizing art than I once was
Knowledge is noble, certainly
But comedy, its copy, is intricate
Hard to analyze
Though its character is curiously trusting[64]

Rather than functioning as an exact reproduction, comedy's mirroring nature is more akin to a conceit. The subject is confronted with the reflector as a physical object, a literal boundary that extends into the outside world. In lieu of naturalizing a process of perfect imitation, the mirror apes and "mortif[ies]," creating distance between what is and what seems. The very preposition "upon" is antithetical to a sense of inwardness. In the passage, hot wax, such as that from a candle, deforms the representation so that the poet suddenly sees a nipple ("another drop of hot wax") over the image of her face. Reality "checks" any narcissistic impulse, not through great travesty, tribulation, or tragedy, but in a visual metaphor that yields laughter: a "nipple on the nose."

Earnestness in these passages moreover betokens a positive link between comedy and realism. When Hejinian writes, "I'm (laughably) an earnest 'I'" and "[comedy's] character is curiously trusting," she evokes her articulation elsewhere that "sincerity is my problem—that and gullibility. I always believe that everything is real."[65] The poet may be gullible, but it is a kind of voluntary gullibility that extends from an honest attempt to believe in the actual. Comedy entails a trust in the world. It is a trust that exists prior to and by definition against any known logical causes or retroactive explanations. For this reason, trust as a comic element is radical because it establishes what Hejinian calls "irreverence," a "capacity for belief without rules."[66] Peter Nicholls, who expresses a similar sentiment in his study of modernist poets from the 1930s, is quoted by Hejinian in her collection of essays *The Language of Inquiry* (2000); Nicholls, in describing sincerity "not as a question of truth, but rather as one of relation and exposure to the claims of others," states that "'sincerity' is not so much a true account of one's inner feelings [. . .] as an acceptance of what *exceeds* the self."[67] For Nicholls, the relationship between sincerity and reality can be traced back to Louis Zukofsky's manifesto "Sincerity and Objectivism" (1931), where the poet defines earnestness as the writer's basic consider-

90   **Chapter Three**

ation for the reality of the world, their "preoccupation with the accuracy of detail in writing."[68] For Hejinian, Nicholls's ideas go further in providing a conduit for comedy. Having quoted him in her essay, she goes on to write that an "acceptance of what *exceeds* the self" can erupt "in disruptive and disordering pleasure, in laughter."[69] The implications are such that we can treat misremembering as a kind of sincere mistake. When forgetting upsets our sense of control over ourselves and others, it nevertheless renews our sense of reality as a space for something other than self-reliance. As a form of comic disorientation that causes us to lose our bearings, it calls attention not only to our external circumstances but also our dependance on strangers.

Comedy—and forgetting, for that matter—only works when we trust that we'll survive whatever risks it poses, when we believe that an alternative or reversal is always available because life is not a singularizing, unalterable force. Through their relationship to realism, the two terms maintain a conviction that the world will never perfectly conform to our thoughts and feelings but that our subjectivities will also participate in something other than ourselves. Though I have mainly been discussing realism in the philosophical sense—that is, something that sits athwart idealism—we can see some of the similarities between these ideas and those from one of literary realism's main interlocutors, George Eliot. A famous definition of realism as genre appears early on in *Adam Bede* (1859) when the novelist writes:

> Certainly I could, if I held it the highest vocation of the novelist to represent things as they never have been and never will be. Then, of course, I might refashion life and character entirely after my own liking; [. . .] But it happens, on the contrary, that my strongest effort is to avoid any such arbitrary picture, and to give a faithful account of men and things as they have mirrored themselves in my mind. The mirror is doubtless defective; the outlines will sometimes be disturbed, the reflection faint or confused; but I feel as much bound to tell you as precisely as I can what that reflection is, as if I were in the witness-box narrating my experience on oath.[70]

The queer theorist Grace Lavery has called attention to the ways in which this definition of realism shifts its weight from a model of imitation to an "oath." The direct apostrophe to the reader is itself a breaking of art's impeccable mimetic surface, as language is used not only to reflect but to address. However odd a pairing, Eliot and Hejinian interestingly both suggest that realism is not bound to literary style but to an underlying orientation or intention. Comedy's contribution is that it celebrates rather than mourns the "defectiveness" of its mirror. Rather than being an exact record of reality or a perfect form of recollection, a work like *A Border Comedy* embraces the ways in which slips of the mind can actually call attention to the "men and things" that encroach on and shape consciousness. As we have seen, things are not mirrored in the self so much as the self is mirrored as one thing among others in the world.

The idea that "two is the minimum required for comedy / which commits subjects to each other"[71] is a testament to Hejinian's rejection of the poet as a lonely figure and her interest in reality as a social, extrinsic space. It also affirms her lifelong interest in artistic collaboration. Pivoting away from *A Border Comedy*, I thus want to spend the remainder of this chapter tracing some of forgetting's residual effects in a later work. In 2008, the poet and her friend Jack Collom published a book called *Situations, Sings*. Collom himself was no stranger to humor, teaching comedy workshops alongside his poetry. Funniness, he thought, could be sought in everyday incongruities, life's "constant reworking of balance."[72] He once told an interviewer, "I think the universe is very funny. [. . .] [T]here are many ways in which they [things] are mismatched."[73] Elsewhere he claimed that he was compelled by the inherent comedy in nature, its "multiple plural bubbling energy type thing."[74]

In any artistic collaboration, forgetting is partly a mode of response. It means letting go of whatever it was you were going to say and adjusting to ever-changing circumstances, including moments of misunderstanding and chance. The title *Situations, Sings* is thus not only reminiscent of lyric song and "situation comedies" but also the communal ideas behind musical improvisation and "improv comedy." Improvisation, as jazz musicians and theorists have averred, does not occur ex nihilo but "derives its particularity from the force of context."[75] When improvising, players are caught up in a simultaneous process of talking and listening, to put it in Steinian terms. Against premeditation, they are tuned into art's contingency as much as they are the organizing structures of forgetting and recalling.

In *Situations, Sings*, Hejinian and Collom offer a philo-poetic dialogue called "On Laughter." Written in a Punch and Judy manner, the two poets demonstrate that in addition to thinking *about*, poetry can think *with*. At one point in the back-and-forth piece, Hejinian's character "A" says:

I have a pebble too and its joke is that it can turn to air. It lodges itself in unlikely places and, as soon as I get near, it disappears, proving that it was never there. But your pebble strikes me as the more jocular of the two; appearance is always more comical than disappearance.[76]

92 Chapter Three

Hejinian's preference for a poetics of presence rather than absence is also a preference for comedy. Appearance here testifies to existence, the very thing that forgetting—when it is a mode of comic affirmation—counterintuitively celebrates.[77] When something appears, it not only generates delight rather than frustration, but it also stresses the very context out of which it emerges. Reminiscent of Freud's own "Fort/Da" plot, the pebble passage suggests that a socially committed poetry might involve a responsibility toward happiness, even in the midst of loss. It's not so much that Hejinian repeatedly masters disappearance and return as a way to make the former tolerable (or even pleasurable) so much as she considers sharing in another's gain. The speaker models her poetics after her collaborator's pebble when her own vanishes.

The language of "On Laughter" further encodes the social nature of forgetting in its allusion to Hannah Arendt. In her dialogue with Collom, Hejinian notes: "Well, it's political—dissimilar but meritorious pebbles make an entry into the public sphere. This is what we should mean by 'an appearance.'"[78] For Arendt, the public sphere is a space for action, speech, and spontaneity. Appearance means "being seen and heard by others as well as by ourselves," thereby "constitut[ing] reality." When we appear, we appear to one another, presuming multiplicity and commonality despite innate inequalities. Without a space for appearance, Arendt argues that "the passions of the heart, the thoughts of the mind, the delight of the senses—lead an uncertain, shadowy kind of existence unless and until they are transformed, *deprivatized*, and *deindividualized*, as it were."[79] A space for appearance therefore cannot survive before or after the very individuals who constitute it. As a public endeavor, it is momentary, allowing subjects to speak and act as if beginning something anew, without the shadow of the past or the overdetermination of memory. Forgetting, as a stimulus to this self-expression, concerns itself with giving room to what can't be prescribed or expected. Throughout Hejinian's work, notions of negative rupture are repeatedly replaced by an Arendtian visibility. Forgetting's social and political power is not only that it redirects our attention from the past to the present, but also that it shifts our gaze from ourselves to those with whom we exist.

In a piece like "On Laughter," the sway of forgetting is this: Try to remember too much and you miss what is going on. Try to link the past with the present and you miss the joke. The unexpected remains happily inexplicable, since nothing destroys a joke (or a magic trick) more than elucidation. This jovial submission to obliviousness points us to one of the most striking things about Hejinian's poetry—namely, how so much of it can sound propositional, interpretive, or explanatory but actually isn't. Her insights, in adopting the form of philosophical claims, frequently confound more than they clarify. At one point in "On Laughter," she says, seemingly out of the blue:

> That laughter is contagious but that emotions can't be shared. But my thinking doesn't end there, it is already on its way to broccoli, Montaigne, and the eclipse of the moon. I have a very strong emotion when reading Montaigne, deep and jocular and suffused with the pathos of fellow feeling, the feeling of sharing emotions that can't be shared.[80]

The passage seems to start on proper theoretical footing. When Hejinian says "[t]hat laughter is contagious but that emotions can't be shared," she evokes a lineage of criticism that theorizes comedy as impersonal and antithetical to emotion. The long-standing argument is that humor appeals to the mind and not the heart; it works best from indifference, for it is hard to find a thing funny when you pity, empathize with, love, or hate a thing. Thus, the ideal audience for comedy is supposedly an objective spectator. But what begins as "thinking" soon gets derailed by "broccoli, Montaigne, and the eclipse of the moon." The humor of the passage is not only in the absurd things she names, but in the idea that somehow the speaker has gotten carried away, not by her emotions, but by her "thinking." Rather than keeping her at a remove, a forgetful logic once again reinscribes Hejinian within comic feeling. When the poet describes reading Montaigne, the experience is "jocular" (comic) but also sympathetic (emotional), even if all this amounts to something seemingly false: "the feeling of sharing emotions that can't be shared." Feeling does not override the reality of difference—namely that none of us can truly experience what another person feels and what we ourselves have not experienced—but happily coexists as a paradox with and within actuality. Comedy accommodates this falsity as a conjunction rather than a set of mutually canceling forces.

Hejinian's poetry moves in the direction of comedy, not because it is necessarily humorous in tone, but because what we think is most personal and biographical must ultimately affirm not the self, but the external and social world. In this very process of committing ourselves to one another, it is the personal that is put at risk, interrupted, destabilized, and depersonalized. Forgetting is the force behind such uncertainties. If traditional autobiography and tragedy each prioritize the individual in its own way, examining how recollection might create a teleology that is either "my life" or "fate," comedy short-circuits memory to create and decentralize various viewpoints. In this process, comedy nevertheless pledges itself to "the real world" so often associated with autobiography. Comedy presents borders between one self and another, one context and the next, precisely

94   **Chapter Three**

to move between them. The nature of this perpetual seesaw, as I have argued, is that of forgetting itself.

Having carried forward my book's argument by asking what it would mean to rethink memory as oblivious, I proceed in my next chapter to argue that one of the ways poets forget is by playing with the paradoxical concept of originality as both "firstness" and "novelty." But before concluding my discussion here, I want to address some final issues, starting with agency. An espousal of self-forgetting might appear to disempower the subject that is central to any account of contemporary life. Thus, in their questioning of lyric subjectivity, Language poets have had to confront and articulate the problems of saying "I don't act; I'm acted by: *things which eat up intentions*."[81] After all, without a sense of "I," what happens to human resistance and responsibility? I hope that in discussing forgetful memory's place in Hejinian's work, I have shown that a resistance to solipsism is not the same thing as a submission to passivity. Nor is poetic freedom a negative liberty from accountability. Rather, the worldliness at work here is one that stresses interaction rather than mere action, reinscription rather than permanent distance. The commitment to happiness is not a utopian or an escapist kind of withdrawal but an engaged form of trial and error. The world is always evolving regardless of whether we like it or not. To change is a human desire that is equally a right. It coexists with our right to be changed by others and differs from a model of conversion that promises too easily to change us once and for all.[82] Whereas effecting change can provide pleasure because it empowers us to see our impact in the world, being changed extends our sense of what is possible, generating pleasure (or displeasure) not out of fulfillment but surprise. This dialectic refers us back to a shared world that is itself dynamic and producing alterations at various, often out-of-sync paces. One of the unique ways in which forgetting reframes transformation—especially with regards to identity, sexual or otherwise—is that it decouples change from linear narratives. It refuses to justify alterations with respect to recognition or conformation to preestablished concepts. If repression has typically been conceived of as a defense, forgetting nevertheless also tests our capacity to tolerate uncertainty, flexibility, and vulnerability. In it, we discover the discontinuity of our realities.

All of these things, I believe, present potential liberatory upshots to Hejinian's forgetful memory. And yet, while I have done my best to shed light on her poetics, I also believe that any poetry committed to social reality faces the borders between art and life. A border, as we have seen, is a set of meeting points, a site of confusion that can be repeatedly crossed. To pretend this border doesn't exist is to suggest that somehow chaos and disorder are as stimulating in everyday life as they are in comedy (even when the reader isn't at a mere spectator but participant). Or it's to think that misunderstanding doesn't also carry with it, in our political engagements, a responsibility toward explanation and communication. Sociality between two art-makers may not, in the end, be remotely close to the models of citizenship that are necessary for functional democratic life (or it may be analogous but nontransferable). Forgetting, in consisting of various speeds and degrees of extremity, can be a form of continuity or interruption, and this in itself represents different models of gradual or revolutionary change, transitional becoming or sudden transfiguration—each of which can be desirable at times and utterly frightening at others. On the one hand, slips of the mind perforate fantasies of omnipotence and sovereignty; on the other hand, they hand us the possibility that in the end, we may have no control over even ourselves, let alone others. Finally, as it becomes more and more difficult to think about excess without considering wealth accumulation's direct relationship to austerity and the human purging of natural resources, Hejinian's amnesia raises the question of just how infinite and renewable our universe is. I state these things not to negate the value of poetic concepts but to emphasize, again, that comedy rejects grand claims for particular negotiations, and that its relationship to reality is not of one-to-one correspondence. Art frequently provides a space for us to do and feel the very things that we might not want to pursue or experience in a different framework. This old and perhaps obvious disclaimer arises precisely out of—rather than against—my thinking about the genre of comedy, which concerns itself at once with the incongruity and coexistence of distinct yet inseparable domains.

Origins and (Un)originality

[CHAPTER FOUR]

It is typically expected of poets to "say something which is original," giving words, as Ralph Waldo Emerson declares, "a power which makes their old use forgotten."[1] Yet, it is also a commonplace idea that poets should court dictionaries and etymologies, having at their side their "own boring philological dinner partner." In crafting this last description, John Hollander once averred that "for a journalist, or writer of instruction manuals, a knowledge of a word's prior meaning and derivation would be crippling; in writing, he or she had best learn to forget what is known about that. But not so for the poet."[2] Poets, in this line of argument, should neither forget nor view language's deep past as obsolete. They should recall and admit the former lives of words.

Beneath this duality is not only the tension between synchronic and diachronic approaches to language, but more salient to our discussion, the Janus-faced concept of poetic originality. When Stein declared in 1928 that "the United States is just now the oldest country in the world" because she "is the mother of the twentieth-century civilization," she capitalized on the paradox that the "newest" of worlds could also be the first of them, the "original" site of modernism.[3] While Ashbery would later praise his predecessor's work for its "profound originality, its original profundity,"[4] the poet Laura (Riding) Jackson had in fact arrived at a somewhat different judgment. Separating Stein's work from the belief that an artist "is obliged to invent" because she "realizes the inadequacy of the usual," Riding argued that Stein "is completely without originality." She went on: "Everybody is unable to understand her and thinks that this is because she is too original or is trying too hard to be original. But she is only divinely inspired in ordinariness. [. . .] None of the words Miss Stein uses have ever had any experience. They are no older than her use of them, and she is herself no older than her age conceived barbarically."[5] Riding's point was that Stein distinguished herself from earlier poets by redefining originality as obviousness rather than exceptionality. Echoing Stein's own critical lexicon regarding the ages of man and civilization, Riding suggested that in using words as if they had no past, the author of *Tender Buttons* rolled innovation back into an elementary and infantile state. The result was a so-called "new barbarism," where "original" could also mean "originary."

In 1983 Hollander articulated this zeugmatic paradox behind originality by identifying it as a "contention of the *primary* and the *prior*, the originalities of the 'now' and the 'then.'" He went on to describe the preference for this year's model to last year's as a particularly modernist and American tendency to "conveniently forget" temporal antecedence and trade it in for innovation.[6] In the last century, a number of significant literary theories subscribed to this split and ongoing displacement of originality's meaning from "first" to "novel" (and vice versa). Paul de Man, for instance, claimed that any genuine new work of art depends on the writer's illusion of unprecedentedness—the false yet necessary belief that all literature generates new beginnings.[7] He argued that when think we are encountering an original work, we are in fact witnessing a reassertion of a failure to originate. "The reader," he wrote, "can very well ignore what the author was forced to forget: that the work asserted in fact the impossibility of its own existence."[8] The idea that writing is a negative trace of what it represses appeared, too, in the Bloomian framework of anxiety and influence, in which "the poet-in-a-poet" who "is desperately obsessed with poetic origins, generally despite himself," must be "strong" enough to assert their own original poetic vision.[9] Indeed, the notion can be cogently traced back to T. S. Eliot's "Tradition and the Individual Talent" (1919). One will recall that in his attempt to resolve the problem of new works and old orders, Eliot begins by identifying one form of poetic originality as

> those aspects of [a poet's] work in which he least resembles anyone else. In these aspects or parts of his work we pretend to find what is individual, what is the peculiar essence of the man. We dwell with satisfaction upon the poet's difference from his predecessors, especially his immediate predecessors.[10]

The significance of the passage, for our purposes, are twofold. First, it already foreshadows what Eliot will argue, namely that creative originality or novelty depends on a sublimation of poetry's origins, its literary past. In taking this stance, Eliot diverges from Futurist beliefs that originality can only come about through rejection of precedence. Second, implicit in Eliot's phrase "what is individual, what is the peculiar essence of the man"

98 Chapter Four

rests the idea that poetic originality depends on a theory of persons. Each person (and each poet) who is born has never existed before. Nor will they exist again after their death. Originality, when it is based on a theory of persons, does not simply mean "first" or "novel," but also "authentic." It is a Romantic, Rousseauian idea, related to man's "peculiar essence," what individuates him. (Emerson, in a less systematic manner, had made a similar presumption when he attempted to link "original action" and original verse to the "Aboriginal Self.") The paradox of modernism, then, was precisely its attempt to simultaneously commit itself to both individuality and impersonality and, in some cases, to dissolve the tension through a theory of originality. Did not Georges Braque say of himself and Picasso, "we were inclined to efface our personalities in order to find originality,"[11] only to be thrust back, after attempts at a common method, into a reassertion of the personal signature? Modernism's attitude of wanting to have its cake and eat it too accounts for how subsequent usurpations of creative originality in the twentieth century regularly tended to track shifting notions of authorial power and function. Uncreative writing rejects self-expression and the idea that the origins of originality are to be found in a preexisting, discoverable self. At the same time, unoriginality has often been reinscribed by genius itself.[12] For instance, the contemporary conceptual poet Robert Fitterman, who is best known for recycling found material, has been called a "plagiarist extraordinaire."[13] To call someone an "extraordinaire" is precisely to differentiate them from everyone else; to call someone a "plagiarist" is to accuse someone of being a mere copy. The oxymoron works by splitting and holding in mind two different meanings of originality: One is not only derivative and innovative. One is innovative precisely because one leans into one's posteriority.

In what follows, I shed light on some of the ways in which various inheritors of Donald Allen's "New American poetry" have harnessed forgetting to explore the paradox of poetry's dual claims to origins and originality. Such uses, I argue, diverge from Eliot's, de Man's, and Bloom's respective notions of sublimation and repression in that they are less concerned with fitting into or toppling literary history than re-creating it as play. In continuously resurfacing, this notion of play bridges Stein's wit (her use of wordplay, play as dramatization, nonsense games) and the comic potentials of Hejinian's work with Tan Lin's quasi-ironic style in chapter 5. The spectrum of cases here ranges from Charles Bernstein's use of cliché to a number of poets' respective manipulations of family trees and origin myths as lively engagements with autogenesis as a trope of originality. I discuss forgetting's subversion of etymological roots and cultural origins in Harryette Mullen's work, and also look at how the return to impossible pasts renders the forgotten as novel in the work of American-born, Vancouver-based poet Lissa Wolsak. Though the examples will be diverse, both in style and in intention, I bring them together to show that forgetting is already adequate to the task of tracking and connecting their various ventures. What binds my examples here is precisely a strategic use of forgetting to disrupt originality's implicit forms of temporality and authority.[14]

*　*　*

The work of Charles Bernstein first emerged in the 1970s and 1980s in concert with Hejinian and other Language environs, but his recent poem "I Don't Remember" (2018) is characteristic of the idiomatic poetics he and his contemporaries have employed in the last fifty years. The poem is neither a successful example of Eliot's model of recalling history in order to transcend temporality nor an example of Emerson's or Marinetti's suppressive models of creativity. Rather, it uses a weak form of forgetting to engineer a bricolage out of the unoriginality of the language of origins. The poem in its entirety reads:

> I don't remember telling her anything. I don't remember if it even happened. I don't remember any stars or even sky. I don't remember the color of the water. I don't remember who I told if anyone. I don't remember the look in your eye. I don't remember what you told me never to forget. I don't remember if I used to remember. I don't remember to write each letter so one glides into another but not enough to become indistinct. I don't remember to remember what I was not remembering—that it was cold or I was paralyzed by an anxiety I don't remember but can still feel. I don't remember the difference between not remembering & forgetting, ideal and the idea of the ideal, game & play, ought and must, wish and want, desire and obsession. Not even now. I don't remember if I am repeating myself or just forgetting what difference it makes.[15]

Sidelining innovation for genericism, Bernstein's poem foregrounds the nature of discourse—how language is used and how it comes to us already used. Forgetting and remembrance generate certain kinds of sentences, which are in turn juxtaposed through their various registers and contexts. The poem is a kind of linguistic machine that filters experience, self, and world through the phrase "I don't remember." The result is a tongue-and-cheek sequence of familiar tropes: there is the sentence spoken by someone who should be keeping a secret ("I don't remember telling her anything"), the sentence that references the self-doubting eyewitness account ("I don't remember if it even happened"), and the use of "I don't

100   Chapter Four

remember" as a cover-up or excuse. Such sentences are clichéd in the sense that they belong to a stockpile of public language rather than the inner life of an individual. They turn inside out what is typically considered a private mental process and cannot be said to correspond to original—that is, earlier and true—feelings.

The engineering behind "I Don't Remember," however, also works by drawing upon a certain tension in the poem's unoriginality. On the one hand, the poem teases how far it can go in decentering its speaker as a single, original source of utterance by forgetting as much and in as many different ways as possible. On the other hand, the work is not actually misremembering anything or concealing its origins. As a collection of pre-interpreted snippets, what claims to be neglecting the past is really a riff on forgetting's discourses. Throughout the poem, the speaker constantly nods to earlier philosophical notions: a few of the sentences entertain the possibility of continuing ad infinitum in a kind of bad regression, while the poet's use of "I don't remember" strikes an echo with how "I don't know" functions in Meno's paradox. When Bernstein writes, "I don't remember the difference between not remembering & forgetting," he plays off the long-standing puzzle of how one can inquire into a certain difference, if one does not already recognize or have the knowledge of that difference.

Perhaps the most conspicuous premise behind Bernstein's unoriginal unremembering is the Augustinian problem of forgetting. By claiming "I don't remember," only to state the very thing (or part of the thing) that the speaker is not remembering, Bernstein leverages the fact that forgetting as a mental limit case is directly linked to the linguistic paradoxes posed by the expression of mis- or non-recollection. The clearest connection to *Confessions* (ca. 400) can be located in the following articulation by Augustine:

> What then? When I mention forgetfulness, I similarly recognize what I am speaking of. How could I recognize it except through memory? I refer not to the sound of the word but to the thing which it signifies. If I had forgotten what the force of the sound was, I would be incapable of recognizing it. So when I remember memory, memory is available to itself through itself. But when I remember forgetfulness, both memory and forgetfulness are present—memory by means of which I could remember, forgetfulness which I did remember.[16]

I want to pause and discuss Augustine because he makes a significant contribution to the question of forgetting and language, and also because his argument stems from a problem of origins. In the passage above, the use of self-referentiality and paradox—which forms the basis of Bernstein's poem as well as a number of classic philosophical riddles, including "this sentence is false" and "be spontaneous"—essentially creates a double bind. How is it, Augustine asks, that "forgetting" deceives us into recognizing a process that should have been, by its very nature, erased? Widening the gulf between the "sound of the word" and "the thing which it signifies," the described crisis is such that as a word, "forgetting" ends up recalling itself, so to speak. Expression and meaning are incongruous, rendering the word "forgetting" both oxymoronic and excessive. And yet, Augustine reminds us that when we forget, we may not forget having forgotten. Presumably, there is an amnesia that one remembers because our true origins in God are imprinted on the human soul and can be recalled even in the depths of sin. Several pages later, he describes the phenomenon of using the knowledge of one's misremembrance in order to produce recall. The mechanism is such that we retain one part of the missing thing, using it to recover the rest of the whole:

> Or perhaps it had not totally gone: part was retained, and was used to help in the search for another part. That would presuppose that memory felt itself to be working with a whole to which it was accustomed; as if limping from being deprived of support to which it was accustomed, it would demand the return of the missing element. For instance, our eyes may happen on a person known to us or we may think of him, and we try to recall his name. Other names that occur will not fit the case, because we are not in the habit of associating them with him, and so we reject them until that one comes up which at once corresponds to the familiarity known and is accepted as correct. [...] If, however, it were totally effaced from the mind, we would not remember even when prompted. When at least we remember ourselves to have forgotten, we have not totally forgotten. But if we have completely forgotten, we cannot even search for what has been lost.[17]

There is a strong and surprising similarity between Augustine's recollective method of trial and error—that is, what names will "fit the case"—and W. H. Auden's description of writing poetry. In his essay "Squares and Oblongs" (1948), Auden had argued that when a poet changes a word in a line, he is not "replacing one emotion by another" or even "strengthening it" but rather "discovering" what the emotion is: "The emotion is unchanged, but waiting to be identified like a telephone number one cannot remember. '8357. No, that's not it. 8557, 8457, no, it's on the tip of my tongue, wait a moment, I've got it, 8657. That's it.'"[18] For Auden and Augustine, writing and thinking begin with what "one cannot remember" and are followed by a consideration of contending options. Bernstein literalizes this by generating a work in which each new sentence begins with "I don't remember."

102   Chapter Four

If Auden and Augustine return to the site of forgetting again and again until the right number, or name, appears, Bernstein's poem seems to work by pressing "refresh" on what the so-called speaker doesn't remember, with the result being ongoing variation. One depends on a process of elimination and the other, accumulation. And yet, here is the irony and tension upon which Bernstein's playfulness depends: in all three cases, forgetting partially acts as a kind of anchor, a false origin that one keeps returning to. Forgetting in "I Don't Remember" works to destabilize and fracture the speaker's perspective while paradoxically grounding the poem with its language. The language of forgetting, which is a placeholder for "original" origins, becomes the source of the poem's meaning, however unoriginal. The mechanism partly relies on synecdoche. In Auden's case, "8," "5," and "7" remain accessible and temporarily stand in for the whole numerical term. In Augustine's case, it is the knowledge of forgetting itself that scores out a part of the whole—the memory of forgetting stands in for the forgotten memory itself. For the theologian, we can say the following: when one experiences forgetting but can still say "I have forgotten," language is a substitute for total absence as well as the discontinuity of the psychic life of the individual. It represses the crisis of reference ironically by naming the crisis. The word "forgetting" emerges as a way to cope with a certain aporia and suspension; we need it in our language in order to cover the various ambiguities of the experience itself. By contrast, in Bernstein's case, the language of forgetting operates as a kind of pseudo-origin of unoriginality. "I don't remember" stands in for a number of interchangeable aspects of cultural discourse. The idioms are commonplace enough that we forget where and how they first surfaced.

The line from Augustine to Bernstein is not entirely tenuous, the obvious intermediary being Ludwig Wittgenstein. The latter—whose writings were a significant influence on Bernstein during his time at Harvard and beyond—began *Philosophical Investigations* (1953) with a passage from *Confessions*. According to Wittgenstein's model of language, we all know what the word "forgetting" means because we can use it correctly, not because we have actually clarified the nature of forgetting as a mental process. And yet, forgetting's hazy and ambiguous conceptual contours are precisely what enable us to use it as we do in its respective language games. In an example comparable with Augustine's own dilemma, Wittgenstein writes:

> I want to remember a tune, and it escapes me; suddenly I say, "Now I know it," and I sing. What was it like suddenly to know it? Surely it can't have occurred to me *in its entirety* in that moment!—Perhaps you will say: "It's a particular feeling, as if it were now *there*"—but *is* it now there? Suppose I

then begin to sing it and get stuck? But may I not have been *certain* at that moment that I knew it? So in some sense or other it was *there* after all!— But in what sense?[19]

If this is a puzzle, it is also Wittgenstein's point. The philosopher underscores the paradoxes in this situation not to resolve it, as Augustine hoped to, but rather to negate the philosophical model it presumes. Forgetting is just one example, but it's an apt one. When we make judgments about whether or not someone "remembers" or "forgets," we often do so without actual knowledge about their inner states. Just as the person who says "she remembers" or "I forget" may use these statements meaningfully without actual confirmation of their verisimilitude, so too is Bernstein's speaker less interested in discovering original (earlier and actual) truths about the self or world than in exploiting that interest to conduct enterprise with the unoriginal language of origins. In the passage above, Wittgenstein's point is that the language of remembering and knowing renders remembering and knowing as types of "feelings" or mental processes, when in fact, upon deeper probing, the connection between one and the other is lacking. It is not that Wittgenstein denies mental processes; rather, he is proposing a language game in which the mental process is irrelevant.

* * *

A poem like "I Don't Remember" suggests that slips of the mind can administer play without ethnically fraught deception, and that forgetting itself is an object of cultural recognition, simultaneously revealed and displaced by its own discourse. One of the ways in which writers have continued to flirt with the relationship between play, culture, and forgetting on the level of poetics is through the construction of pseudo-genealogies. As Foucault argued in his 1971 essay on Nietzsche and history, a genealogical method counterintuitively "opposes itself to the search for 'origins,'" seeking in unpromising and neglected places, places we tend to think and feel are without history. If origins ask to be recovered, remembered, and connected to the lines of succession that they father, the genealogist instead rejects this quest, understanding the past as both descent and diversion without seeing it as an active determination of the present. "What is found at the historical beginning of things is not the inviolable identity of their origin," Foucault writes. "It is the dissension of other things. It is disparity."[20] Genealogy, in other words, moves "up time," not "down time."[21] Against chronology, it is the present that begets the recent past and the recent past, a more distant one.

As a form of genealogy, the myth of creative origins goes a long way back: the nine classical Muses were themselves the daughters of Zeus and Mnemosyne, a tale whose fictive nature nevertheless reminds us that poetic inspiration is not inherited or recalled but constructed. Subsequently, poets have taken this to mean potential ancestral play. The oft-neglected avant-garde writer Tom Weatherly, for instance, fabricated a mixed-race family tree when he described himself as "the grandson of Wallace Stevens and Hilda Doolittle, Jimmy Rogers and Sippie Wallace, and first cousin to Paul Blackburn."[22] Alice Notley, while composing the prose-manifesto "Doctor Williams' Heiresses" (1980) ignored actual literary history to paint a queer fable of origins: "Poe was the first one, he mated with a goddess. His children were Emily Dickinson & Walt Whitman—out of wedlock with a goddess. Then Dickinson & Whitman mated—since they were half divine they could do anything they wanted to—& they had 2 sons, William Carlos Williams & Ezra Pound."[23] The poet Robert Duncan[24]—whose actual adoption by his parents was conceived of as an appointment inspired by the consorting of astrological charts—was particularly fond of inventing mythical origins where historical ones were unavailable. While his peer Ed Dorn recalls that Duncan had the "presumption that he was the son of Ezra Pound and H.D.,"[25] elsewhere, Duncan identified Kenneth Rexroth as "a big brother." And when asked about Stein, the Black Mountain School poet once said in a fake southern accent, "You're referring to my mother."[26] The examples, as you can see, are nearly infinite. To offer just a few more recent ones, consider how the late Tyrone Williams has called the poet Erica Lewis the "granddaughter of O'Hara, Koch and the New York School as well as granddaughter of Ginsberg, Kerouac, Kaufman [. . .] count[ing] among her sisters and brothers Gina Myers, Brenda Iijima, Michelle Detorie, Sampson Starkweather and Dana Ward."[27] Even more common than this kind of family networking is the implicit tendency to describe any given poet's style as the begetting of X writer meets Y writer. Describing the contemporary Los Angeles-based poet Carlos Lara, who sometimes writes under the alter ego Losarc Raal, Kirsten (Kai) Ihns writes: "No one else is quite the 'cold ornamental cardboard and rising Teflon god' that Raal undeniably is. Maybe if Keston Sutherland were also a Mean Girl TM, or if Ashbery had listened to trap music, but still, probably not. [. . .] It's Tristan Tzara and Unica Zürn and Amiri Baraka and Sir Philip Sidney and Osvaldo Lamborghini and Rimbaud and . . . Saddam Hussein(?), to name just a few."[28]

Such fictional genealogies, kinships, and clans are not instances of pure poetic forgetting, but they do disregard fidelity to a factual past. Their lightheartedness moreover suggests that their creators are more interested in toying with, than taking seriously, the Romantic notion of autogenesis, the idea that poets can replace history, or the actual event of parental naming, with the writer's self-baptism as a creator. Previously, the act of originating oneself in light of engendering literary tradition might have been considered a formidable task. Paul Valéry, in writing about Stéphane Mallarmé, began with an anxiety regarding repetition—"what can I say [. . .] that I have not said before, or that everyone has not said?"—only to claim that originality is merely what's forgotten: "We say that an author is *original* when we cannot trace the hidden transformations that others underwent in his mind."[29] In his comprehensive study *Romantic Origins* (1978), Leslie Brisman reads Samuel Taylor Coleridge's concern with the self as origin as involving particularly high stakes: if an individual can be the source of a truly original thought, they are also capable of free will, of being the originator of their actions. And as I have already outlined, de Man's sense of forgetting origins remained both the precondition for writing *and* evidence of the writer's self-deception, a sign that modernism failed to erase the past *and* a definition of modernism in terms of this failure. (When Arthur Rimbaud says, "If only I had one predecessor in French history! But no, none," we witness modernism's performative impulse and its illusion of eternal youthful rebellion.[30]) The examples I congregate above, however, forget that the project of origination is supposed to be profound. In explicitly inventing for themselves literary lineages—rather than suppressing them—poets ironically *seem to forget the deeper forgetting* that is supposed to motivate the forward movement of literary tradition. Notley goes a step further to even dismiss the origins of her own origin story: "I can't remember anything about what I was thinking about Williams & women writers. Years ago it was just a crackbrained theory so I could write some works then."[31] The statement evokes Ron Padgett's writing on Joe Brainard: "I don't remember the genesis of *I Remember*."[32] In both these cases, drawing a blank serves as a gesture of irreverence.

As a final case, consider the work of poet and playwright Rochelle Owens, most often associated in poetry with writers like Jerome Rothenberg and the 1960s small magazine *Yugen*. For Owens, the re-creation of genealogy is a satire on the sanctity of origins and legacies. In her collection *The Joe 82 Creation Poems* (1974), she reworks creationist tales from biblical scripture. In *I Am the Babe of Joseph Stalin's Daughter* (1972), genealogy is volatile, not stabilizing. Lines like "I came from   Judea" and "I came from Palestine" coincide with the other fictionalized histories: "i was brought out / of Egypt i came out / of Egypt I was brought / out of Egypt I came out / of Egypt I went to rome, / mainz, flatbush, New York."[33] In the collection's eponymous poem, Owens turns to the USSR and hyperbolically empowers the figure of Svetlana Stalin. In escaping her father's political grip, Svetlana embodies a queer overthrowing of Joseph Stalin's sexual and militaristic potency. Stalin's "huge occidental" penis gets replaced by

106 Chapter Four

his "huge occidental / daughter Svetlana," who subsequently unleashes chaos by parodying an act of begetting:

> & then cracking open
> my eyes, banging in like a fat
> shoe, is an image of Joseph
>   Stalin's huge occidental
> daughter Svetlana! she has given me
>   birth!   I swam out
>   of her fresh salty womb[34]

Owens take aim at patrilineality as well as Western art's hypermasculine claim to genius, which has historically been synonymous with originality. Leaning into both Judaism's and America's obsessions with genealogy and the myth of "the melting pot," she nevertheless disrupts the seriousness of efforts to retrace ancestry. The speaker recasts personal lineage as a kind of outrageous birth-of-Venus legend, where the speaker paradoxically becomes an exile of sorts. Elsewhere, Owens takes equal pleasure in poking fun at bourgeois repression. In her poem "Bernard Fruchtman in Town & Country" (1972), she begins: "I have suppressed / Bernard Fruchtman a long time / & now he leaps out." She continues: "I could've been born / a man   or a bedbug [. . .] with / a diabolical antenna / to tune in on girls!"[35] A parody of motivated forgetting, the poem detonates the true and primitive self that might be released through analysis and reconstruction. The Freudian notion of penis envy, or having a "diabolical antenna," becomes a comic reversion into the phallic phase. At the same time, Owens's choice of title and evocation of "Rockefeller" with his "white / -haired Grand Dad" lampoons "WASP" culture's claim to "Old" America.

Misreading and misremembering have often been associated with intentional repressive strategies, but the fictional genealogies above present one way in which poets after the postwar period have creatively appropriated the terms of autogenesis. Yet another method can be found in the trope of poetic incarnation, whereby a poet claims that their identity is really another earlier writer. A traditional example might be Pound's "Histrion" (1908). Using the past to strategically stress his own authorial genius, Pound starts:

> No man hath dared to write this thing as yet,
> And yet I know, how that the souls of all men great
> At times pass through us,
> And we are melted into them, and are not

> Save reflexions of their souls.
> Thus am I Dante for a space and am
> One François Villon, ballad-lord and thief[36]

While the opening of the poem claims unprecedentedness, the subsequent lines compound Pound's own voice with earlier figures. Incarnation here is used to exploit both forms of originality, to justify one's authority by way of literary history, and to be an inventor at the same time. As Pound goes on to evoke other historical figures—"Christus, or John, or eke the Florentine"—the poem emerges as a scene of perpetual rebirthing. The ambiguity of whether the past produces the modern artist, or whether he himself begets and possesses the identities of his forebearers is part of the trope's forgetful mechanism. Disrupting sequentiality and distorting creativity's dependency on individuation, it works in the following way: the later poet is said to "really" be the earlier original poet reappeared in a new form; the later poet is at once the metaphorical child of their predecessor *and* the progenitor of the born-again predecessor. One can illuminate this metaleptic complexity with some additional examples. For instance, John Dryden once described Edmund Spenser's inheritance of Chaucer through a peculiar anachronism: "Spenser more than once insinuates, that the soul of Chaucer was transfus'd into his body; and that he was begotten by him two hundred years after his decease."[37] In Notley's essay collection *Coming After*—which is titled to acknowledge belatedness—she describes how "Frank O'Hara was the first poet I read who 'sounded like me.'" She goes on to qualify that "[o]bviously he doesn't sound at all like me [. . .]: he was a gay man from Massachusetts born in 1926, I'm a straight woman from the Southwest born in 1945"; regardless of actual biographical origins, though, O'Hara "got right into my . . . the part of my head that has a silent tongue, and his waggled like mine"[38] (ellipsis in original). Framing what might otherwise be seen as influence as equivalence, incarnation here works by having both poets share a metaphorical brain and body.

In his ongoing project *The H.D. Book*, posthumously published in 2011, Duncan maintains that H.D.'s reading of Charlotte Mew and Robert Browning "is related to older religious concepts of reincarnation—the *metempsychosis* or transmigration of soul, the *metangismos* or transfusion."[39] He quotes from H.D.'s review of Mew's *The Farmer's Bride* (1916) in *The Egoist*, which I reproduce more fully:

> Originality is now rare, if not extinct. That is why we overestimate it. But in this, our present day, literary Alexandria, even the most "original" among us may take a sort of perverse delight in finding a new writer daring to

discard his personality to follow, remotely or unconsciously perhaps, the tradition of an earlier generation. [. . .] When one reads of "the white geraniums in the dusk," one feels that [Mew's] Madeleine has wandered in that same garden where the moth and the moth-kiss brushed the heavy flower-petals—and the "portrait of my mother at nineteen" brings to one's over-sophisticated imagination [Browning's] Duchess with her unappreciated, wan smile and her branch of cherries. It is part of our pleasure in art in these days to imagine such things.[40]

Classically speaking, the model of reincarnation depends more on forgetting than remembering. When the men and women of Plato's *Republic* choose their subsequent lives, they must first pass through the "Plain of Oblivion" and drink from the river that Virgil later names Lethe. Though H.D. does not invoke this directly, she imagines transplanting Mew's Madeline into the past, admitting that doing so is a "pleasure" rather than an occasion for anxiety. Against a theory of originality based on separate and distinct personalities, H.D. says that to "discard" one's uniqueness can lead to an appreciation of the richness of origins and itself be a kind of "bold" gesture. In the poet's description, there is again an ambiguous directionality of influence. Mew's language causes Browning's duchess to come to mind for H.D., even though the duchess technically foreshadows and precedes Mew's character. The word "follow"—which I discussed briefly in the last chapter—seems to approximate the strangeness: what comes after moves backward in time by recalling an earlier figure. At the same time, it follows the forward movement of their predecessor into the here and now. The force of the past always has a presence, but the present is also "Alexandria" in a new form. While Coleridge had protested this very form of reminiscence, stating that "nothing can be baser than Parallelisms, when brought to invalidate the originality of a certainly original mind,"[41] H.D. suggests that forgetting the differences between the Duchess and Madeline and imagining corresponding lives can disturb origination in an inspired manner.

A recent and more clear-cut case of forgetting as it undermines authorship and originality occurs in Lisa Robertson's *The Baudelaire Fractal* (2020), a poet's novel in which the main character Hazel Brown wakes up with the sense that she has written all of Baudelaire's works. Robertson, upon whom the novel is based, says in an interview:

I opened my copy of Baudelaire and had the totally uncanny experience that I had written the text I was reading. [. . .] Much later after I'd begun writing the novel I learned that Baudelaire had that experience himself when he was first reading Poe as a young man. [. . .] It's the kind of internal readerly sensation that anybody can have. [. . .] I didn't have the feeling that I was Baudelaire, nor that I wanted to be him. Only that I had written his work.[42]

Like Notley on O'Hara, Robertson is addressing the proximity of reading and writing, what Georges Poulet once compellingly described as being on loan or forgetting one's own self for another. The experience is "uncanny," a description that depends on two senses of originality, namely that what is forgotten is both surprisingly unfamiliar (or novel) *and* familiar in that it leads back to origins. In the description above, Robertson notes how her unique experience turned out not to be special at all: she eventually discovered that Baudelaire himself had a similar feeling when it came to Edgar Allan Poe's work. Indeed, when Jean-Paul Sartre wrote about the two male poets, he stressed how Poe significantly allowed Baudelaire to inherit and become an embodiment of a past order: "It was then that the resemblances acquired their full value; they transformed Poe, as it were, into an image in Baudelaire's past. [. . .] Baudelaire leant over the depths of the years, over the distant, hated America, and suddenly he caught sight of his own reflection in the gray waters of the past. That's what he *is*."[43] Whereas chronology collapses into a single identity in Sartre's depiction, Robertson nevertheless rejects the idea that she and Baudelaire are one; rather, what is stressed is the strangeness of having *two* origins. The phenomenon is one in which a work feels so natural to a reader that it seems to have as two authors, between whom there is an "involuntary transmission":

[. . .] I believe that there was no active sequence of cause and effect, no organic arc of development that could explain the transmission. I simply discovered within myself late one morning in middle age the authorship of all of Baudelaire's work. I can scarcely communicate the shock of the realization.

What then of this authorship, this boisterous covenant? I either received it entire, as one slips into a jacket and assumes its differently accented gestural life, or I uncovered it within myself, which is to say inwardly I fell upon it. I felt it as both purely external and self-identical. Perhaps these two things are not very different from one another. Life is apparitional. Fashion, as I have said, had initiated me into the untimeliness within the timely; after a period of forgetting, garments transcribe garments, unfurling a secretive negation within apparent semblance. We feel this slight vibration as the new. The art of psychoanalysis has demonstrated that a pure repetition of priorness *will* erupt in the present, so that the past and the present, for the potent duration of such an iconoclastic event, become self-identical.[44]

110 Chapter Four

Priorness and simultaneity are central to Robertson's disruption of linear time.[45] In the above passage, authorship falls into Foucault's definition of authorship as being produced after the fact of writing. The "original" works of Baudelaire result in Hazel-the-author, not vice versa. And yet, the peculiarity of the experience depends on a lack of memory. There is no earlier event of literary creation that Robertson's protagonist can recall. Typically, the feeling of having written something stems from a memory of having *actually* written it; but here, the book's protagonist experiences a feeling of possession without memory, a possession that comes to her as if through "a period of forgetting." William James's claim that recollection must evoke not only a sense of pastness but also a sense of intimacy, a sense of "*my* pastness," gets revised. For Robertson and Hazel, there is a sense of "my-ness" without anteriority. This feeling cannot be causally traced back to memory or the past; rather, the nature of the feeling is produced and entailed by a present that has forgotten how it came to be. When Hazel wakes up with the discovery that she has written all of Baudelaire's works, the feeling is authentic not because she remembers writing them but because self-knowledge in the present tends to entail privileged epistemic certainty. Just as a person who feels an emotion does not typically question whether it is really "they" who feels or whether it is really such-and-such emotion they are experiencing, so too does Hazel's feeling emerge as a kind of self-knowingness that does not depend on whether she can remember creating Baudelaire's works but merely the fact that she feels she has done so.

*   *   *

By way of family trees, authorship, and identity, one naturally arrives at nomenclature as a tool for misremembering origins. On the one hand, accounts from Augustine, Freud, and everyday life show that names, in being somewhat arbitrarily assigned, are particularly privy to forgetting. On the other hand, names play a significant role in how we think about and remember the past. Monuments, memorials, and signatures are one example: through acts of naming and inscription, they tend to preserve various forms of originality, whether that be the first founders of an institution or some remarkable figure who should be remembered for their unprecedented or extraordinary contributions. A second, albeit wildly different, case of nomenclature's relationship to memory can be found in Saul Kripke's causal theory of reference. Responding to Wittgenstein, Kripke claimed that each use of a person's name directly refers to an earlier use of their name, which refers to an even earlier use, until we arrive at an

Origins and (Un)originality   111

original "dubbing" event (typically occasioned by a person's parents). Yet another, third example might be the simple, mundane fact that names, even when they don't have definitions, have histories and meanings—histories and meanings that we may or may not enjoy fulfilling. A child who is named after their father may struggle all their life to differentiate their personality or, conversely, long to replicate certain life paths.

In the work of Harryette Mullen—a contemporary of Hejinian and Bernstein best known for her blend of conceptual writing with investigations into gender, race, and culture—forgetting is a way of capering with nomenclature and ancestry while functioning as a mode of cultural critique. Generally speaking, slips of the mind are pervasive in Mullen's world. In her poem "All She Wrote" (2002), she uses forgetting to dodge rather than communicate meaning: "Forgive me, I'm no good at this. I can't write back. [. . .] Now I'm unable to process words. I suffer from aphasia. I've just returned from Kenya and Korea. Didn't you get a card from me yet? What can I tell you? I forgot what I was going to say."[46] Elsewhere, in an interview, she describes amnesia as part of her working process: "It probably has to do with how I synthesize information because a lot of times I actually forget where I have read something and who said it."[47] The poet's most sustained engagement with forgetting, however, is borne out at the level of the history and origins of names and words. In an anagram based on her nephew William Otis's name, which resounds of the American baritone singer Otis Williams, Mullen composes a whole poem out of lines like the following:

> —Is it Otis?
> —I'm . . .
> —Otis, so it is.
> —Am I?
> —'Tis Otis.
> —I am . . .
> —So, it's Otis.
> —I am William.
> —O, Otis sit.
> —O, I am Will.
> —Sit, Otis.
> —It's Will.
> —Is Otis to sit?
> —Otis?
> —Is Will, so sit!
> —O, will I?

112   Chapter Four

—Will Otis sit?
—I'm William!
—O, will Will sit?[48]

Instead of using assonance and consonance to improve recall, Mullen's speaker slips and slides into a Beckettian absent-mindedness.[49] The constant confusion of the first and last name—the name of familiarity and the name of descent—mirrors a kind of game in which history and personal identity constantly get misrecognized for one another. Because the reference and meaning of "it" and "I" are dependent on their respective deictic situations, what begins as a dialogue at times morphs into a monologue and then back out of it. The monologue—a literary form meant to link a particular character's identity with inner profundity ("O, will I?" is Hamletesque) or epiphany (the speaker later says, "O, I am!")—becomes a kind of joke when the sound *O* is overly repeated. One doesn't perceive emotional insightfulness so much as the sound of forgetfulness, as in the phrase "Oh, oh, oh" when one is trying to recall something. The poem, in being aphasic, harkens back to one of modernism's key contributions: that crucial aspects of subjectivity are shown to be dependent *not* on the Romantic soul but on a material and neurological organization.[50]

Elsewhere, Mullen resists giving priority to proper names over common nouns, suggesting that particular identifications of places, groups, or people do not necessarily grant us privileged access to different kinds of originality. In "Zen Acorn" (2002), she writes:

a frozen
indian acorn

a frozen
indiana corn

afro zen
indian acorn

afro zen
indiana corn

a zen fro
in diana corn

frozen fan
in zero canadian

indian corn for
arizona nonradiance

a narco dozen
faze an african[51]

Transmuting common nouns into prepositions, names into adjectives,
and so forth, Mullen plays with the fixity of labels by breaking words down
into false prefixes, roots, and suffixes, only to reassemble them in altered
forms. This deconstruction is not methodologically sound in the sense of
relying on the official "records" of language, but it is a kind of haphazard
process that relies on both sound and sight. Scholars have tended to view
orality as a dominant way of understanding the history of African American art, with literacy being a more neglected form, but Mullen shows that
each mode recovers and forgets what the other often doesn't. Rather than
having us read according to pronunciation, which traditionally links sight
with sound, Mullen permits us to temporarily forget the sound of a word
in order to see it in a new way and vice versa: in the third couplet, the letter "a" surprises us by shifting from being a long vowel to a short one in
"afro." But when Mullen moves from "canadian" to "nonradiance," she
does so sonically, both words being four syllables long, with a stress in the
second syllable. Not unlike N. H. Pritchard's collection of concrete poems
The Matrix (1970), Mullen asks us to literally peer inside a word, not to discover a more genuine meaning but to see another word altogether.

Mullen's slant method of reworking language directly challenges Western obsessions with etymology's authenticating force. Coleridge, for instance, had argued that "in disciplining the mind one of the first rules
should be, to lose no opportunity of tracing words to their origin."[52] For
writers like Pound and Charles Olson, etymology was a form of memory linking the present to an origin that would bear the truth of language
and meaning, while offering a claim to cultural capital. The former had
translated Ernest Fenollosa's statement that "only scholars and poets feel
painfully back along the thread of our etymologies and piece together our
diction, as best they may, from forgotten fragments."[53] In a 1956 letter to
Larry Eigner, Olson even expressed his frustration that Duncan had engaged in what he called "arbitrary etymologies," "etymologies *one makes
up*." He claimed instead that "what's most needed right now is an *Indo-
European* Dictionary—*roots*, so one can feel that far back along the line
of the word to its first users."[54] By contrast, Mullen's clever subversion
of serious philological study replaces linguistic hierarchy with irreverent
permutation and, in doing so, calls attention to the relationship between
naming and history. Might "Zen Acorn" be a play on the "Indianapolis"

114 Chapter Four

passage in Stein's *Everybody's Autobiography*, then? Recounting her visit to a collection of Indigenous artifacts in Indianapolis, Stein described her excursion with the words "Indiana Indianapolis and Indians," stating that the state capital "had in no way been a disappointment." Critic and writer Astrid Lorange attributes this judgment to the fact that Stein's fantasy of America had been confirmed by her museum visit, that the city of Indianapolis "had delivered on the promise of its name by providing access to a historicized Indianness."[55] But if Stein's treatment of "Indiana Indianapolis and Indians" feels uncomfortable because historical violence accords all too well with upholding aesthetic philosophy, Mullen highlights the intentional misfit between the English language and American history. "Indian" refers at once to Indigenous populations *and* to history as a site of misrecognition and misnomers, since "Indiana"—meaning "Land of the Indians"—was a construction of the US Congress in 1800, when lands were paradoxically being appropriated by white settlers. History as a human project is thus exposed as a history of types. "Afro" and "zen" are signifiers that serve as racial shortcuts, but Mullen sheds light on their constructed nature precisely by breaking down a name not to uncover some original, essential meaning but something different and equally surface altogether. "Indian" can become "african" as much as it can become "arizona" or "canadian."

Since the eighteenth century, the dual genres of the dictionary and encyclopedia have constituted evolved forms of external memory, relying on a sense of "pure referentiality, self-enclosed, in the sense that every entry could be seen to refer to every other entry [. . .] in such a way that nothing is undefined within the work of reference."[56] In "Jinglejangle" (2002), Mullen uses the index behind these forms to present a number of soundwords. But in using language in an aphasic manner, she also pushes back against the dictionary's fantasy of meaning and totality. Aphasia, which disrupts memory, takes the form of telegraphic speech. Inverting Stein's stylistic method, Mullen's eliminates words with grammatical functions and prevents words from combining into simple or complex sentences:

> ab flab abracadabra Achy Breaky Action Jackson airy-fairy airfare
> Asian contagion analysis paralysis Anna banana ants in your pants
> Annie's Cranny Annie Fanny A-Okay ape drape argle-bargle
> artsy-fartsy awesome blossom
>
> backpack backtrack Bahama Mama balls to the wall bam-a-lam
>   bandstand
> Battle in Seattle beat the meat bedspread bee's knees behani hani best
>   dressed

best in the West BestRest Best Western Betsy Wetsy Better Cheddar Big
  Dig bigwig
bird turd black don't crack blackjack blame game boho boiling oil[57]

Referencing the lyric form, a "jingle" typically uses its sonic elements as
a mnemonic lure. A jingle is meant to be easily stored and recognized.
It gets stuck in our heads. We find ourselves singing it when we least intend to. Yet Mullen's use of sound is less straightforward. Sometimes a
certain syllabic structure or rhyme will do the work of what Philip Sidney called "knitting up of the memory."[58] Other times, though, more ir-
regular rhythms or the spilling of words into one another refuses facile
comprehension, approximating instead a kind of tongue twister. The poem's oscillation between language as material signifier, on the one hand,
and language as the storehouse of cultural knowledge, on the other hand,
furthermore works to constantly redistribute power. The reader who
knows what "achy" and "breaky" mean, respectively, may not necessarily know what "Achy Breaky" refers to. By emphasizing the gap, Mullen
moves words out of linguistic memory into other kinds of memory, often social. She rewrites the relationship between literacy and comprehension.

Forgetting in Mullen's poem has to do with what one does or does not
call to mind. One way of navigating the work is through forgetting as a kind
of process of elimination. Initially, "ab" could mean a number of things:
there is the option of reading it as a prefix, a babbling unit of sound, the
beginning of the alphabet, and so forth. Once we encounter "flab," however, the latter tends to suppress certain meanings so that we reread "ab"
as "abdominal." The process of *return* or *rereading* is not rooted in remembering proper but in forgetting as a method of selection.

The seemingly innocent, childlike pastime of singing a "jingle" also
rides up against a reader's racial unconscious. "[. . .] airfare / Asian con-
tagion analysis paralysis" and "black don't crack blackjack blame game
boho," for instance, foreground the kind of associative work that occurs
in the process of racial stereotyping. The dictionary and the ABC book are
based on arbitrary indexes, but the question "what does this word make
you think of?" never is. In other words, Mullen rejects the notion implicit
that alphabetic structure can "communicate objectivity without hierarchy."[59] At the same time, the poet's work resists race as the sole way
of entering into her language. In an interview, Mullen has said that the
phrase "the other side of far" suggests *for her* Zora Neale Hurston. "For
other people," though, "it comes from Larry Neal. It's both; Larry Neal
may have gotten it from Zora Neale Hurston originally—I don't know.
[. . .] Most of what I'm using doesn't really belong to any one person or

116   **Chapter Four**

any one group. Some material I think of as African American, and I will go somewhere else and find out it is Irish, or German, or Italian! I think that it's mine. And I realize that I have to share it."[60] Language—in being transcultural, learnable, and full of surprises—questions the notion that history is something one has an exclusive "right" to. It can also reveal the myth of assumed origins, marring the notion of language as a personal or private, rather than communal, inheritance.

*   *   *

While I began this chapter by suggesting that origination and originality are riven by a temporal spectrum—what is oldest cannot be newest— I want to conclude with a possible alternative conceptualization. In the relatively unknown work of American-born poet and Vancouver resident Lissa Wolsak, one encounters a unique fusion of the two poles. In contrast to Bernstein and Mullen, poets typically associated with the "linguistic" turn in postwar American poetry, Wolsak—who is also a goldsmith and energy field therapist—has been called "mystical," "spiritual," and "profoundly etymological."[61] To end on her work is thus to partly expand our notions of the experimental while suggesting that part of her radicalness depends on two kinds of forgetting: first, a kind of regressive forgetting, not *of* origins, but *into* them and, second, the appearance of the forgotten as something new.

The originality of Wolsak's work seems to arise not from a model of progress, whereby one calls up literary tradition in order to surpass it, but a model of regression, "a movement of thinking toward primordial thought."[62] When Charles Altieri says, "I am still learning to read Lissa Wolsak,"[63] he captures the sense of returning to something vexingly elemental, not as a form of recollection but forgetting—a learning that entails unlearning other things. In Wolsak's poems, we are never quite sure what age or time zone we're in, but the feeling is that we are beyond the capacities of human memory. The deeper into the past we go, the more things appear new. Freshness and agedness each commission a kind of distance by refusing to assimilate into a contemporary lexicon with which we are acquainted.

Take, for instance, the fact that what appears ancient and esoteric in Wolsak's work can often lead to neologism. Reflecting upon her work, the poet has made up new descriptors such as "trans-gypsy," "peri-feral," and "interthronging."[64] The paradox of this kind of linguistic work is that these words ask to be searched up, but in fact they have no past record of use. Their various parts might direct us to useful histories, but a degree of speculation remains. Readers often end up pursuing increasingly diver-

Origins and (Un)originality 117

gent routes. In *Pen Chants* (2000)—a title that itself seems to be an invention made from the word "penchant"—she writes:

> at neap tide   a bow-ride,
>
>   quant . . . through
>
> peach-fed ancestors   whose ancestors were fish[65]

Characteristic of Wolsak's work, these lines entail what Kent Johnson has called her "secret-seeming vocabulary flavors," as well as her Mina Loy-esque span of "archaic-modernist-futurist memory."[66] Just as "Pen Chants" could be an invented etymology *or* a descendant of "penchant," so too does the word "quant" in the above lines entail a mixed sense of time and origins. Given the poem's water imagery, "quant" could refer to the English word used to describe a pole that propels a boat. Given the poet's interest in modern physics, it could also refer to a light quant. Looking up the word's sources does not clarify its meaning but actually perplexes it: the linguistic origin for the first kind of "quant" is unknown, while the other comes from the Latin "quantum."

In using caesurae and referencing aspects of Anglo-Saxon poetry, Wolsak evokes the form of the riddle, that early genre that makes objects and animals speak and ask "What or who am I?" Evidence of the Anglo-Saxon influence can be found in the use of "fish"—which nestles the riddle's bestiary interest within evolutionary time—and the use of "bow-ride" as a kind of kenning. The kenning, as I have been alluding to, is a constant device or inspiration in Wolsak's work. As a writer who also works as a goldsmith, she has welded phrases such as "spike-train," "spin-glass," "slink-lily," "light-cones" while extending this linguistic category to more modern and commonly used terms such as "sleep-mask" and "speech-blows." Unlike Mullen, who plays with linguistic origins in order to deconstruct language, Wolsak's return to earlier forms of English verse leads to new linguistic constructions within it. Such constructions also mark a departure from Steinian regression, whereby diction is simplified rather than specialized.

However much Wolak's diction—her use of obsolete terms and her pervasive interest in Latin—might tempt us to seek an end point in etymology, there is often no definite solution to meaning by way of linguistic ancestry. If the reader searches up "neap," they will uncover yet another word that has no known origin. Infinite gaps, then, lie within words just as they lie between them in the white spaces of the page. A hyphen may appear to bridge this gap at the same time it stresses it. This aporia, which cannot be

118   **Chapter Four**

fully resolved through philology or through internal or extrinsic memory, allows words to resemble traces whose links to the present and to each other are not always accessible. The history of words does not guide us, as it does for so other etymological poets, "into fairly obscure areas, but not actually untraceable areas."[67] It instead leads to linguistic inventions, or the forgotten qua forgotten—the forgotten as unassimilable trace. In the latter case, words appear to us as fragmentary fossils, remnants from the expansive realm of lost time:

came to be

birds

for their cloaks   kapu

depend   from the trunk

rice bird

cattle   egret[68]

Here, Wolsak presents the language of evolution and the history of land cultivation. The presentation of monosyllabic words and concrete rather than abstract nouns is especially reminiscent of certain modernist aesthetics, as well as the twentieth century's interest in anthropological and scientific origins. There *is* the sense that, as Eliot says, the "poet is older than other human beings,"[69] that the poet is involved in antiquity. In fact, it is surprising that few if no readers have connected Wolsak to Pound, who was also interested in polyglotism and preoccupied throughout his career with merging new and old, especially through "'primitive' signifiers" like the kenning or ideogram. At the same time, origins are neither justifications of the present nor markers of primitiveness in Wolsak's work. The language of the past is full of aporia, as creature and artifact both precede and outlast humankind, and "kapu" and "cattle" appear as indexes of missing *Homo sapiens*. Against Eliot's notion that "poetry begins [. . .] with a savage beating a drum in a jungle,"[70] history and civilization cannot be sequenced into a progression of temporally distinct stages. "Progress" into modernity is always blurred with a return into origins. Symbols are converted into paratactic signs *and* vice versa; a Babel-like spread of language alerts us to both postmodern difference *and* early myths of a universal language.

In Wolsak's model of origins and originality, what is excavated can of-

Origins and (Un)originality 119

ten expose a chasm, defining the past as a radical absence rather than an integrable one. Her creative regression is thus not conclusive but inconclusive. The sense is that both past and future are infinite and indefinite, arriving from opposite directions at once. This complex temporality and conflation of old and new, first and latest, generates notable aesthetic effects for the reader. Consider the following passage, which begins with more normative, linear grammatical forms only to disrupt any sense of forwardness:

lies of origin

avoid speaking . . . . . the

new thing is to skip

generations

licks like   before   while

within   sometimes I   or we

here and now[71]

. . . .

I hollow   or dig   echopraxia

expellee   evacuee[72]

To move through this passage is to confront the difficulty of an increasing preference for simultaneity over temporal linearity. There is the air of pastness, but one that is preserved in a kind of opaque monolith, where bygone ages can never be fully accessible, only glimpsed through displaced fragments. Even temporally charged words like "before" and "while" have the feel of being spatialized, coexisting suddenly in the temporally suspended vacuum of the page. When Wolsak brings together two preexisting words to form a new compound—or when an outdated word appears without an identifiable source, or when the specific connotations of "before" abut those of "while"—what is stressed is the concurrence of absence and presence, origination and originality, what she calls "link   or not." Sometimes, etymology aids in binding words to a single poetic logic:

120   **Chapter Four**

frondage   frondescent   frondose[73]

But many times, it doesn't:

probab   voltage   dipthong[74]

Like the "hollow—dig—echopraxia—expellee—evacuee" sequence, such characteristic passages disrupt originality by playing with homologous versus analogous structures. Do words, which mean radically different things, appear together because of a shared linguistic ancestry? Or do words, which appear dissimilar and are etymologically unrelated, nevertheless share meanings and functions because they exist in similar poetic environments? As an example of the latter case, the words "hollow," "dig," "expellee," and "evacuee" emerge as manifestations of one semantic cluster of meaning, though they have different histories. "Echopraxia," which means the involuntary imitation of another's actions, requires a sonic association, since "echoes" are typically produced in hollow, dug-out, evacuated spaces. Each word in the semantic cluster appears simultaneously the way objects do in space, with the effect being that the normative temporality of verbs is sucked out, making them appear noun-like. The sequence "probab   voltage   dipthong" is a bit more elusive, since there is no semantic glue. On the one hand, all three words are disyllabic and share an "o" sound. On the other hand, the use of gaps—including the missing letter in "diphthong" that renders "dipthong" a neologism—is significant in creating the effect that there might have once been connections that are now unrecoverable. Just as the "new thing is to skip / generations," so too does Wolsak's negative space "blunt / the tenacity of links" available in language.[75]

Emphasis on what is irrecoverable ultimately gives the impression that the fabric of Wolsak's writing approximates that of an erasure poem. As if revolving around the simultaneity of a source text and the writer's later redaction, the emphasis falls less on the relationship between sign and referent, or appearance and reality, and more on the relationship between a glimpsed part and an ungraspable whole. Erasure is never a matter of simple disappearance but leaves traces of its own vanishing act, resituating the new within the old and vice versa. In Wolsak's work, forgotten words appear defamiliarized when they are suddenly free-floating, when we can't trace how they got there in the first place. An entire history of language may be needed to read this poetry, and yet it is precisely the suppression of the totality promised by dictionaries and encyclopedias, the partial concealment of it that endows the sedimentations of forgetting—a "language / unearthed by a kiss"[76]—with its illuminated qualities.

Ambient Forgettability [CHAPTER FIVE]

Among the many observations in Russian neuropsychologist A. R. Luria's 1968 case study of "S.," a man with hypermnesia, one set of details stands out. When called to remember a discombobulated series of letters like "TMOFAM," S. was able to succeed because he didn't "remember" the letters per se but instead "perceived" them in his head in real time. The mechanism was such: words were "converted [. . .] into *visual images*"[1] so that all S. had to do was visualize where he had placed the image, look, and identify what he was seeing. At times, S. would place the to-be-recalled items in dim and obscure places and at other times along a clearly perceived walk. Each of these sites activated a system of memory that theorists, following Cicero, have long-called *loci*—mental spaces intended to hold images.[2] As a result, whenever S. committed the rare act of forgetting, the occurrence had to do with the surrounding ambience. "Once I had the word *omnia*," S. recalls, "it got entangled in noise and I recorded *omnion*. [. . .] Other times smoke or fog appears . . . and the more people talk, the harder it gets, until I reach a point where I can't make anything out."[3] Smoke, fog, and sound were all contributors to an informational noise that collapsed S.'s ability to distinguish a background from the foregrounded object of recollection. Things as simple as "bad lighting" or "puffs of steam" led the subject to describe the process of remembrance as "exhausting."[4] Yet, given his extraordinary and overwhelming memory, such defects in ambience were interesting in their own right, since as far as Luria was concerned, they solved a major problem. "Many of us are anxious to find ways to improve our memories; none of us have to deal with the problem of how to forget," he wrote. "In S.'s case, however, precisely the reverse was true. The big question for him, and the most troublesome, was how he could learn to forget."[5]

However atypical a literary pursuit,[6] the question of how to make

122   Chapter Five

something forgettable is a chronic preoccupation in the poet Tan Lin's "ambient" work. While a gravitation toward information and technology characterizes some aspects of ambient writing as a genre—making it akin to flarf—other art forms such as ambient music, fluxus, architecture, and minimal and post-minimal light and space work also provide points of reference. As Timothy Morton has suggested, ambience marks a shift in discourse from a determined environment to something more open, in which the subject might be absorbed into the background, thereby collapsing the distinction between the two.[7] Borrowing from a much earlier use of the term by Leo Spitzer in 1942 and Philip Kotler in 1973,[8] ambient poetry implies a shift from autonomous works to networks, systems, and flows, from fine arts to total lifestyle, from centers to peripheries, from intrinsic to extrinsic, even algorithmic, forms of writing. Speaking to the last of these points, Craig Dworkin and Adam Dickinson, respectively, describe the frequent use of "preestablished rules and parameters" by ambient poets and "the appropriation, involvement, and reframing of found texts and other environmental influences."[9] The decentralized role of the author we saw in the last chapter coincides with an additional investment in certain affective and aesthetic effects: diffusion, relaxation, synesthesia, softness, mood, surface, inattention, and, central to this chapter, forgettability.

Most ambient poets, however, are not like Luria's S. They do not possess unlimited or extraordinary memories. Why, then, is there the need or desire for amnesia? Observing forgettability's role in Lin's work, Paul Stephens has written that "Lin makes it difficult to source the information contained in his indexical poems. The effect [. . .] is one of erasure, which mimics a larger cultural amnesia."[10] Admitting a degree of ambivalence into her response, Jennifer Scappettone has called attention to Lin's fascination with planned obsolescence, arguing that any poetry as relaxing and smooth as Lin's "releases traces of what is missing from the sentencing of the historical artifact; it exudes effluvia of the forgotten as if passively—though we cannot be sure whether Lin's ultimate, echoing sentences accord with an exposure of historical powerlessness, an escapist fantasy, or a posthistorical verdict."[11] Such observations accurately describe the trickiness of forgetting's status, the sense that ambient forgettability is simultaneously complicit and subversive within larger cultural, historical, and socioeconomic systems. They also track the tonal ambiguity in Lin's writing. Not quite satirical, not simply sincere, truisms like "one reads, as everybody knows, to forget not to remember," "to read is to forget the meaning of reading," or "a poem, like a disco hit, is designed to be immediately forgettable"[12] feel at once facetious and provocative. There's irony, but there's also the collapse of irony—the destabilization of the gap between what something seems to mean and what is actually meant.

In an attempt to give an account of Lin's ambient forgettability, this chapter is driven by two intuitions: my first hunch is that Lin's "unmemorable" works do more than raise consciousness about the pervasive amnesia in contemporary culture or use forgettability to resist the rarefication and "long-term" value of fetishized art goods. Going beyond the functions of social reflection and critique of elitism, forgettability is a mild aesthetic effect that grants the writer license to invert capitalism's permeation of everyday life by way of attention economies. While avant-garde poets have traditionally recanted economic capital for "cultural" capital (with a general disdain for mass consumerism and an effort to assert an outsider position), Lin leans into the possibilities of an attention economy in order to turn it inside out and generate *in*attention. Second, I sense that in Lin's work, forgettability is Asian, not as an essentialist trait of actual persons or a proclivity of certain cultures, but precisely as a kind of ambient aesthetics. Forgettable things turn out Asian, and Asian things embed a degree of amnesia. Thus, while general skepticism about ambient poetry has stemmed from the "anxiety [. . .] that ambient poetry negatively forgets the issues of race, gender, sexual orientation, etc.,"[13] this chapter resituates Lin's use of the genre in appropriate social contexts—literary, economic, and personal.

*   *   *

To situate Lin's memory lapses within a conceptual lineage, we can turn to the history of ambience, not simply as a scene of forgetting but one that also harkens back to modernism itself. In her work on shadows and "the structure of ambient light,"[14] Elaine Scarry recalls that for Marcel Proust, "the mere change of lighting was enough to destroy the familiar impression I had of my room [. . .] the anaesthetic effect of habit being destroyed."[15] For Stéphane Mallarmé, such links between memory and environment came into focus through ambient features like Luria S.'s "fog" and "smoke." Sharing with Duchamp an affinity for the ambience created by pipes, cigars, and cigarettes during his Tuesday salons, Mallarmé felt that these objects were more than mere accessories. They participated in "the work of memory,"[16] specifically, the eddying dispersion of it. As the critic Tierry Davila notes, the pipe's smoke was alone "capable of making him [Mallarmé] forget for an instant what he referred to as 'the important books I had to write.'"[17] It transported him to another realm. Smoke, like memory, presented a kind of illusion of materiality, a following of what was there into what was suddenly, or gradually, not. It was an index for how forgetting or disappearance could itself be sensuous and vivid.

Years after Édouard Manet painted Mallarmé resting against a couch

124 **Chapter Five**

with a cigar rather than a pen in his hand, Henri Matisse would speak of an art that could forget the grinding reality of an industrial society. In "Notes of a Painter" (1908), Matisse writes:

> What I dream of is an art of balance, of purity and serenity, devoid of troubling or depressing subject-matter, an art which could be for every mental worker, for the business man as well as the man of letters, for example, a soothing, calming influence on the mind, something like a good armchair which provides relaxation from physical fatigue.[18]

Where Matisse alludes to forgetfulness's kinship with the Greek word *lēthargos*, he also provides a historical example of ambience's interest in relaxation and forgettability. He suggests that decor, furniture, setting, and background can induce calmness in the form of temporary memory loss. Inspired by Matisse's statement, the composer Erik Satie would go on to father the earliest versions of ambient music. Coining the term *musique d'ameublement* or "furniture music," he set the stage for its universally commodifiable offspring, Muzak, also known as "architecture music."[19] Along with Claude Debussy, who was exposed to Javanese music at the Paris Exposition of 1889, composers such as Satie discovered what David Toop calls "an ethereal culture, absorbed in perfume, light, silence and ambient sound," an aesthetic energy that would eventually respond "to the intangibility of twentieth-century communications."[20] What these artists all shared was a fascination with the diffusion of an art object into something more elusive: an influence, a sound-space, something abstract. With intangibility replacing concreteness, such ambient precursors decoupled the conflation of medium and resistance, which was to figure so strongly in modernism's self-image and legacy.[21] They offered an alternative genealogy of relaxation, one that actually spoke to an earlier tradition of poetry's restorative and leisurely functions.[22] The goal was not to struggle and revolutionize society with aesthetic destruction and creation, but rather to disperse and distribute art in a way that exceeded the object/subject divide, permeating the "atmosphere" or "environment" in a totalizing way. Such an artistic totality did not depend on a sense of closure or unity, but rather porousness and "culture" or "lifestyle" at large.

While the move from relaxation to forgettability in works by Satie and Mallarmé assumed a degree of passivity, ease, and non-cognition, this very move ironically risked devolving into forgettability's other modernist extreme: boredom, where the dissolution of a subject-object attachment becomes total detachment and non-relation. Here, it is Stein who represents ambient poetry's matriarch, although Poe, beloved by the French modernists, was one of the first to push repetition, a marker of ambient style, to its somnambular and opiate end.[23] After dedicating nearly a decade to composing her first magnum opus, which was to be a complete documentation of everyone who is, has been, and will be, Stein reflected in her subsequent memoir *Everybody's Autobiography* that *"The Making of Americans is a very important thing and everybody ought to be reading at it or it."*[24] Stein's striking phrase, "reading at" a book, is shadowed by the more common phrase "looking at." It reminds us not only of S.'s own conversion of words into images, but also the artist Robert Smithson, who from 1966 to 1967, composed *A Heap of Language* and wrote his statement "Language to Be Looked at and/or Things to Be Read." Collapsing the distinction between literal matter and environment, on the one hand, and figuration and materiality, on the other, Smithson blurred the line between what Richard Sieburth calls "*things* and *language*,"[25] just as Stein had blurred the line between "reading at" and "reading."

Contrasted with a reading process that is immersive and absorbing, "reading at" can refer to a linguistic surface that is just dull or impenetrable enough to be merely skimmed. Yet, just as "looking at" something may imply more focus than merely seeing it, "reading at" also assigns to attention the problem of forgettability. In his review of Stein's *The Making of Americans*, the critic Harvey Eagleson wrote:

> There are reasons for Miss Stein's use of repetition. The artistic effectiveness of it is another matter. Margaret Anderson has stated the usual [. . .] when she says, "I like it when she [Stein] says, 'a woman who had not any kind of an important feeling to herself inside her.' This seems to me interesting and important material. But when, in a book of six hundred thousand words like 'The Making of Americans,' she repeats this description every time the character appears—which is probably six hundred times—I find the system uninteresting. I don't deny that it gives weight, but to me it is the weight of boredom."[26]

Repetition here induces a kind of monotony, putting Stein's work in proximity with a number of other art forms—drone and ambient music, serial art, and Smithson's entropic content, which moves toward indistinction and uniformity. Across these various modes, forgettability is a key aesthetic effect, one that transpires when a "system" replaces a more human "method" and when excess produces a draining of attention, interest, and importance. In the case of Stein, recurrence stalls time while highlighting our awareness of it passing, however slowly. In other cases—for instance, in some ambient music—waiting for something to happen manifests itself as a tedium that causes us to forget where we are located relative to a beginning and end. Sianne Ngai attributes this kind of boredom to "the

126 Chapter Five

absence of a 'sequence of cause and effect,' producing the effect of delay, fatigue, or 'temporary paralysis.'"[27] Recursive language emphasizes how a routine that replaces itself again and again blurs each reiteration with all others, often with no memory of having already transpired that day.

In this version of modernism, a pendulum swings between relaxation and boredom. But a third historical contribution to ambient forgetting can further be identified: the issue of source material. In publishing *The Waste Land* (1922), T. S. Eliot "had at first intended only to put down all the references for my quotations, with a view to spiking the guns of critics of my earlier poems who had accused me of plagiarism."[28] Famously, he chose to expand the notes, in order to provide a few more pages of printed matter. By 1957, the mounting scholarship on his citations led Eliot to seemingly retract his decision: "my own preference would be to abolish the notes to *The Waste Land*."[29] The use of disparate materials here raises the problem of forgettability—less in relation to one's state of mind than to matters of authenticity and source. Citation works by functioning as a mnemonic trace, while plagiarism is the deceptive elimination of origin by reproduction. The extent to which Eliot could or could not have used footnotes—and the extent to which his work was edited by Pound—created what Peter Ackroyd calls "a continual oscillation between what is remembered and what is introduced, the movement of other poets' words just beneath the surface of his own."[30] As an ambient poem, *The Waste Land* opened itself up to an ongoing conversation and collaboration among its (potentially lost) sources, the "primary" text, and the reader. It became a kind of "allusive network much closer to the surface,"[31] underscoring Eliot's understanding that immature poets imitate and mature poets steal.[32] The use of collage and allusion offered the writer "a perfect mechanism to pass over inspiration as an artistic problem and position the writer's task as one of ordering."[33] Such ordering in Eliot's work redefined the artist's role from content creator to content mediator.

Given that relaxation, boredom, and the problem of source figured as three ways in which ambience was already a site of forgetting in the early and mid-twentieth century, the pieces of this genealogy were available, in the first decade of the twenty-first century, as cornerstones for Lin's thinking. When Lin writes that poetry should aspire to "the condition of variable moods, like relaxation and yoga and disco,"[34] and that it "ought to be replaced by the walls that surround it [. . .] camouflaged into the feelings that the room is having, like drapes, silverware, or candlesticks,"[35] he evokes Matisse's description, suggesting that what is camouflaged cannot be singled out or recalled. When he asks, "What would it be like to look at a poem? It would be the most beautiful thing in the room that could stand to be looked at. [. . .] A beautiful poem is a poem that can be repeated over and over," he inherits Stein's idea of "reading at" poems that are always beginning again.[36] Elsewhere he even explicitly says: "the beautiful book should not be read but merely be looked at."[37] In his fifteen-minute PowerPoint video made from his PhD dissertation's bibliography, Lin pushes Eliot's use of footnotes to its logical extreme. The work shifts our focus from the indexed to the index itself, from the archived to the archive. For Lin, Eliot is the first ambient poet, the first "DJ" of ready-made, sample-friendly material. Referencing Eliot's theory of impersonality in numerous texts, Lin argues that for the modernist, "things like voice or personality don't get remembered; they get remixed and accessed."[38] Remixing acts as a method of outsourcing artistic creation, of using older media as one's primary material.[39]

Such a cast of modernist figures, however, would be incomplete without Lin's crucial interest in an additional forgetful interlocutor: Andy Warhol. In *The Philosophy of Andy Warhol* (1975), the pop artist famously describes his tendency to ask friends what happened at a party the night before, because either he "missed" or "forgot" it. In the passage immediately after, Warhol states:

> I have no memory. Every day is a new day because I don't remember the day before. Every minute is like the first minute of my life. I try to remember but I can't. That's why I got married—to my tape recorder. That's why I seek out people with minds like tape recorders to be with. My mind is like a tape recorder with one button—Erase.
>
> If I wake up too early to check in with anyone, I kill time by watching TV and washing my underwear. Maybe the reason my memory is so bad is that I always do at least two things at once. It's easier to forget something you only half-did or quarter-did.[40]

As critics have noted, Warhol's "wife" of a tape recorder eliminates the need to remember. As a device, the tape recorder not only compensates for a bad memory but also encourages a bad memory by espousing the activity of forgetting.[41] Forgettability furthermore works in tandem with the "non-selectivity" of the tape recorder, which as Gustavus Stadler writes, "doesn't get overly focused [...] doesn't make many choices about what is more and less important as it listens."[42] Decades earlier, in 1935, the critic Porter Sargent had associated such receptivity with ambience in poetry: "Just as most the perfume of the flowers escapes upon the desert air, little of the poetry about us is caught and fixed because too few of us are receptive, recordant, true poets," he wrote.[43] As a kind of replacement for the ideal "receptive, recordant, true poet," the tape recorder is totally nonjudgmental, with a tendency to flatten the value of its content. It overlooks

128 Chapter Five

differences in value and is instead good at "noticing or creating resemblances."[44] It absorbs and assimilates.

The nonselective, total recall of the tape recorder reminds us of how Warhol's serial artworks tend to welcome a sense of erasure and are constructed by a constant process of undoing and redoing. In 2014, Lin—who would go on to be a recipient of an Andy Warhol Foundation Arts Writers Grant—dedicated an essay to the pop artist's *Shadows* (1978-79), a work that showcases abstract panels showing a total of fifty-six "peaks" and fifty-six lower "caps." For Lin, the 360-panoramic, ambulatory experience of the serial artwork proposes a model based on "nonlinear absorption, mindlessness, trance states, relaxation, the extended interval, liking things, forgetfulness, and the random accessing of material in real time."[45] The best way to experience Warhol's work is "not to track the images methodically, painting by painting, but to surrender to a more leisurely movement of the retina across a series of canvases, rendering looking into a mood-based computation."[46] The ambience of Warhol's work or "such mood-based shifts" are what Lin calls "largely antithetical to memory." The poet drives home his point when he asks: "Who remembers whether one saw a cap or peak five panels back?"[47]

As a narcotic effect, forgettability here renders aesthetic experience at once impersonal and comfortable. The more one spends time with a piece, the more it evacuates itself of meaning and the more unmemorable it becomes. Across Warhol's work, this logic extends into a Steinian sociology: "people will be repeating the same models," which means "that there are going to be people out there who look like your fantasy, and that there is a good chance someone will like the look that you bought too."[48] Warhol, of course, is not alone in his serial seriality. Poets such as Alan Davies have attributed this lineage of "left to right 'flatness'" and "adherence to system" to Arnold Schoenberg and Anton Webern, distinguishing the ambient aspects of the serial poem from the poem or sonnet cycle.[49] What has been taken for granted, however, is that this "experimental" facet of Lin's work that embraces Warholian notions of reproduction, technology, appropriation, boredom, et cetera, remains separate from the more "identitarian" facet of later works that seem to prioritize questions of heritage, mourning, and family. I want to push the idea that even in Lin's early thinking, ambience has a racial, ethnic, and cultural component. It is not only that relaxation, boredom, and repetition call to mind a whole history of Western appropriation of Zen Buddhism, meditation, reincarnation, and Daoism, but also that this appropriation has itself become clichéd, raising the question of what it would mean for an Asian American writer to appropriate someone else's appropriation. Or, to flip the coin onto its other side: Does assimilation make Asian Americans more white (because that is the purported goal of assimilation)? Or more Asian (because Asians are purportedly "good" at assimilation)?

In light of these questions, Lin's interest in Warhol prompts us to consider the 199 Mao Zedong silk-screen paintings that the visual artist made between 1972 and 1973, as well as the artist's visit to Hong Kong and China a decade later.[50] To read Warhol through Lin and vice versa is to observe a cultural paradox. On the one hand, there has been the global celebration of Warhol's genius, the re-inscription of mechanical reproduction into a signature style that has been praised as the work of a "truly revolutionary artist."[51] On the other hand, there is the Asiatic stereotype of post-revolution Communist China as being conformist, homogeneous, and endlessly reproducible in its ideology and subjecthood. Lin's work constantly ironizes these readings of East and West. The joke is something like this: Did Warhol's Chinese methods of flattening and homogenization make Mao more Western (and expensive) than ever? Or did Warhol's American methods of capitalist mass production make Mao more Chinese (and reproducible) than ever? Such questions situate forgetting, repetition, and redundancy squarely in the problem of subjecthood. How are certain cultural, racial, and economic subjects—and for that matter, objects—produced? And what means of production are available to any experimental writer working within contemporary life's contradictory fantasies of individualism, on the one hand, and behavioral market predictability, on the other?

One way of working through these questions is to consider how the switch from producing objects to producing subjects has played a key role under late capitalism through the rise of attention economics. Attention economies are closely linked to the totalizing yet immaterial aspect of ambience because they aim to put the totality of life, not just labor, to work. Capitalism, as we all know it, produces not just physical objects or goods, but whole worlds or environments, which in turn give rise to certain subjects, objects, and relations between the two. World-making requires a whole slew of services such as marketing, research, and communications to transform the capitalist enterprise into one that is equal to relationship enterprises.[52] Thus, to sell goods also means to construct a clientele, which requires intervention into a person's values primarily by way of attention, memory, and habit. Maurizio Lazzarato writes, "The capture of a clientele and the building of its loyalty means first and foremost capturing attention and memory," with "*attention* and *memory* [being] the forces of creation."[53] But even more than shaping a consumer subject, retention of information becomes "productive by means of the reception that gives the product 'a place in life.'"[54] The exchange of something like information does not lead to the renunciation of it on the part of the transmitter, but

130 Chapter Five

rather the increase of that information's value through diffusion and sharing.[55] Attention economies reveal how the public's memory constitutes not only a kind of consumer but also a means of production.

To create something forgettable, then, is also to trade in an attention economy for an inattention economy. It is to create a work that can be repeated precisely because it has been forgotten, repeated in a way that reproduces some information in the work endlessly and in mass. In Lin's work, this replication at once uses and misuses the logic of capitalism: like an ad that is deliberately designed to be reproduced, his ambient writing renders materials redundant—but in a way that escapes memory. As such, it constantly approximates a form of kitsch, since kitsch, as a derivative form, relies on the wholesale packaging of instantaneous and general rather than "earned" and "individually subjective" emotional effects.[56] Kitsch is the result when a poet replaces the spatial and temporal aura of an object with ambient forgettability.

By way of example, Lin's *Heath Course Pak* (2012, fig. 5.1) operates as kind of "a text and image environment"[57] as well as an economy of inattention. As the second edition of Lin's earlier book *Heath*—whose ISBN was registered in 2007, even though the book clearly wasn't finished until 2008—*Heath Course Pak* already represents its own derivative, its own untimeliness in the world of poetic innovation. A text compilation in the broadest sense, it draws upon Eliot's "remixing," Genette's influential work on paratext, and core ideas from Foucault and Barthes. The book's use of visual text, e-text, printed text, scanned texts, copy/pasted text, digital text, hypertext, annotation, transcription, and so on all accentuate the tension between *Heath Course Pak*'s nonliterary content, "elevated" to the status of a hermeneutic object, and the literary form of a book, "reduced" to mere paratext and stripped of an original or central text. Examples of content that exhibit "weak" author functions include SMS messages, screenshots of Google search results, things that belong to the public domain, and parts of an annotated and redacted version of the book's first edition. Even more examples include emails, publishing contracts, online shopping catalogs, the legal small print preceding Project Gutenberg's version of *The Diary of Samuel Pepys*, reprinted index cards with handwritten "biographies" by Lin's students at the Asian American Writers' Workshop, and excerpts from an "unread novel" (fig. 5.2).

Within this environment, forgettability makes itself available in various forms, functioning as a mild aesthetic effect. Lin compiles items that traditionally act as forms of interference or distraction, but recontextualized as a sort of "course pack," what exactly do these things interfere with? The book lacks a centering focus. The reader cannot locate an adequate "beginning" to the book, which confuses its own copyright material with the

Ambient Forgettability 131

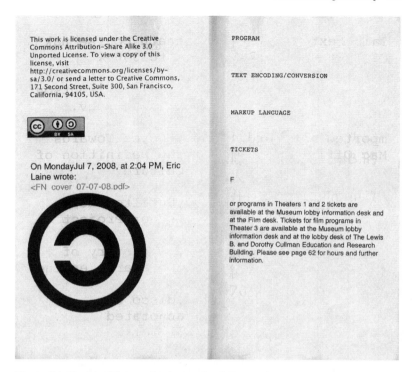

Figure 5.1. Tan Lin, "This work is licensed ..." Excerpt from *Heath Course Pak* (Denver: Counterpath Press, 2012). By permission of Tan Lin.

paratext it has remixed. Without any page numbers, the reader's inability to recall the location of certain passages also mirrors the inattention paid to the sources of various materials. As a result, content tends to recede into the background, with Lin creating a series of minor disruptions in attention that do not distract from one singular object, but rather merely occur through the act of shifting between lateral terms. This shifting makes each text quickly forgettable, but such fissures in attention and lack of recall do not really represent what Lin calls "radical disjuncture" or a "montage/shock effect" in relation to the historical or neo-avant-garde. They are less consequential precisely because the attention is so shallow in the first place. When Lin writes, "I wanted You or me or her to read it like web surfing, or a mash up or something we do all day long,"[58] he suggests that any kind of formal erasure through redaction, poor scanning, or visual hindrance can be seen as merely effacing what was already forgettable.

At times, *Heath Course Pak* appears indifferent to whether its contents are memorable or not. At one point Lin includes a Gutenberg warranty: "If you discover a Defect in this e-text within 90 days of receiving it, you can

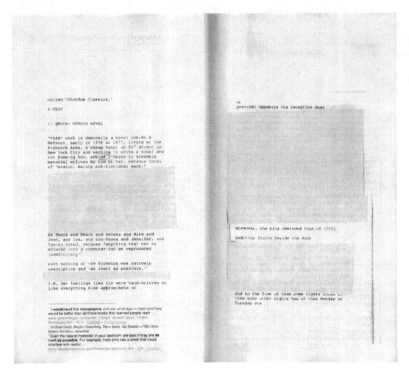

Figure 5.2. Tan Lin, "... called 'Chandos Classics.'" Excerpt from *Heath Course Pak* (Denver: Counterpath Press, 2012). By permission of Tan Lin.

receive a refund of the money [if any] you paid for it by sending an explanatory note within that time to the person you received it from." Here, the irony of procuring a financial return for having exchanged one's attention for outdated information produces only a momentary feeling of amusement. Similarly, Lin includes hyperlinks only to emphasize how they can't be shared or clicked on. J.Crew promotions may be eye-catching, but Lin's inclusion of a "final sale" is clearly antiquated (fig. 5.3). This is also the case with a copy-and-pasted web page selling György Lukács's *The Theory of the Novel*, followed by the sentence "Get it by **Tuesday, Jul 15** if you order in the next 27 hours." In each of these cases, recontextualization forces material to lose its ability to exchange meaningful information for one's attention. Attention can't be focused according to marketing logic, and the kind of value anything accrues in Lin's book is again the kind attributable to kitsch—the familiarity of a certain, near-universal language (like Amazon's) or the comfort of knowing that J.Crew's homogeneous, algorithmic style hasn't changed at all over the years. Lin couches consumerist lan-

Ambient Forgettability   133

guage within poetic ideas and vice versa, but the affective register is kept supple, as he asks what poetry might do to the language of advertisement that the latter hasn't already done to poetry.

The feelings of recognition offered by familiar images and corporate language are in themselves brief, unsustainable, and unremarkable. While they don't demand anything enduring like Kantian contemplation, they also can't lead to the purchasing action and engagement their producers would like. This isn't to say that their recontextualization in *Heath Course Pak* isn't strange. Part of the downright weirdness of *Heath Course Pak* lies in the direction of its appropriation and paradoxically, its embrace of averageness. After all, it is the world of luxury that typically reinscribes the "priceless" aura of art: in 2021, for instance, Valentino launched a campaign that asked influential contemporary writers to fill a single page with writing. Included in this was a romantic poem/ad by Ocean Vuong, written from the perspective of Gian Giacomo Caprotti to Leonardo da Vinci. The idea was that one could flip through the *New Yorker* and come across the "sponsored" lyric. A year later, Louis Vuitton celebrated its two

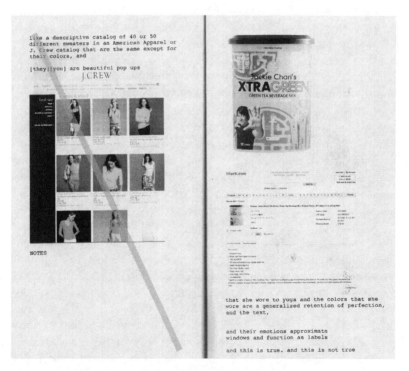

Figure 5.3. Tan Lin, ". . . like a descriptive catalog . . ." Excerpt from *Heath Course Pak* (Denver: Counterpath Press, 2012). By permission of Tan Lin.

134 Chapter Five

hundredth birthday by asking two hundred creative visionaries—poets, architects, visual artists—to construct unique versions of the brand's classic trunk. But when Lin reverses the direction of this process, replicating the logic of advertisement in a way that involves an extra step of appropriation (art's reappropriation of capitalism's appropriation of art), the effect is both recognizable and not.

But what exactly does this mean? How does Lin's work produce the effect of being both recognizably obvious (therefore sidestepping the need for retention) *and* unintelligible (therefore being difficult to process and keep in mind)? For one, the more you look at the images and reproductions in Lin's work, the odder they feel because you realize they weren't initially designed to actually be looked at. Are you "reading" advertisements or "browsing" poetry? And if what the reader is looking at is poetry—because the context and reading environment generates certain expectations for modes of engagement—what does a women's catalog for J.Crew have to do with a Chinese American experimental writer in his fifties? It seems that by using the brand as a piece of Americana, Lin appropriates upper-middle-class white culture in a way that is neither fully cynical about its consumerist and racial ideology nor cooperative with it. In fact, as I write this, it occurs to me that the natural counterpoint to J.Crew is the rise of Uniqlo, the Japanese casual-wear line that was formed two years after the American company in 1949 and began to expand rapidly and internationally around the time of *Heath Course Pak*'s publication. Both fashion brands claim to subscribe to the myth of "Made for All" while in reality constructing the image of a certain generic subject: suburban, American, and upper-middle class, on the one hand, and cosmopolitan, urban, and ageless, on the other. Yet neither brand is race-free. Uniqlo's minimalism, like Marie Kondo, revolves around a projection of "Japanese-ness," with its self-branding of fashion as "technology" and "life-wear" making it a form of ambience. With seemingly interchangeable textile colors and swatches, the brand's "Japanese-ness" feels at once culturally identifiable *and* nonspecific and thus global. As for Lin's use of the J.Crew catalog, the simultaneous forgettability of the ad's contents *and* the strangeness of its recontextualization capture a certain historical conception of Asian Americans as being both invisible and different. The commodified object gets blurred with the authorial subject, the J.Crew image with an image of what Asian Americans are like. To put it another way, the ambient confusion between recognition and nonrecognition, forgettability and strangeness is produced through a series of underlying transformations rendering the textual environment racially ambivalent: the concept of American individualism is turned into homogeneity, which has historically been launched against racial others who all "look the same," which in turn allows an Asian American writer to paradoxically claim affinity with a J.Crew ad. The mechanism achieves its complexity not by probing psychological depths but by trading surfaces for other surfaces, by doing what Anne Cheng has called invoking but displacing the human. Part of the slipperiness of Lin's work is that irony is never about the differences between how things seem and how they are but how these two collapse in a metaphysics of social construction, whereby somewhat arbitrary things nevertheless offer real modes of identification and non-identification. Furthermore, his use of the ad suggests that authenticity and assimilation, the dual notions of the "melting pot" and "multicultural difference," are not opposites but two sides of the same coin. Self-fashioning paradoxically makes you like everyone else; "blending in" makes you more American *and*, by the same token, more assimilationist—that is, Asian or "non-American." It is for this reason that I am claiming that forgettability as an ambient effect is Asian—and Asianness is an ambient effect—in Lin's work. The subtlety lies in how Lin uses certain markers to stress race as an effect of signification. Race isn't already there to be read but is produced in certain intensive or non-intensive processes of reading. And indeed, the more skimmable, the more Chinese. Only in Lin's work can an overtly white ad from J.Crew end up producing a feeling of Asianness. (Similarly, Uniqlo's use of Mickey Mouse or Andy Warhol in its graphic tees somehow makes it feel *more*, not less, Japanese.)

The unmemorable nature of *Heath Course Pak* additionally arises from two other facts. First, what is specific in content is often general in form. Throughout Lin's oeuvre, the generic is most conspicuous in two areas: genre, and the grammatical construction of categorical standpoints—for example, "as any child knows . . . ," "as anyone who has eaten can tell you . . . ," "as anyone who has been to an airport can tell you . . ."[59] In *Heath Course Pak*, however, the generic is platform-based: most readers would recognize track changes on a Word document or screen captures, hence "understanding" what they were looking at without having to actually read the particular details, which at times are also reproduced in too indecipherable a print size anyway. Rather than having desire or economic demand form in relation to a specific, rare object, Lin draws from ubiquitous or widely available forms to disperse attention rather than to focus it. Through generality, he encourages unmemorable "poetry," forgetting rather than fixation. In the world of kitsch, this phenomenon falls under the condition that the work be "instantly and effortlessly identifiable,"[60] that it appeal to the "common denominators of experience."[61] When a word document or screen capture references itself as a general and transparent form, it is forgettable because it is highly available, ubiquitous, and ambient.

136 Chapter Five

Second, much of Lin's outsourced content survives poorly in the sense that it has not evolved in real time. Lin recontextualizes digital content, but in the framework of an even older technology, the book. Such recontextualization reveals the opposite of enhancement: content translates poorly across media, failing to preserve all sense of presence. Lin describes this phenomenon at one point in *Heath Course Pak* when he writes about the media documentation surrounding an art piece called Hamster's Nest:

> In Japan, the article from *New York Magazine*, sent to a different printer, would look different, ancillary, even awkward in the way that tropical cultures once looked to Gauguin; the difference is platform-based rather than anthropological: faces and expressions would appear pinkish and too bright, like a cartoon with no shadows, and white expanses of paper would look cleaner, more sharply defined like sunlight passing through salt crystals or snowflakes. In Europe the event would appear "cooler" and less instantiated, more conceptual, like the documentation for an event that it resembles. In the 50's, in America, pictures would be warmer and muddier, like flickering, super-8 footage of the Viet Nam war.

Here, events cannot be preserved and transported faithfully across platforms and are instead partially forgotten and distorted. Forgettability creates minor differences out of duration, emerging when there is a certain delay between an event and its reproduction, and then another delay between that reproduction and the next. In the passage above, this process is bound up with the construction of race. Race surfaces the more removed it is from actual persons, when presence is replaced by reproduction, authenticity by glitch, reality by picture. The fact that the same faces appear in different hues dovetails with the rendering of race as a form of generic approximation ("pink*ish*," "cooler") that depends on comparing relative "mistakes" ("too bright"). Race doesn't reflect the racial subject as much as it does the viewing experience and the technology of imaging and perception.

One of the most well-cited parts of *Heath Course Pak* involves clips of the "real-time" news surrounding the death of the actor Heath Ledger. These news clips are inevitably outdated, referencing a kind of memory that is stored in general culture rather than in any of our actual experiences of the event. The low-energy conditions of the book come to absorb the highly charged event of the actor's death by dispensing with timeliness. Met with once-relevant material, the reader experiences the forgettability of even the most alarming occurrences, which are characterized by their obsolescence as news but also as a kind of mortality. Headlines and blog entries, which were initially designed for circulation and reproduction, fail to grab one's attention when the replication takes place too slowly or surfaces only after a lag of time. By reproducing them according to the timeline of book production, Lin suggests that ambient poetry enacts "an endless rehearsal of things in order to forget them."[62] This rehearsal is something like the opposite of Freud's *Nachträglichkeit*. The second appearance of an event, or the appearance of a second event, does not introduce trauma belatedly; rather, when it appears as a part of Lin's book, the shock of Ledger's tragic death is totally nontraumatic. It appears as something that has always been very forgettable and that can now be forgotten again.

At one point, Lin uses the unremarkable spectacle of the celebrity's death to produce a new relation: he describes a hallucination of Ledger—an actor known for his "aura" of mystery, distance, and introspection—as the Hong Kongese actor Jackie Chan. The confusion is not between actual selves but reified types. Ledger's "subjective inwardness" gets blurred with Chan's "clownishness,"[63] as Ledger's own cowboy mystery appears suddenly sentimental and cheesy. The stereotype of the unexpressive Asian gets repackaged as the stereotype of the repressive homosexual and stoic cowboy, at the same time that Chan's corniness blends with Ledger's melodrama. When Lin includes and juxtaposes the two actors' autographed movie stills, he underscores that even the precious and authentic memorabilia of "true" artists' signatures can be reproduced to form a kind of kitsch (fig. 5.4). While autographs usually operate as testimonies to exceptional, in-person experiences, a reproduction of an autograph resembles a more general and surface fondness for actors that might be accessible to anyone using a search engine. Subsequently, *Heath Course Pak* does not demand that readers emotionally invest in Ledger's uniqueness but that they experience it as something codifiable. Ledger, in being conflated with his performance in *Brokeback Mountain*, becomes precisely that: a cultural role or avatar that anyone, including Chan, can somehow come to inhabit.

For Lin, things are always partially forgotten when they are reproduced, when they fail to endure in meaning across time or space. This is less of a tragedy about portability than a feature of art as a medium of communication and dispersion rather than singularity and creation. Objects that are forgettable are also shallow and highly available; they invite inattention with their generality and obsolescence. Even when we, at last, admit the general framework of language as a recording medium, we are faced with the incongruities of *Heath Course Pak*'s archival premise. True, the materials in *Heath Course Pak* are time-stamped, extracted from

138 Chapter Five

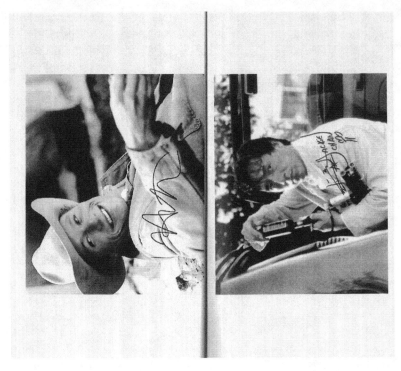

Figure 5.4. Tan Lin, signed photographs of Heath Ledger and Jackie Chan. Excerpt from *Heath Course Pak* (Denver: Counterpath Press, 2012). By permission of Tan Lin.

Lin's browsing history within a certain biographical period and cultural milieu. But not unlike Borges's imagined *Don Quixote*, written anachronistically during the twentieth century, or Lin's "unread novel" in which characters "rewrite the newspaper every day" (a bit that Lin takes from the conceptual poet Kenneth Goldsmith), *Heath Course Pak* consistently reproduces distant pasts as 2012. If *Heath Course Pak* acts as Lin's quasi-diary, it also contains parts of Samuel Pepys's *actual* diary from the seventeenth century, demonstrating a confusion of experiences that leads to the recurring question: to whose memory does this archive belong? The derivative quality of Lin's text erases, replaces, and outlives its original sources. Even if one raises the prospect that the very derivation depends on an acknowledgment of succession, the relationship between original and reproduced material revolves less around origins than distribution. When Lin reproduces a celebrity events blog, recalling the source is beside the point when the source is not really an author, but a set of cultural assumptions, interests, and demands within an attention economy that dictates what might be interesting for a consumer. And this set of as-

Ambient Forgettability 139

sumptions is always ephemeral. If language records, it also reflects what constitutes short-term memory and transcends or falls out of individual retention altogether.

* * *

That ambient forgettability's aesthetic and theoretical lineage need not be excluded from a social consideration of forgetting ought to be increasingly apparent. Such a consideration—which I have begun to emphasize above—finds its fullest expression in Lin's later work, where amnesia is a way of thinking about his Chinese American upbringing. Rather than weakening familial bonds, forgetting is seminal to Lin's understanding of and fondness for his Fukienese father, Shanghainese mother, and sister Maya. For one, when we are faced with the impossible preservation of the people and experiences that matter to us, alternative objects like photographs or television can save what Lin calls the *surface* of such things. By becoming a substitute for memory, these objects actually point to the forgettability of what lies beneath their surface. For another, the mistakes and forms of misunderstanding implicit in misremembrance strengthen Lin's love for his elders—a relationship that is always defined by gaps at once generational, cultural, and epistemological. Out of such gaps, forgettability produces a proliferation of different but similar versions of an absent referent, all of which approximate one another while undermining the notion of a singular history.

In his 2011 digital essay-memoir "The Patio and the Index, Or 'The Anthropology of Forgetting in Everyday Life.' A sampled novel. Alt: A field guide to a family,"[64] Lin uploads childhood photographs, maps, and images of heirlooms onto the Web. Such an archive invites us to understand the repetitive experience of what remembers *us*—purchased items, databases, memorabilia, brands, et cetera—while already being steeped in amnesia. After all, Lin's essay about his so-called "roots" reflects upon the life of a Chinese family living in Athens, Ohio—which is to say, a family that has been precisely *up*rooted from their country of ethnic origin in order to live in a place that itself conjures up the displacement of antiquity with the strange novelty that is American imitation. His focus on childhood is also the focus on a highly ambient period, the outgrowth of what Freud once called infantile amnesia. What is true regarding our earliest memories, studies have shown, is that many of them are in part false. Lin leans into and extends this into adolescence, suggesting that factual errors can nevertheless be fundamental to authentic feelings.

In his meditation on shopping as his family's ultimate pastime, Lin is not concerned with recalling singular events that get at objective truth

140   Chapter Five

but general habits, manifested as feelings detached from autobiographical fact. He describes his family's consumerism in a highly decontextualized way, presenting childhood as a welter of mass-produced affects and images:

> . . . my father accumulated things that were, photographically speaking, misunderstood and blind, and this blindness reminded me not so much of objects as the ambivalence of objects, the scenery in someone else's genealogical chart, or the tiny numerological captions (order numbers) of objects in mail-order catalogues. To my sister and me, it seemed as if we had been deposited on a cruise ship whose interior walls had been demoed by J. Crew in the '80s and replaced with American Apparel tank tops in the 2000s. As we half-lived and -shopped in this ship for a good many years, we discovered that the cruise-ship mentality and then the voyage itself had achieved a muteness associated with cotton-poly blends. The ship was like a description of a description on a clothing-care label, and the description allowed us to become American children in Ohio (after we had become adults), fall in love in restaurants in New York, and eventually have children of our own. [. . .] [A]ll these items [bought and revamped by Lin's father] looked like the remains of some lost history that had washed up in Appalachia and was stamped MADE IN CHINA.

The past exists within an economy of literal goods, where commodities become storage containers for memories themselves. But even within this discourse of remembrance—which in Lin's work always veers closer to reminiscence than recollection proper—there is a kind of built-in haziness, an inherent forgettability that presents childhood itself as a form of isolation, displacement, and remove. Just as the "magic" of commodities depends on forgetting the labor that made them, so too does a childhood "MADE IN CHINA" somehow make fugitive its source, getting recontextualized, alienated, and lost along the way. Where, for instance, are the '90s in Lin's description of this "lost history"? The feeling of being on a cruise ship entails both the limbo of family vacation time and the disconnection from a grounded world. Is the ship imagery one that Lin and his sister shared at the time? Or is it a retrofitted replacement for what can be only partially remembered? Assigning a number of possible sources to his father's purchases, Lin loses track of where these objects and memories come from: mailed catalogs, number captions, or "someone else's genealogical chart." The passage echoes a moment in Lin's novella *Insomnia and the Aunt* (2011), when the poet recalls an image and says, "I don't know if this memory is based on something my aunt wrote me in a letter or said to me or whether I clipped the picture from a magazine many years later."[65] Memory, in other words, does not bring Lin closer to a single version of the past, but closer to various potential sources. Memories work by conjuring up other memories rather than reality per se.

Forgettability in such moments acts as a sort of feedback loop among various versions of the past, which are informed not just by how things were but also how things might have been, how they seemed to be, what they were *like*, and how they were changed over time. Continuing in "The Patio and the Index," Lin writes:

> This shopping had very mixed results for the look of our family, for nature, and for our house. During this period of life in Ohio, maybe a decade or more, I never remember our family ever once running out of toilet paper, D-size batteries, Yard Guard, spray starch, flashlights, mothballs, kerosene, ice, Miracle-Gro, or aluminum foil, and I never ever once remember visiting a neighbor to borrow sugar or butter or eggs. In our household, there was never shortage; there was always surplus and redundancy, along with a vague sense of the unnecessary. Our storage and pantries looked a little like shelves at Murphy's Mart or Buckeye Mart, and both Maya and I had closets filled with clothes, mostly from Sears, that were one or two sizes too big and that—because fashions for adolescents change *much* more rapidly than adolescents can grow (both Maya and I were and remained skinny for most of our childhoods)—we never ended up wearing. And so one family, and here I mean the private, slightly embarrassed look of a family, the family that only the family knows, was produced not principally by the things we shopped for and I wore but by the large number of outfits my sister and I would not be caught dead wearing. This is part of a family that is not documented in any family photo albums. In the photographs you see here, there are no photographs whatsoever of Maya wearing one-piece corduroy jumpers . . .

As Lin writes about the "mixed results" of his family's shopping, he uses the phrase "I never [once] remember" in lieu of the affirmative "I remember." Recollection exists in a suspended state between what actually happened and what didn't. The representation of the past is a collage of heterogeneous absences as well as cultural bits. Earlier, when Lin compares childhood to "a description of a description," he equates memory with something twice removed, translated as if once from Chinese thought to spoken English and then a second time from that broken English into an original Chinese intention. Such transpositions risk losing accuracy in translation, thereby threatening to result in false memories. But the loss or misunderstanding itself *also* comes to constitute Lin's sense of childhood. The result of trying to recall his youth becomes a meditation on the

142 **Chapter Five**

diversity of memory practices and the kinds of forgetting that each practice implies.[66] Rediscovering and losing track of the past are not just acts of consciousness. They are also interactions with material and immaterial environments, consisting of spatial markers, pieces of memorabilia, and digital information. They extend the Warholian interchangeability between people and things by objectifying the most ephemeral and most human of mental processes. What is forgotten by some forms of memory in this instance is salvaged by others: the clothes Maya and Lin never ended up wearing and the family "that is not documented in any family photo albums" together represent a slippery relationship between the nonexistent image of a certain memory (what wasn't documented in a certain form) and the memory of absence itself (that which couldn't have been documented).

The embedding of mental processes into endless, at times out-of-date, troves shows just how close Lin's interests in race and ambience run. Reading the passage above, I am struck by its similarity to Anne Cheng's analysis of a nineteenth-century picture of Afong Moy, otherwise known simply as the "Chinese Lady" when she was imported into the United States to "tour" major cities. Cheng writes: "The immobile lady's ontological promise, her imagined interiority, is not just framed but also deeply infused by the built environment. [. . .] She accessorizes the furnishings, while the furnishings accessorize her."[67] A juxtaposition of this with Lin's family purchases stresses how ambience, as a mode of Asianness, results in forgettability as figures disappear into the background. In Lin's description, there are more things than people. And yet, the objects are an index for the Chinese family that couldn't be fully captured in terms of what American items it bought. A correlation is made between the hoarding Lin describes and the vanishing that constitutes childhood, between the forgettability of ever-changing fashion trends and the enduring value of what isn't recorded or what is lost in the material environment. If our earlier discussion of attention was based in an economy that aims to produce subjects rather than objects, the reverse transformation of people into things evinces a racial complexity regarding how certain subjects are constructed precisely through their vanishing into objects. Environments are not opposed to figures but consist *of* them.

Halfway through his essay, Lin compares the English spoken by his father to "tokens." He then reattributes this "memory" to a scholarly source: "Yuen Ren Chao, my mother's teacher at Berkeley and the linguist who most influenced the preceding paragraph and from whose book *Language and Symbolic Systems* I have borrowed my recollection of my father's speaking habits, has said that 'length is usually a measure of the amount of meaning.'" Borrowed memories, as Lin seems to suggest, are memories that are not quite yours. At worst, they are instances of plagiarism and lying; at best, they are instances of identification. Borrowed memories are also memories that never quite belong. They are memories that come to the aid of those who have forgotten, who have dispossessed or misplaced pasts. They are the memories of second-generation immigrants.

As Lin attributes his memory of his father to a variety of sources, he undermines the accuracy of recollection as well as the uniqueness of speech's source: one's voice. The memory that Lin claims to borrow is none other than one of his father's "speaking habits." In the same essay, Lin writes, "Whereas my aunt's was a kind of voice I heard intermittently on television, my father had the voice of a very long playing record or a Wollensak tape recorder." This evocation of the Warholian recorder stresses a kind of indifference and redundancy on the part of Lin's family. His father's lack of discernment among objects as long as they were all "American" allowed him to take a good and make it "into something that it wasn't but in fact was." This play on identity, not as exact replication, but as a plural category of identities, depends on a proliferation of similarities as opposed to a stark individualism. It shares with camp "a love of things being what they are not,"[68] but whereas camp is a deliberate exaggeration of this difference, the ambient confusion here produces a sense of love out of its unintentionality. Note that Lin doesn't compare the tape recorder to his father's memory; he compares it to his father's *voice*. A voice that is a tape recorder speaks by playing its surrounding noises back to itself. It doesn't have any memories or intentions of its own.

Like the confusion of tape recorder and voice, the reincarnation of a Chinese, motel-owning aunt into a television in Lin's *Insomnia and the Aunt* is indicative of how forgettability functions as an effect of familial love. In the 2011 novella, we see how Asiatic femininity, constituting "the life of a subject who lives as an object,"[69] engages questions of amnesia. Even more so than the tape recorder, the television as a piece of technology has been conceptualized as "the annihilation of memory."[70] Regarding its various contents, which oscillate between market and aesthetic effects and are made up of ever-changing broadcasts or replays of the same material, "one can simply forget it."[71] And yet, gathering around the TV has also been one of the iconic images of postwar American family life. Until perhaps recently, it occupied an essential place in recollections of childhood. Situated in the aunt's motel rather than a middle-class home, the television in Lin's novella thus provides access to an experience akin to love. This approximation is less an impoverishment of a cultural ideal—

144 **Chapter Five**

the motel could be read as a poor version of the white picket-fence home—than it is a copy, a duplicate, an *extension* of the nuclear family as replicated in a broader family context. At one point, recalling his and his aunt's pastimes, the protagonist says:

> I have watched hundreds of movies with Asians and fake Asians in them, and the one thing that makes them all the same (except the white Asians) is that the Asians never stare into your eyes through the glass of a TV screen and you are never allowed to look too deeply into theirs. I think it is for this reason that whenever I think about my aunt, and TV for that matter, I can never remember my aunt's eyes (they appear to belong to someone else), and think instead of Robert Redford [...]. For my aunt, TV can never really lie because it is on all the time, unlike the theater, where there are all sorts of changes of scenery and which as a result goes on and off and is thus the perfect medium for telling lies one after another.[72]

He goes on:

> Having someone else laugh on TV for my aunt was the most relaxing of things because it allowed someone else to have her feelings while she was watching. TV, and I think all TV is great, is not about having emotions but escaping from your least predictable emotions. Of course, only someone who watches a lot of TV like my aunt knows what it means to escape from an emotion.[73]

Here, family memories paradoxically revolve around the forgettability of "hundreds of movies with Asians and fake Asians in them," which is seconded by the more stereotypical notion that Asians are in fact the most "surface" of minorities since they refuse visual "depth" and are therefore difficult to recall. Note that familial bonding does not arise through mutual recognition. It does not emerge from peering into the "windows to one's soul," but rather through an acknowledgment of blankness and blindness, which are paradoxically central to the visual activity that the protagonist and his aunt share. The passages foreshadow the later conversion of the aunt into a TV, whereby she literally becomes something one sees *through*. Like the other "hundreds" of Asians, she is impenetrable because she is invisible; she is transparent ("TV can never really lie") but only because depth collapses into surface, singularity into a generic, anonymous, Chinese "auntie."[74] Love here is represented by the substitution of the aunt's eyes with Robert Redford's, or somebody else's entirely. Less an example of double consciousness—what W. E. B. Du Bois had described as the "sense of always looking at one's self through the eyes of others"[75]—the moment is suggestive of a certain Asiatic inexpressibility. But this is not because the Chinese aunt's feelings are repressed; rather, feeling undergoes an almost extreme form of sublimation. It becomes someone else's. In this sense, the aunt is not unlike an author who generates and distributes emotions for her readers to feel, lives for them to experience. The interchangeability of the Asians in the movies establishes the theme of vicariousness: the protagonist recalls things that didn't actually happen to him as much as his aunt forgets firsthand emotions. The model of family love above is the complete opposite of what has been called, since the 1980s, the setting of "emotional boundaries" and, indeed, Lin's description might be read as a form of codependency. And yet, to recall others' memories and to forget one's own by giving their expressions away is also to experience things at lower intensities, to diffuse our sense of the personal.

The "greatness" of television notwithstanding, the aunt's flatness and forgettability remain tinged by a certain racial melancholy involving lost objects and broken ties. When her character dies, and the protagonist shows a photograph of her to his mother, she says that she remembers nothing in the picture. Alchemizing the aunt into a television is thus a way of bringing back the dead through images of other people, a way of replaying the same content again and again. Objectification becomes a substitution mechanism by which one might reserve one's feelings as another's, one's own forgetfulness as another's memory. The aunt's personhood, in being linked to a medium and object, is animated precisely through people playing other people, actors having feelings that are and aren't their own. As a television, she can display both "live" events and recordings of the past, but neither are exactly hers. Both her livelihood and her death revolve around a literal and metaphorical selflessness.

Near the end of the novella, the protagonist describes removing photographs of his aunt from a family album, in which the photos appear in reverse chronology. He says to the reader: "what you are reading no longer contains some of the things I have been telling you about."[76] Rather than needing to control the objects of memory, the author here relinquishes and gives greater mobility to the facts and fictions that constitute family. Erasure is part of letting go, as Lin writes:

> People say you cannot imagine a thing like love coming from a TV set, but I think most of our family's feelings for each other started and ended there. [...] Now that they are dead, my aunt and father exist inside a place where the less-than-honest ravages of the world can finally be made to unfurl without the violence of the feelings that normally attaches to them. People like my aunt don't need to be remembered; they need to be forgotten

inside a TV set. The era of forgetting isn't over, it just needs to be reinvented by databases.[77]

Lin's protagonist isn't upset by forgetting the dead because forgetting here is presented as a kind of storage and protection rather than abandonment. To forget something inside a TV set is in some senses to leave it behind but also to leave it alone, to preserve rather than to alter it. Underlying these passages is the sense that amnesia further releases the dead from the rehearsal of trauma. Forgetting the deceased is a way of facilitating their escape, withdrawal, rest, and refuge. The passage revises the typical process of mourning by converting a key symptom, the loss of worldly interest, into something else: "a place where the less-than-honest ravages of the world can finally be made to unfurl without the violence of the feelings that normally attaches to them." Escapism is not defined by a disappearance of reality but a renewed mode of contact with it, in which *the self* is what disappears, this time into the world. The end is not disintegration but reintegration. It involves a kind of free flow of introjection and projection, whereby the dead can both absorb and evacuate distressing experiences without harm, and the living can have a relationship with loss that involves accepting what goodness can still be taken in from the outside. By becoming part of a television, the aunt and father don't just become or disappear into objects, thereby becoming more ambient and more Chinese; they are also transformed into television in the sense that they are now the thing the viewer absorbs. They provide objective correlatives that produce real emotions in the living, endlessly distributing, relinquishing, and producing something like love. Forgetting involves a series of transfers where letting go, in the end, is merely the beginning of something shareable.

A Reading Affair [CODA]

In Denise Levertov's poem "The Secret" (1964), two girls tell the poet that they've discovered the secret of life in one of her lines of poetry. They don't disclose, however, what it is they've learned or where it was they first unearthed it. More than a week later, they forget the contents of their finding, along with the title of the relevant poem. The knowledge the two girls share becomes a secret even to themselves. As the poem goes on, obscurity comes to undergird and condition curiosity and intimacy, illuminating the pleasures of hiding and seeking. The secret's significance is replaced by the significance of its loss, and forgetting becomes a kind of testament to what forever binds the three figures in unknowability. By the end of the poem—which is itself a secret of a secret—misplacing and displacing things becomes a way for a lifelong commitment to art to consist still of spontaneous pleasure. The speaker says of the girls:

> I love them
> for finding what
> I can't find,
>
> and for loving me
> for the line I wrote,
> and for forgetting it
> so that
>
> a thousand times, till death
> finds them, they may
> discover it again, in other
> lines

148 **Coda**

in other
happenings. And for
wanting to know it,
for

assuming there is
such a secret, yes,
for that
most of all.[1]

Slips of the Mind has largely been about writing, but failures in memory have also given shape to the process of reading. Forgetting in Levertov's poem is both the logic and reason for devouring poetry as an ongoing pursuit. The point is that "the secret" in question isn't sacred; or else, it is only sacred because it is vital, not scarce, because it can be left behind without any real travesty. The threat of having something fall into oblivion remains absent. Levertov's work isn't a poem about extinction but forgetting as a way of paradoxically re-creating the experience and intensity of firsts—those otherwise "unforgettable" moments in life—until lastness, as death, claims us. Is forgetting not then also a way of returning to girlhood? The preciousness of the two girls' experience lies precisely in their carelessness, mimicked in the poem's quickening *for*s. Amnesia restores a childhood sense of belief and wonder—a state in which the world is not past but still before us, waiting. Whatever losses might weaken confidence as a feeling of certainty about life's truths become the basis of confidence as a condition of trust and sociality. What about the secret, in Levertov's poem, entails an instruction to forget? What about it suggests that there might be a perverse pleasure in allowing such secrets to slip through our fingers?

The art historian T. J. Clark has written compellingly about this kind of sensation, about how art embeds amnesia and therefore a return to what has inevitably changed in and for us. The desire for certainty in life and in art is ongoing, but certainty itself is momentary and subject to flux. Forgetting things partially fuels the desire to see, to stand before, to feel them again. Can it be, Clark asks, that there are certain things "that simply cannot be retained in the memory, or fully integrated into a disposable narrative of interpretation; so that only the physical, literal, *dumb* act of receiving" can suffice?[2] And again, "certain new combinations of form and content [. . .] make us want to return to them, perhaps in order to remember what it was like to encounter them for the first time: this just *is* the aesthetic, and as such profoundly ordinary."[3] But return is precisely not the same as remembering; the first time can only be re-created as the first second time, the first umpteenth time. Return is what happens when we are led by memory's insufficiency to want the thing itself, when we are driven both by the answers we are convinced by and the questions that remain. Returning to the aesthetic object renders recollection superfluous. Even the long-standing association of poetry with memorization undervalues how poems so often escape us because they exist in and through time rather than all at once. Most of the time, when we "remember" the poems we've read, what we really remember is a kind of feeling. Impressed in us is some residual effect of beauty or astonishment over what happens "plot-wise." (The Boston-based poet Stephen Jonas once wrote: "There've been / so many poems / i can't remember/ them all: // the bright ones / w/ fair hair / strident intellects / eyes dark & keen."[4]) But even if and when we remember the words verbatim, there is no way of calling them up without returning to the poem itself, not just the memory of the poem. And *even this* seems to ignore half the pleasures of reading poetry: the best poems cannot be absorbed or digested as a whole; the words pull apart as much as they cohere. The notion that verse resists paraphrase is linked to the fact that memory cannot abbreviate poetic meaning without costing us some part of its allure. When we read or listen to a poem for the first time, we are meant to miss much of it. Again: it is almost as if the best poems return us to those moments in youth when we read books far too advanced for us. We finish these works for the eventual reason that what is lost on us makes as much of an impact as what we immediately comprehend.

The poet and critic Richard Howard, in an essay on Robert Creeley, once described the latter's poems as works that weren't meant to be "murmured, remembered, but rather encountered, confronted."[5] He attributed this aversion to memory to the poems' avoidance of "patterns." Such avoidance might be read as a contribution to complexity—not at the level of contradiction (which informs much of what entices Clark) but at the level of an indescribably stubborn, forward insistence. Reading Creeley's work, I know that this insistence emerges from a syntax that, in being manipulated, still has to result in sense, still has to abide by some principle—in part grammatical and in part psychological—as if to ultimately justify the manipulation. His poems, despite their short lines, remain organized by the sentence and, moreover, a kind of sentence that refuses tautology. In literature, some kinds of poems are difficult because they appear easy, because they approximate the state of something natural. Creeley's poems, by contrast, want us to feel—and perhaps they even exaggerate—the effort involved in their making. Something about their highly wrought appearance opposes their assimilation into memory. It is as if the intricacy and compactness of the poetic constructions are already at such a limit that the poem cannot yield any more of itself to be more easily retained.

150 **Coda**

Creeley's poems know that memory wants to take shortcuts and actively thwart this process.

Other poems in the English language are still best read with a certain evacuating energy. I have already alluded to adjacent phenomena in my discussions of Stein's "gist" and Lin's lateral shifts in inattention. But even outside these single-author examples, forgetting is essential to how poems direct and regulate their own speed. W. H. Auden alludes to this when he writes of Lord Byron: "Unlike most poets, he must be read very rapidly as if the words were single frames in a movie; stop on a word or line and the poetry vanishes."[6] Or as Lin writes: "7 is generally thought to be the number of things the human brain can readily remember. [. . .] 7.2 seconds is hopefully just along enough to get the reader/viewer into a groove."[7] That every poem has its own optimal, internal pacing is at once cognitive and poetic. Auden's description of Byron suggests counterintuitively that some words need to be read swiftly enough for something else to be grasped, that somehow *not* retaining words is the best way of getting at the poetry. This is largely true of poems that are made up of long lines, for length is one way of having words be carried by their own momentum.

It is with the language of forgetting that John Keats, in an 1817 letter to Benjamin Bailey, defended the merits of the long poem: "Do not the Lovers of Poetry like to have a little Region to wander in where they may pick and choose, and in which the images are so numerous that many are forgotten and found new in a second Reading: which may be food for a Week's stroll in the Summer?"[8] The kind of reading painted by Keats's rhetorical question veers closer to a form of labor than to the kind of work that might culminate in a final, finite product. In a dialectic with its audience, the poem both renews and exhausts our readerly energy. Forgetting depends on the bounty of the described bucolic setting. Speaking to poetic assortment, letting go scores time in a way that isn't anxious. The poet's choice of "lovers" significantly places amnesia in relation to romance and stage of life: acts of relinquishing are associated with endless choice, not the inevitabilities of old age, which are, by contrast, characterized by the ease and frequency with which one forgets, but at the very period when one has the most memories stored. The image that appears in the Keats passage is that of young lovers in no rush to complete the affair of reading. Wandering as a mode of turning and wending—rather than directing oneself in a straight fashion—is their primary state. They are not lost travelers trying to recall their way home, but drifters who indulge in not knowing their precise way forward and back. Indeed, as representatives of readers, they seem not to have any sense of ending at all. This is telling, for while poems can't be created a second time in a strict sense, they can be read again and again. Forgetting is why we reread; it is also an object of knowledge that surfaces during this process. A map of the things we can't remember in a poem or book would reveal and constitute, as the writer Julien Gracq once suggested, a kind of shadow or double text in relation to the primary work. What escapes from our mind, and how, can thus end up tracking the very connections between images or phrases. It can call attention to how loosely or tightly those links have been made. More than a negative index for formal and thematic motifs, forgetting itself might be a unifying structure, giving definition to poems through varying degrees of porousness.

Acknowledgments

Over the years, this book was inspired and improved by conversations and correspondences with many individuals. Most directly and significantly, it grew out of the ongoing support and readership of Susan Stewart, Joshua Kotin, and Diana Fuss. I am especially indebted to Susan for coining the phrase "slips of the mind" when I was in a conundrum over my title; the phrase quickly became the most memorable of my various options.

Matthew Bevis, Keston Sutherland, and Michael Wood each shaped my thinking at various stages in this project's evolution. Anna Moser and Orlando Reade read late drafts of chapter 4 and offered valuable commentary. Many thanks are owed to Ted Rees for first introducing me to the work of Lissa Wolsak and to Nick Sturm for his various pointers regarding the New York School. Between 2019 and 2021, attendance at the Twentieth Century Graduate Workshop in the Department of English at Princeton University aided the project's development. In particular, I am grateful to workshop members and friends Janet Kong-Chow, Oli Browne, Cate Mahoney, Eli Mandel, Liora Selinger, Kimberly Bain, Ian Davis, Reuven L. Goldberg, Elspeth Green, M. (Emmy) Kumar, Ryan Zaluzec, and Mary Nayden. I appreciate those who offered feedback at relevant presentations at the Northeast Modern Language Association in 2019 and 2021 and the readers at *Modernism/modernity* and *Journal of Modern Studies* who commented on article versions of chapters 1 and 2.

I happily acknowledge the additional influence, at Princeton, of Esther Schor, Anne Cheng, Bill Gleason, Jeff Dolven, Erin Huang, Kinohi Nishikawa, Meredith Martin, Claudia Johnson, Bob Perelman, Nathan Ashe, Emily Eyestone, Elias Kleinbock, Catie Crandall, Matthew Ritger, Alex Lin, and Kate Thorpe. At the University of Oxford, I met many brilliant people who shaped my thinking: Kathryn Murphy, Nicholas Gaskill, Jack Parlett, Michael Kalisch, Alexander Roberts, Michelle Taylor,

154 Acknowledgments

and Charlotte Terrell. I am also grateful to my colleagues at the University of Denver for fostering an environment in which I could finish *Slips of the Mind*. I especially want to thank Bin Ramke, R. D. (Ryan) Perry, Menglu Gao, Graham Foust, Patrick Cottrell, Kimberly Jones, Michael Greenberger, and Wayne Yeung for their friendship and camaraderie. And to those earliest graduate students who inspired joy in my work and gave me weekly conversations to look forward to—especially Monroe Lawrence, Mary Helen Callier, Jane Huffman, Jason Lipeles, and Briana Hanratty—thank you.

To the team at the University of Chicago Press, I am most indebted. Alan Thomas guided this manuscript into its final form with the utmost grace. Anahid Nersessian and Nan Da were nothing but encouraging: I thank them for taking this project on. Randolph Petilos was an invaluable source of knowledge and, along with Erin DeWitt, a key part of the production process. I am also grateful to my two anonymous readers for their invaluable insight, enthusiasm, and commentary.

My deepest thanks to Charles Bernstein and Tan Lin for allowing me to reproduce their work, and to Alice Notley, David Kermani, and Ron Padgett for permission to reproduce written and visual texts by Ted Berrigan, John Ashbery, and Joe Brainard, respectively. Pat Nolan kindly provided a scan of Berrigan's "Things to do today" postcard, which originally appeared on the New Black Bart Poetry Society site.

I would not have been able to write this book without the enduring love of my friends and family. The number of poets who have expanded my realm of thinking and experience—and have thus shaped *Slips of the Mind* indirectly—is countless. Christopher Frugé not only accompanied me from this project's conception to its end but also, on a daily basis, continues to make me a better and happier thinker. I am grateful for Emily Soong's care and ongoing encouragement. Finally, I dedicate this book to my loving parents, 福欽 and 郁南, who allowed me my curiosity and expression, and who and gave me the childhood, education, and freedom to be who I am today.

*   *   *

Grateful acknowledgment is made for permission to reprint the following: "The Ecclesiast," from *Rivers and Mountains*, copyright © 1966, 1985, 2008 by John Ashbery, all rights reserved, by arrangement with Georges Borchardt, Inc. for the Estate of John Ashbery; "Zen Acorn," from *Sleeping with the Dictionary* by Harryette Mullen, © 2002 by the Regents of the University of California; Joe Brainard's drawing "Things to Do Before I Move," from *Some Drawings of Some Notes to Myself* (1971), by permission of the Estate of Joe Brainard; "I Don't Remember," from *Near/Miss* (University of Chicago Press, 2018), © 2018 by Charles Bernstein, all rights reserved, by permission of the author and the University of Chicago Press; "Things to do today" (ca. 1970), by Ted Berrigan, by permission of the Estate of Ted Berrigan, and reproduced with help from and permission of Pat Nolan and the New Black Bart Poetry Society; and pages from *Heath Course Pak*, copyright © 2012 by Tan Lin, by permission of the author.

Earlier versions of portions of chapter 1 first appeared as "Forgetting, Knowledge, and Action: Gertrude Stein's Modernist Terms," *MODERNISM/MODERNITY*, Vol. 9, cycle 1 (Fall 2024), © 2024 by Johns Hopkins University Press; and earlier versions of portions of chapter 2 first appeared as "The 'To-Do' List Poem: Prospective Memory and a New York School Genre," *Journal of Modern Literature* 43, no. 4 (Summer 2020): 91–107, © 2020 by The Trustees of Indiana University.

Notes

Introduction

1. Friedrich Nietzsche, *The Birth of Tragedy and Other Writings*, trans. Ronald Speirs, ed. Raymond Geuss and Ronald Speirs (Cambridge: Cambridge University Press, 1999), 17.

2. Søren Kierkegaard, *Either/Or: Part I*, trans. and ed. Howard V. Hong and Edna H. Hong (Princeton, NJ: Princeton University Press, 1987), 185-86.

3. Fernando Pessoa, *The Book of Disquiet*, trans. Margaret Jull Costa, ed. Jerónimo Pizarro (2017; reprint, London: Serpent's Tail, 2018), 374.

4. For studies of forgetting's thematic appearance, consult books by Harald Weinrich, Lewis Hyde, Douglas J. Herrmann and Roger Chaffin, and Christopher Ivic and Grant Williams.

5. Svetlana Boym, *The Future of Nostalgia* (New York: Perseus Books, 2001), xiv.

6. Rebecca Bryant, "Nostalgia and the Discovery of Loss," in *Anthropology and Nostalgia*, ed. Oliva Angé and David Berliner (New York: Berghahn, 2014), 155.

7. Francis Yates, *The Art of Memory* (London: Routledge, 1966); Pierre Nora, *Realms of Memory*, vols. 1-3, trans. Arthur Goldhammer, ed. Pierre Nora and Lawrence D. Kritzman (New York: Columbia University Press, 1996-98); Maurice Halbwachs, *Collective Memory* (1950), ed. and trans. by Lewis A. Coser (Chicago: University of Chicago Press, 1992); Mary Carruthers, *The Book of Memory: A Study of Memory in Medieval Culture* (Cambridge: Cambridge University Press, 1990).

8. Maurice Blanchot, *The Infinite Conversation* (1969), trans. Susan Hanson (Minneapolis: University of Minnesota Press, 2003), 315.

9. Marc Augé, *Oblivion*, trans. Marjolijn de Jager (Minneapolis: University of Minnesota Press, 2004), 20-21.

10. Christopher Ivic and Grant Williams, introduction to *Forgetting in Early Modern English Literature and Culture: Lethe's Legacies*, ed. Christopher Ivic and Grant Williams (London: Routledge, 2004), 2.

11. A more recent example might be that from the Gettysburg Address: "The world will little note, nor long remember what we say here, but it can never forget what they did here."

12. "He who forgets himself because of women or children shall come upon an evil place unless God is merciful to him."

158   **Notes to Pages 5–7**

13. Mary Carruthers, *The Craft of Thought* (Cambridge: Cambridge University Press, 1998), 82.

14. Cicero includes memory as one of the five pillars of rhetorical prowess, foregrounding it in his tale of Simonides. When Cicero writes that memory is "the firm mental grasp of matters and words," he draws attention to memory's transition from the realm of the oratory to the ethical. Cicero, *De Inventione*, 1.9. See Yates's *The Art of Memory* for more on how the Middle Ages solidified this transition.

15. It is useful to track the terminological constellations formed around memory and forgetting. In everyday use, memory almost always stands in for remembering, not a mixture of remembering and forgetting. For clarity, this book is consistent with this common usage unless otherwise noted. Writing about seventeenth-century literature, Ivic and Williams intentionally choose the stronger term "oblivion" over "forgetfulness," writing, "Oblivion resonates with Death and Envy, while Memory generates meanings with History as well as with Justice and Prudence." Ivic and Williams, introduction to *Forgetting*, 22. Augé, who also uses the term "oblivion" but in a more liberal fashion, notes: "I am now going to pronounce some 'enormous' words: the word *oblivion* first of all, and those that oppose it merely by being linked with it, such as *memory* and *remembrance*; a few other that are harmonics, deformations, or outgrowths of the first ones more or less—like *pardon, indifference*, or *negligence* on a line with oblivion, *remorse, obsession*, or *resentment* on a line with memory; and then there are two more words: *life* and *death*." Augé, *Oblivion*, 13.

16. Friedrich Nietzsche, *On the Advantage and Disadvantage of History for Life* (1874), trans. Peter Preuss (Indianapolis: Hackett, 1980), 29.

17. See Friedrich Nietzsche, *On the Genealogy of Morals*, trans. Douglas Smith (Oxford: Oxford University Press, 1996). It was forgetting's connection to genealogy that came to define Nietzsche's philosophical legacy in the mid- and late twentieth century. If genealogy converted the question of transcendental beginnings to moments of human invention, forgetting's relationship to origination—both as its upset and its substitution—appealed to later twentieth-century thinkers. For instance, when Michel Foucault writes that for Nietzschean genealogy, "what is found at the historical beginning of things is not the inviolable identity of their origin; it is the dissension of other things. It is disparity," we witness a poststructuralist moment, whereby both a Derridean philosophy of difference and a Deleuzean philosophy of fissure are at stake. Michel Foucault, "Nietzsche, Genealogy, History" (1971), in *Language, Counter-Memory, Practice*, trans. Donald F. Bouchard and Sherry Simon (Ithaca, NY: Cornell University Press, 1977), 139–43. Derrida, in *Spurs* (1978), was particularly interested in forgetting as a double movement—what concealed an absent origin while concealing misremembrance's own meaning. Because oblivion was a kind of paradox—its "essence" being "non-essence"—Derrida argued that it "not only attacks the essence of Being" but also "belongs to the nature of being" at the same time. Jacques Derrida, *Spurs*, trans. Barbara Harlow (Chicago: University of Chicago Press, 1978), 141. Chapter 5 in this book will pick up a discussion of genealogy.

18. Gino Severini, "Plastic Analogies of Dynamism: Futurist Manifesto" (1913), reprinted in *Futurism: An Anthology*, ed. Christine Poggi, Lawrence Rainey, and Laura Wittman (New Haven, CT: Yale University Press, 2009), 165.

19. Umberto Boccioni, "The Plastic Foundations of Futurist Sculpture and Painting" (1913), in *Futurism*, ed. Poggi, Rainey, and Wittman, 139.

20. Bruno Corr, F. T. Marinetti, and Emilio Settimelli, "The Futurist Synthetic The-

Notes to Pages 7–11 159

atre" (1915), reprinted in *Manifesto: A Century of Isms*, ed. Mary Ann Caws (Lincoln: University of Nebraska Press, 2000), 191.

21. D. Burliuk, Alexander Kruchenykh, V. Mayakovsky, and Victor Khlebnikov, "Slap in the Face of Public Taste" (1912), reprinted in *Words in Revolution: Russian Futurist Manifestoes, 1912–1928*, ed. and trans. Anna Lawton and Herbert Eagle (Washington DC: New Academia Publishing, 2004), 51.

22. Marcel Duchamp, *Salt Seller: The Writings of Marcel Duchamp*, ed. Michel Sanouillet and Elmer Peterson (New York: Oxford University Press, 1973), 167.

23. Ezra Pound, *Guide to Kulchur* (London: Faber and Faber, 1938; repr., New York: New Directions, 1970), 51, 134.

24. See Michael North's "Where Memory Faileth: Forgetfulness and a Poem Including History," in *Ezra Pound: The Legacy of Kulchur*, ed. Marcel Smith and William Andrew Ulmer, 145–65 (Tuscaloosa: University of Alabama Press, 1988).

25. See Robin Gilmour, *The Victorian Period: The Intellectual and Cultural Context of English Literature, 1830–1890* (London: Longman, 1993).

26. Alfred North Whitehead, "The British Association at Newcastle. Section A. Mathematical and Physical Science: 'The Organisation of Thought,'" *Nature* 98 (1916): 81.

27. Henri Bergson, *Memory and Matter* (1908), trans. Nancy Margaret Paul and W. Scott Palmer (London: George Allen & Co., 1913), 74, 34.

28. See Messay Kebede, "Action and Forgetting: Bergson's Theory of Memory," *Philosophy Today* 60, no. 2 (Spring 2016): 347–70.

29. Sigmund Freud, "Fragment of an Analysis of a Case of Hysteria (1905 [1901])," in *The Standard Edition of the Complete Psychological Works of Sigmund Freud*, vol. 7, trans. James Strachey (London: Hogarth Press, 1953), 15, 16, 17.

30. Wilfred Bion, *Attention and Interpretation* (Lanham, MD: Rowman & Littlefield, 2004), 42.

31. Wilfred Bion, "Notes on Memory and Desire" (1967), reprinted in *Melanie Klein Today: Developments in Theory and Practice*, vol. 2: *Mainly Practice*, ed. Elizabeth Bott Spillius (New York: Routledge, 1988), 18. Psychoanalyst Philip Bromberg reiterates a similar point in his essay "Staying the Same While Changing Reflections on Clinical Judgment," *Psychoanalytic Dialogues* 8, no. 2 (1998): 225–36.

32. Bion, "Notes on Memory and Desire," 18.

33. Arguably, there is a bit of a chicken-and-egg problem. Remembering itself might impart significance to an event, rather than supposing an event's innate significance.

34. Harald Weinrich, *Lethe* (Ithaca, NY: Cornell University Press, 2004), 134, 234.

35. See Daniel Wegner, David Schneider, Samuel Carter, and Teri White, "Paradoxical Effects of Thought Suppression," *Journal of Personality and Social Psychology* 53, no. 1 (1987): 5–13.

36. Henry D. Thoreau, "Walking" (1862), in *The Essays of Henry D. Thoreau*, ed. Lewis Hyde (New York: FSG, 2002), 158.

37. Ralph Waldo Emerson, "Self-Reliance" (1841), in *Emerson: Essays and Lectures* (New York: Library of America, 1983), 270, 265.

38. Louis Menand, *The Metaphysical Club* (New York: FSG, 2001), 88.

39. John Dewey notes: "[H]abits must intervene between wish and execution in the case of bodily acts [. . .] but in fact, formation of ideas as well as their execution [also] depends upon habit." In other words, we do not form a pure idea of conduct and then execute it irrespective of habit. Rather, habits—our sense of what we do—support our ideas of conduct and what is possible: "[T]he act must come before the thought, and a

160 Notes to Pages 11–17

habit before an ability to evoke the thought at will." Dewey, *Human Nature and Conduct* (New York: Henry Holt, 1922), 80.

40. William James, *Pragmatism: A New Name for Some Old Ways of Thinking* (1907; repr., New York: Cosimo, 2008), 109. This reliance on "previous human thinking" finds a parallel in Charles Sanders Peirce's work, where changes in habits indicate an evolution of our ideas in a non-deterministic world. For Peirce, habits constitute a broad array of conventions, from our use of symbols to that of rules of reasoning and dispositions.

41. William James, *The Principles of Psychology* (New York: Henry Holt, 1890), 650.

42. Paul de Man, *Blindness and Insight* (New York: Oxford University Press, 1971), 40.

43. Paul Ricoeur, *Memory, History, Forgetting*, trans. Kathleen Blamey and David Pellauer (Chicago: University of Chicago Press, 2004), 412.

44. Allen Grossman and Mark Halliday, *The Sighted Singer: Two Works on Poetry for Readers and Writers* (Baltimore: Johns Hopkins University Press, 1992), 11.

45. Richard B. Miller, "The Moral and Political Burdens of Memory," in *Friends and Other Strangers: Studies in Religion, Ethics, and Culture* (New York: Columbia University Press, 2016), 231.

46. David Rieff, *In Praise of Forgetting* (New Haven, CT: Yale University Press, 2016), 55.

47. Ernest Renan, "What Is a Nation?" (1882), reprinted in *Nation and Narration*, ed. Homi Bhabha, trans. Martin Thom (London: Routledge, 1990), 11.

48. Nicolas Russell, "Collective Memory Before and After Halbwachs," *French Review* 79, no. 4 (2006): 794.

49. W. James Booth, *Communities of Memory: On Witness, Identity, and Justice* (Ithaca, NY: Cornell University Press, 2006), 155, 149.

50. Nora, *Realms of Memory*, 1:3.

51. Sue Campbell, *Our Faithfulness to the Past: The Ethics and Politics of Memory* (Oxford: Oxford University Press, 2014), 12.

52. Campbell believes that our sense of the past changes depending on the present. According to her, this is not a bad thing and has too often been considered a "distortion" of faithfulness or accuracy by memory theorists. She criticizes the emphasis on accuracy for both "over-individualizing" memory and "preventing us from seeing the value in how memory changes over time and in response to our need." The distinction that Campbell makes is similar to one that Tzvetan Todorov makes between "exemplary" and "literal" remembering. However, Todorov sees the desire for moralizing in exemplary memory as what makes memory vulnerable to political instrumentalization. Campbell, 35.

53. Procedural memory is our memory of how to do things, contrasted with propositional/semantic memory, which is our memory of facts and common knowledge. Episodic memory is our memory of our personal past experiences. Popular memory is a type of collective memory (either in an oral or written form) that is often contrasted with the published historical accounts of official institutions; folk memory similarly refers to stories passed down through oral tradition across generations and is often used to refer to a more distant past. Institutional memory refers to any knowledge that is held and preserved by an institution, e.g., a company, a religious institution, a government. Artificial memory, unlike pure memory, is memory that has been trained, sculpted, exercised, and cultivated. Prosthetic memory denotes any "memories" we might have acquired vicariously; it has become a more popular concept since the development of cinema and television.

Notes to Pages 17–22   161

54. See Rieff, *In Praise of Forgetting*; Augé, *Oblivion*; and Krondorfer, Björn Krondorfer, "Is Forgetting Reprehensible? Holocaust Remembrance and the Task of Oblivion," *Journal of Religious Ethics* 36, no. 2 (2008): 233–67. Paul Connerton's and Frank R. Ankersmit's respective categorizations also come to mind. Connerton, "Seven Types of Forgetting," *Memory Studies* (2008): 59–71; Ankersmit, "The Sublime Dissociation of the Past: Or How to Be(Come) What One Is No Longer," *History and Theory* 40, no. 3 (2001): 295–323.

55. Krondorfer, "Is Forgetting Reprehensible?"

56. I briefly discuss Canadian poet Lisa Robertson in chapter 4.

57. W. H. Auden, *The Dyer's Hand and Other Essays* (London: Faber and Faber, 1963), 321.

58. Gertrude Stein, *Writings, 1932–1946*, ed. Catherine Stimpson and Harriet Chessman (New York: Library of America, 1998), 220, 222.

59. The titles of Donald Allen's *New American Poetry* (1960) and Ron Silliman's *In the American Tree* (1986) both attest to this national interest. See also de Man's essay "Form and Intent in American Criticism" (1971) for a discussion of how American poetry has been defined by a preoccupation with a divide between form and intent.

60. Gilles Deleuze, *Nietzsche and Philosophy* (New York: Columbia University Press, 1983), 113.

61. Jacques Derrida, *Given Time: I. Counterfeit Money*, trans. Peggy Kamuf (Chicago: University of Chicago Press, 1991), 17.

62. Umberto Eco, "An *Ars Oblivionalis*? Forget It!" trans. Marilyn Migiel, *PMLA* 103, no. 3 (May 1988): 258.

Chapter One

1. Gertrude Stein, "Many Many Women," in *Matisse Picasso and Gertrude Stein, with Two Shorter Stories* (Mineola, NY: Dover, 2000), 119.

2. Readers will find that in this chapter, I do not follow the division of the writer's work into "two Steins" (an experimental one seemingly devoid of a "personal history or a cultural background" [B. F. Skinner] and a more conventional one). Instead, the development of her work might be seen as taking the following trajectory: the writing of *The Making of Americans* from 1906 to 1908, directly following *Three Lives*, represented one of Stein's first breakthroughs; it was followed by a radical phase of experimentation with portraiture, poems, and plays from 1908 through the 1920s (this includes *Tender Buttons, Four Saints in Three Acts, Lifting Belly, Cezanne*), with its most intense phase 1909–12. In writing *The Making of Americans*, Stein developed her method of "talking and listening" as a way of feeling the rhythm of individuals and exhausted her project to typify every kind of human being. Her transition to shorter works began when Stein realized complete description is in fact possible, thus, no longer in need of doing. From there, the publication of *The Autobiography of Alice B. Toklas*, written in 1932, launched Stein as an international controversial celebrity, who conducted her series of lecture tours in the United States 1934–37, a period that also saw the writing of *The Geographical History of America; or, The Relation of Human Nature to the Human Mind* (1936). Stein's interest in autobiographical writing would appear again in *Everybody's Autobiography* (1937) and the 1945 memoir of WWII, *Wars I Have Seen*.

3. Gertrude Stein, *The Making of Americans: Being a History of a Family's Progress* (1925; repr., Normal, IL: Dalkey Archive Press, 1995), 520. At the start of the book, Stein

162 **Notes to Pages 22-23**

admits that the American family, being only three generations old, has the "privilege" of not having to recall much.

4. *The Making of Americans*, 33-34.

5. Gertrude Stein, *Everybody's Autobiography* (1937; repr., Cambridge: Exact Change, 1993), 142.

6. See "Portraits and Repetitions," where Gertrude Stein writes, "There can be no repetition because the essence of that expression is insistence, and if you insist you must each time use emphasis and if you use emphasis it is not possible while anybody is alive that they should use exactly the same emphasis." Stein, *Writings, 1932–1946*, ed. Catherine Stimpson and Harriet Chessman (New York: Library of America, 1998), 288.

7. Concerning visual artists, Stein once said: "[P]ainters have nothing to do with memory, they concern themselves only with visible things." Stein, *Picasso*, in *Writings, 1932–1946*, 507.

8. Examples include everything from Ezra Pound's interest in the ideogram as the verbal idea of action to Charles Olson's disposition of energy as an exercise in willing inert material into action. There is Paul Valéry's "Poetry and Abstract Thought" (1939), where he speaks of "the poem's action" and "the power of verbal action," as well as the language of mechanical models and thermodynamics in William Carlos Williams's *Kora in Hell* (1920), Robert Creeley on action and movement, and, later on, the "I do this, I do that" poetry of the New York School. Harold Rosenberg's understanding of action painting likewise stems from this modernist tradition.

9. Jane Beckett, "Dada and Surrealism," in *The Art Press*, ed. Trevor Fawcett and Clive Phillpot (London: Art Book Company, 1976), 33.

10. Ian F. A. Bell, "The Real and the Ethereal: Modernist Energies in Eliot and Pound," in *From Energy to Information: Representation in Science and Technology, Art, and Literature*, ed. Bruce Clark and Linda D. Henderson (Stanford, CA: Stanford University Press, 2002), 124.

11. Ronald Martin goes so far as to describe writers of modernist action as "knowledge destroyers," though the destruction is often bound to a desire for the creation of new knowledge. In his account of Williams, he says "every common thing has been nailed down, stripped of freedom of action and taken away from use" because of "rationalist inquiry." Martin, *American Literature and the Destruction of Knowledge: Innovative Writing in the Age of Epistemology* (Durham, NC: Duke University Press, 1991), 4, 274. Elsewhere, Henri Lefebvre writes, "There is certainly a major problem here: how are we to recapture the natural and spontaneous life forces dislocated by the society of the machine, dissipated by the division of labour, and lost by the processes of accumulation (technology, knowledge, means of production)?" The youthfulness of modernity "is the opposite of the experience which is gained through accumulated knowledge. From this angle, human life would appear to be a process in which, rapidly or slowly, spontaneity and presence waste away: a squandering of youth." Lefebvre, *Introduction to Modernity*, trans. John Moore (London: Verso, 1995), 159.

12. See also Joel Nickels, *Poetry of the Possible: Spontaneity, Modernism, and the Multitude* (Minneapolis: University Minnesota Press, 2012); and Daniel Belgrad, *The Culture of Spontaneity: Improvisation and the Arts in Postwar America* (Chicago: University of Press, 1998).

13. See Jennifer Summit and Blakey Vermeule, *Action Versus Contemplation: Why an Ancient Debate Still Matters* (Chicago: University of Chicago Press, 2018).

Notes to Pages 23–26   163

14. Jean-Paul Sartre, *Baudelaire*, trans. Martin Turnell (New York: New Directions, 1950), 163.

15. For a critique of presentism, see François Hartog's *Regimes of Historicity: Presentism and Experiences of Time*, trans. Saskia Brown (New York: Columbia University Press, 2003). For theories of the present, I recommend Michael North, *What Is the Present?* (Princeton, NJ: Princeton University Press, 2018); Lauren Berlant, *Cruel Optimism* (Durham, NC: Duke University Press, 2011); and Benjamin Morgan, "Scale, Resonance, Presence," *Victorian Studies* 59, no. 1 (Autumn 2016): 109–12.

16. Friedrich Nietzsche, *On the Advantage and Disadvantage of History for Life* (1874), trans. Peter Preuss (Indianapolis: Hackett, 1980); Williams Carlos Williams, *Kora in Hell*, in *Imaginations* (New York: New Directions, 1970), 17.

17. Paul de Man, *Blindness and Insight*, 2nd ed. (London: Routledge, 1983), 142.

18. Ezra Pound, *Selected Prose, 1909–1965* (New York: New Directions, 1973), 455.

19. Charles Bernstein, "The Art of Immemorability," *Journal of Philosophy* 2, no. 6 (2006): 33.

20. Mallarmé once wrote to Villiers de l'Isle-Adam: "I was dumbfounded by your letter because I really *wanted* to be forgotten." Stéphane Mallarmé, *Selected Poetry and Prose* (New York: New Directions, 1982), 86.

21. Sascha Bru, "Avant-Garde Nows: Presentist Reconfigurations of Public Time," *Modernist Cultures* 8, no. 2 (2013): 273.

22. Gertrude Stein, *The Geographical History of America; or, The Relation of Human Nature to the Human Mind*, in *Writings, 1932–1946*, 380.

23. Stein, "Poetry and Grammar," in *Writings, 1932–1946*, 334.

24. Stein, *Narration: Four Lectures by Gertrude Stein* (1935; reprint, Chicago: University of Chicago Press, 2010), 20.

25. Paul Ricoeur notes that growing out of the Renaissance's feats of artificial memory, there was a subsequent backlash against rote memory. "A critique of memorizing memory coincided with the praise of ingenium—genius, spirit," he notes, citing a strain of thought which runs through Rousseau's work while reaching an apex during Romanticism. Ricoeur, *Memory, History, Forgetting*, trans. Kathleen Blamey and David Pellauer (Chicago: University of Chicago Press, 2004), 67. See also Bob Perelman, *The Trouble with Genius* (Berkeley: University of California Press, 1994), for more on Stein and genius.

26. Natalia Cecire, *Experimental: American Literature and the Aesthetics of Knowledge* (Baltimore: Johns Hopkins University Press, 2019), ix.

27. Linda Voris, *The Composition of Sense in Gertrude Stein's Landscape Writing* (Washington, DC: Palgrave Macmillan, 2016), 25.

28. Johanna Winant, "Explanation in Composition: Gertrude Stein and the Contingency of Inductive Reasoning," *Journal of Modern Literature* 39, no. 3 (2016): 95.

29. Jennifer Ashton, *From Modernism to Postmodernism: American Poetry and Theory in the Twentieth Century* (Cambridge: Cambridge University Press, 2005), 35, 52. See in particular the chapters "Gertrude Stein for Anyone" and "Making the Rose Red: Stein, Proper Names, and the Critique of Indeterminacy."

30. Elizabeth Freeman, "Hopeless Cases: Queer Chronicities and Gertrude Stein's 'Melanctha,'" *Journal of Homosexuality* 63, no. 3 (2016): 337.

31. Liesl M. Olson, "Gertrude Stein, William James, and Habit in the Shadow of War," *Twentieth-Century Literature* 49, no. 3 (Autumn 2003): 328–59; Omri Moses, "Gertrude Stein's Lively Habits," *Twentieth-Century Literature* 55, no. 4 (2009): 445–84.

32. Sharon Kirsch, *Gertrude Stein and the Reinvention of Rhetoric* (Tuscaloosa: University of Alabama Press, 2014).

33. Gertrude Stein, *Wars I Have Seen* (New York: Random House, 1945), 3.

34. *Wars I Have Seen*, 3.

35. *Wars I Have Seen*, 6, 4.

36. For an example from literary history and one from psychology, see Mary Carruthers, *The Book of Memory: A Study of Memory in Medieval Culture* (Cambridge: Cambridge University Press, 1990); and Gabriel Radvansky, *Human Memory*, 3rd ed. (New York: Routledge, 2017), respectively.

37. The replacement of memory and historical knowledge with science's emphasis on direct observation was vital in Stein's academic training between 1893 and 1902, first as a student of psychology, then as a medical student at Johns Hopkins University. The split between direct and indirect knowledge, memory and perception, is inconceivable in Aristotle's model, since memory for him is still a sense-perception faculty. When we move into the twentieth century, memory and perception no longer vary in degree but rather in kind.

38. Stein, *Everybody's Autobiography*, 197.

39. Stein, *Stanzas in Meditation*, in *Writings, 1932–1946*, 89.

40. Stein, *Everybody's Autobiography*, 70.

41. Cecire, *Experimental*, 83.

42. Stein, *Everybody's Autobiography*, 142.

43. Stein, "What Are Master-Pieces and Why Are There So Few of Them," in *Writings, 1932–1946*, 359.

44. Because the present is seen and heard but not remembered, remembering not only prevents the creation of masterpieces and carries with it the danger of overdetermination, but also is fundamentally antithetical to the clarity that writing must espouse. For eighteenth-century philosophies on "clear" versus "confused" ideas, see works by G. W. Leibniz, Christian Wolff, and Alexander Gottlieb Baumgarten.

45. Stein, *A Long Gay Book*, in *Matisse Picasso and Gertrude Stein, with Two Shorter Stories* (Mineola, NY: Dover, 2000), 41.

46. Kirsch, *Gertrude Stein and the Reinvention of Rhetoric*, 76.

47. Ulla Dydo and William Rice, *Gertrude Stein: The Language That Rises, 1923–1934* (Evanston, IL: Northwestern University Press, 2003), 39.

48. See Birgit Van Puymbroeck, introduction to "'Let Us Save China': Gertrude Stein and Politics," by Gertrude Stein, *PMLA* 132, no. 1 (2017): 201.

49. Stein, *Stanzas in Meditation*, 80.

50. The idea that the difference between 501 and 502 appears negligible compared to that between three and four is also known as Weber's Law.

51. Following the various associationist accounts given by David Hartley and later figures William James and Sigmund Freud, Umberto Eco posits that mnemotechnics, or the art of memory, is essentially a connotative semiotics rooted in drawing similarities; a system of lexical units activates, evokes, or "reminds" one of a corresponding system of images, which in turn, activates another system of content or res memorandae. See Eco, "An *Ars Oblivionalis*: Forget It!" trans. Marilyn Migiel, *PMLA* 103, no. 3 (May 1988): 254–61.

52. Stein, "An Acquaintance with Description," in *Writings, 1903–1932*, ed. Catherine Stimpson and Harriet Chessman (New York: Library of America, 1998), 530–31.

Notes to Pages 31–36 165

53. "An Acquaintance with Description," 532.

54. Thornton Wilder, introduction to *Four in America*, by Gertrude Stein (New Haven, CT: Yale University Press, 1947), vii.

55. Stein, *The Geographical History of America*, 385.

56. *The Geographical History of America*, 385.

57. I am thinking in particular of John Ruskin's employment of metaphor/simile in his distinction between the "reflective" poetry of Wordsworth, Tennyson, and Keats, who all supposedly perceived wrongly because of feeling, and the "creative" work of the epic poets, who did not confuse the emotionally colored appearances of things with the physical fact of things. Edmund Burke makes a similar distinction between clear and strong statements almost a century earlier in "How Words Influence the Passions." There, he argues that the difference between things as they are and things as they are felt to be is that the "former regards the understanding, [and] the latter belongs to the passions." Ruskin, *Modern Painters*, vol. 3 (London: Smith, Elder, & Co., 1872); Burke, *The Works of the Right Honourable*, vol. 1 (Boston: Wells and Lily, 1826), 217.

58. Stein, *A Long Gay Book*, 20.

59. *A Long Gay Book*, 20.

60. Stein, *Stanzas in Meditation*, 94.

61. Stein, *Everybody's Autobiography*, 76.

62. Stein, "Lecture 3," in *Writings, 1932–1946*, 343.

63. "Lecture 3," 350.

64. Stein, "Portraits and Repetition," 297.

65. "Portraits and Repetition," 287.

66. Stein's desire to rethink action as an activity or state is a result of shifting notions of history. If historicist action traditionally took complete past accomplishments and achievements as its content, a new notion of writing that could "make history" had to draw from other conceptions of actions. As the extended organization of memory in its collective form, history always posed a puzzle for Stein. On the one hand, the importance of forgetting would make it seem as though Stein belongs to a camp of ahistoricism. On the other hand, she was adamant about "making history" and constantly interested in history as a generic and cultural project. What only seems like a paradox points to the shifting ideas of history during the modernist period, in which historical accounts, formerly magistrate vitae, became no longer instructive of action, but actually obstructive of it. Behind this dismantling of history's didactic potential was the replacement of history's repetition with its singularity, its sequencing of distinct, individual events. Unlike the nineteenth century, which Stein viewed as outdated because it conceived of history as progressive, hence connected and linear, the twentieth century emphasized the loss of progressivism and its replacement by the singularity of the event and non-successive nature of knowledge as nonhistorical. The preoccupation with "make it new" thus mapped onto the demand to actively "make history." For more on this, see Hannah Arendt, *The Portable Hannah Arendt*, ed. Peter Baehr (New York: Penguin, 2000); Richard Terdiman, *Present Past: Modernity and the Memory Crisis* (Ithaca, NY: Cornell University Press, 1993); and Reinhart Koselleck, *Futures Past: On the Semantics of Historical Time*, trans. Keith Tribe (New York: Columbia University Press, 2004). Given that the rise of reproductive means such as the gramophone and color reproduction during this time made possible an instantly accessible past, the actual act of recollection was also problematized: with no temporal distance to

166   **Notes to Pages 36–40**

traverse and discover, one had to figure out how the present could be distinguished from the past.

67. States also fall into the paradoxical space of occupying two modes of being. Like material objects that are said to exist, states are to a certain degree static. But like events, they also seem to occur, happen, or take place. While generally accepted as kinds of event, states and activities may extend over time, but duration and culmination remain irrelevant. Activities such as breathing or seeing, for instance, seem to remain homogeneous and constant. Aside from their shared sense of temporality, states and activities also confront the agential question of mixed voluntariness and involuntariness. An activity like breathing might be seen as purely behavioral, biological, or habitual (in this case, not involved with the will), while one like running is often seen as intentional. States, too, can switch back and forth between something that seems to happen *to us* and something that occurs *by* us, *in* us. Whether these states take place in us, or whether they are externalized so that we are "in a state" remains a part of the flexibility with which we refer to them.

68. See Wendy Steiner for a theory of a three-stage portraiture development in Stein's works from 1908 to post-1925. Steiner, "The Steinian Portrait," in *Critical Essays on Gertrude Stein*, ed. Michael Hoffman (Boston: G. K. Hall, 1986), 130–38.

69. Stein, "Many Many Women," 119–20.

70. In the philosophy of language, the distinction between individual-level and stage-level predicates is that the former is expressive of permanent and essential qualities and the latter denotes transitory and accidental states. Greg Carlson's 1977 dissertation was a major contribution to the field when it located the question of stage-level and individual-level interpretations at the transition between individual and kind. A classic example is the sentence "Firemen are available," which is read as meaning *some* firemen, while the alternative sentence "Firemen are altruistic" entails a universal claim about *all* firemen. Carlson argued that bare plurals like "firemen" (bare because it doesn't have a preceding quantifier like *any, a, one*) might be ambiguous, but that the context always selects one meaning over another, so that we make either a universal or an existential interpretation. Our intuitive grasp of different adjectives colors how we quantify the word "firemen." For Carlson, bare plurals are individuals in their own right—not individual objects, but individuals as *kinds*. A kind of thing, he argued, is that "whatever-it-is" that ties a series of stages together to make them stages of the same thing. Like a proper name, bare plurals give continuity and identity to different appearances across time. Unlike the proper name of an object, bare plural as kinds can function to appear in many places at any given time, too. Carlson, "References to Kinds in English" (PhD diss., University of Massachusetts Amherst, 1977).

71. Orazio Toscanella, *Modi di studiare le pistole famigliari di M. Tullio Cicerone*, quoted in Lina Bolzoni's *The Gallery of Memory: Literary and Iconographic Models in the Age of the Printing Press*, trans. Jeremy Parzen (Toronto: University Toronto Press, 2001), 59.

72. Stein, *Stanzas in Meditation*, 90.

73. Stein, "Making of *The Making of Americans*," in *Writings 1932–1946*, 279.

74. Stein, *A Long Gay Book*, 21, 24.

75. Even in her most "historical" works set during wartime, Stein's texts focus on eating, trading, and walking on roads but without much plot development or causal connections. With no completion of a dramatic sequence, the actions in *Wars I Have Seen* provide little continuity between present, past, and future. There are no chapters

or formal stopping places except for paragraphs. Dates are occasionally mentioned but these mentions are irregularly paced; when indicated, they usually demonstrate the disjuncture between regularized calendar time and the irregularity of long or short mental states and activities.

76. John Goldsmith and Erich Woisetschlaeger, "The Logic of the English Progressive," *Linguistic Inquiry* 13, no. 1 (1982): 79–89.

77. Stein, "Poetry and Grammar," 320–21.

78. E. L. McCallum, *Unmaking "The Making of Americans": Toward an Aesthetic Ontology* (Albany: State University of New York Press, 2018), xxii–xxiii.

79. Stein, "Portraits and Repetition," 303.

80. Responding to B. F. Skinner's article "Has Gertrude Stein a Secret?" (1934), Stein denounced the possibility of true automatic writing. See Richard Bridgman, *Gertrude Stein in Pieces* (New York: Oxford University Press, 1970), 135–36. In an interview with Robert Hass, she notes: "I made innumerable efforts to make words write without sense and found it impossible. Any human putting down words had to make sense out of them." Stein, "Gertrude Stein Talking—A Transatlantic Interview," by Robert Hass, *UCLAN Review* (1962–64), reprinted in *Gertrude Stein: A Primer for the Gradual Understanding of Gertrude Stein*, ed. Robert Haas (Los Angeles: Black Sparrow Press, 1971), 18.

81. For more on practical knowledge, see Gilbert Ryle, "Knowing How and Knowing That," *Proceedings of the Aristotelian Society* 46 (1945–46): 1–16.

Chapter Two

1. Aristotle, *On Memory and Reminiscence*, trans. David Bloch (Leiden: Brill, 2007).

2. Mark A. McDaniel and Gilles O. Einstein, *Prospective Memory: An Overview and Synthesis of an Emerging Field* (Los Angeles: Sage, 2007), 2; Jonathon D. Crystal, "Prospective Memory," *Current Biology*, 23, no. 17 (2013): 750.

3. Lawrence Halprin, "The RSVP Cycles" (1969), reprinted in *Theory in Landscape Architecture: A Reader*, ed. Simon Swaffield (Philadelphia: University of Pennsylvania Press, 2002), 43.

4. Liz Kotz, *Words to Be Looked At: Language in 1960s Art* (Cambridge, MA: MIT Press, 2007), 49.

5. Kotz, 64.

6. James Schuyler, "An Interview," by Mark Hillringhouse, *American Poetry Review* 14, no. 2 (1985): 11. Schuyler claims in the interview that he invented the form. Alternatively, Terence Diggory cites, via Larry Fagin, Gary Snyder as the "to-do" poem's originator. Diggory, *Encyclopedia of the New York School Poets* (New York: Facts on File, 2009).

7. Frank O'Hara, *The Collected Poems of Frank O'Hara*, ed. Donald Allen (Berkeley: University of California Press, 1995), 341.

8. Williams Carlos Williams's "tabular account of specimens found in this well" in Book IV of *Paterson* is a good example of how this tradition has lived on in American poetry. Williams, *Paterson* (1946–58) (repr., New York: New Directions, 1995), 139.

9. Kotz, *Words to Be Looked At*, 6. Ted Berrigan cites Cage's method of composition in "Tambourine Life" (1965): "thank you they were composed / excuse me / I mean not composed / using the John-Cage-Animal-Cracker / Method of Composition (this seems to be mushrooming into a / major work of high /seriousness)." That same year,

168 **Notes to Pages 46–50**

Berrigan also conducted a made-up interview with Cage. Berrigan, *The Collected Poems of Ted Berrigan*, ed. Alice Notley, Edmund Berrigan, and Anselm Berrigan (Berkeley: University of California Press, 2007), 125.

10. See David Lehman, *The Last Avant-Garde: The Making of the New York School of Poets* (New York: Anchor Books, 1999); Diggory, *Encyclopedia of the New York School Poets*; Alan Golding, "Faking It New," *Modernism/modernity* 16, no. 3 (2009): 474–77; and Kenneth Koch, *Wishes, Lies and Dreams* (1970; repr., New York: Harper Perennial, 1999).

11. Larry Fagin notes that the ideas in *The List Poem* "came out of my work as poet-in-residence at public schools in New York City," though the "list" also gained traction as part of New York poets' revival of Sei Shōnagon's *The Pillow Book*. Fagin writes, a "virtue of the list poem is its usefulness in teaching beginners how to write in poetic lines." Because schools abound in lists, "the familiarity and simplicity of the form encourages students." This has since been reaffirmed by illustrated poems for children, such as Elaine Magliaro's "Things to Do If You Are a Pencil" and Bobbi Katz's "Things to Do If You Are a Subway." Fagin, *The List Poem: A Guide to Teaching and Writing Catalog Verse* (New York: Teachers & Writers, 2000), 1.

12. Libbie Rifkin, "'Worrying about Making It': Ted Berrigan's Social Poetics," *Contemporary Literature* 38, no. 4 (1997): 640; Richard Howard, "John Ashbery," in *John Ashbery*, ed. Harold Bloom (New York: Chelsea House, 1985), 40; Michael Clune, "'Everything We Want': Frank O'Hara and the Aesthetics of Free Choice," *PMLA* 120, no. 1 (2005): 183.

13. Others who read against futurity are Christopher Schmidt and Tatiana Sverjensky. For Schmidt, Schuyler's work is a queer challenge to reproductive futurism. Schmidt, *The Poetics of Waste: Queer Excess in Stein, Ashbery, Schuyler, and Goldsmith* (New York: Palgrave Macmillan, 2014). For Sverjensky, Ashbery's description of Frank O'Hara's poetry as "hav[ing] no program" is an indicator of Ashbery's poetics of resistance. Having no promise or obligation to dicta liberates "the inoperative" from capitalist productivity, Sverjensky argues. Sverjensky, "John Ashbery's Inoperative Poetics," *College Literature* 43, no. 2 (2016): 281.

14. François Hartog, *Regimes of Historicity: Presentism and Experiences of Time*, trans. Saskia Brown (New York: Columbia University Press, 2003), 112.

15. Since the 1960s, the term "intention" has often been negatively associated with the subject's ego and "authorial intention." However, intentionality is in fact very much a part of the "to-do" poem, not in a way that emphasizes a "means-to-end" but in a way that speaks to intentionality as the prerequisite for possibility rather than actualization.

16. O'Hara, *The Collected Poems*, 413.

17. John Searle, "What Is a Speech Act?" in *Philosophy in America*, ed. Max Black (Ithaca, NY: Cornell University Press, 1965), 236.

18. James Schuyler, "Things to Do," in *Collected Poems* (New York: FSG, 1993), 59–60.

19. Kenneth Koch, *Wishes, Lies, and Dreams* (1970; repr., New York: Harper Perennial, 1999), 20.

20. This is of course not always the case. In Schuyler's "Things to Do When You Get a Bad Review" (1969), he starts composing a reply: "Dear Meager Sack of Shit, / forget it / but remember to / leave windpipe / 'hanging over pot.'" Schuyler, *Other Flowers: Uncollected Poems*, ed. James Meetze and Simon Pettet (New York: FSG, 2010), 186.

Notes to Pages 50–56   169

21. In an endnote to Berrigan's collected poems, Alice Notley writes: "Ted was particularly interested in '10 Things I Do Every Day.' [. . .] Ted later used the 'list' as a framework for an expansive, discursive poem, opening the space between 'items' into a talking, pondering space." *The Collected Poems of Ted Berrigan*, 678–79.

22. In describing their collaboration, which emerged out of a scheduled reading on Memorial Day at the Poetry Project, Waldman uses the language of instruction: "[W]e sent & exchanged pages back & forth to each other regularly that spring of 1971. I took on *the final task* of 'arrangement' with scissors, tape and paste in hand, laying cut-up sections out on the floor [. . .] to collage the poem together" (emphasis mine). A number of "to-do" instructions end up running through the poem: "Dear Mr. Postman / Please take this from me / to me," "Forget it! / Piss on it! / Kiss my ass!," and even, potentially, "Tomorrow you die." Denise Duhamel, Maureen Seaton, and David Trinidad, *Saints of Hysteria* (New York: Soft Skull Press, 2007), 38–42.

23. There is a connection here to Martin Heidegger, who claims death as the ultimate possibility, arguing that death individualizes Being while making its finitude known. An authentic Being-toward-death recognizes that one's death is always one's own—never the experience of others' deaths—and because of this, it represents the possibility of one's inexistence. Whether Berrigan explores some version of this is less important than what his speaker is constantly aware of: that what the genre moves toward is also what limits it. The instructions to "disappear," "Jump off a roof on the lower East Side," or "go away" all appear in Berrigan's poems, finding an echo in Alice Notley's work when she writes in *In the Pines*: "the point of literature is to court her daily and go away." Notley, *In the Pines* (New York: Penguin, 2007), 11.

24. Ted Berrigan, "Things to Do in Providence," in *The Collected Poems of Ted Berrigan*, 376–80.

25. Henri Bergson, "Laughter" (1900), translated by C. Brereton and F. Rothwell (1911), reprinted in *Comedy: "An Essay on Comedy" by George Meredith. "Laughter" by Henri Bergson*, ed. Wylie Sypher (Baltimore: Johns Hopkins University Press, 1956), 101.

26. Leslie K. Arnovick, "The Expanding Discourse of Promises in Present-Day English: A Case Study in Historical Pragmatics," *Folia Linguistica Historica* 15, nos. 1–2 (1994): 177.

27. Schuyler, "December," in *Collected Poems*, 13–14.

28. By the 1970s, the cultural sentiment of "forget the future" became that of "no future" at all. Such a theme would carry over to various poets' works as they dealt with the end of time, literalized both by the early deaths of Frank O'Hara and Ted Berrigan at ages forty and forty-eight, respectively, and what futures were soon rendered nonexistent by the AIDS crisis. Prospective memory recedes into the background, for instance, in a work like Ashbery's *April Galleons*, which confronts how futures were stolen from the forgotten and neglected victims of AIDS. For more on the collection's concern with lasting, conservation, and its related "network of remembering, sheltering, redeeming, preserving for later, and keeping," see John Shoptaw, *On the Outside Looking Out: John Ashbery's Poetry* (Cambridge, MA: Harvard University Press, 1994); Susan Stewart, "The Last Man," *American Poetry Review* 17, no. 5 (1988): 9–16; and John Emil Vincent, "*April Galleons*: Forgetting, Evading, Holding Off," in *John Ashbery and You: His Later Books* (Athens: University of Georgia Press, 2007), 26–46. Describing the possibility of some architecture or shelter, Ashbery writes in "Song of the Windshield Wipers": "this / Dream too was taken away, forcibly, as though by hand" (*Collected Poems*, 845) while elsewhere in "Letters I Did or Did Not Get," forgetting is the problem of historical

170 Notes to Pages 56-66

neglect: "There are too many of us ever / To be remembered let alone recorded" (*Collected Poems*, 841). John Shoptaw, "Saving Appearances," review of *April Galleons* by John Ashbery, *Tremblor* 7 (1998): 172-77.

29. Schuyler, "The Morning of the Poem," in *Collected Poems*, 262.

30. Ron Padgett, "Inaction of Shoes," in *Collected Poems* (Minneapolis: Coffee House Press, 2013), 625.

31. Berrigan, "Things to Do in Anne's Room," in *The Collected Poems of Ted Berrigan*, 219-20.

32. Joe Brainard, quoted in Ron Padgett, afterword to *I Remember* by Joe Brainard (1970; repr., New York: Granary Books 2001), 171 (emphasis mine).

33. Brainard, quoted in Padgett, afterword to *I Remember*, 173.

34. Bernadette Mayer, "From: A Lecture at the Naropa Institute, 1989," in *O/two An Anthology: What is the inside, what is outside?*, ed. Leslie Scalapino (Oakland: O Books, 1991), 93.

35. Bernadette Mayer, *Studying Hunger* (Berkeley: Big Sky, 1975), 7.

36. Georges Perec, *Species of Spaces and Other Pieces*, ed. and trans. John Sturrock (New York: Penguin, 1997), 145. See in particular "Some of the Things I Really Must Do Before I Die" and "The Objects That Are on My Work-Table."

37. Brainard, quoted in Padgett, afterword to *I Remember*, 173.

38. Padgett, afterword to *I Remember*, by Brainard, 174.

39. John Ashbery, "The Impossible," review of *Stanzas in Meditation*, by Gertrude Stein, *Poetry* (July 1957): 250-54, available at https://www.writing.upenn.edu/~afilreis /88/stein-per-ashbery.html.

40. Bernadette Mayer, *Memory* (Plainfield, CA: North Atlantic Books, 1975), 36, 41.

41. Mayer, *Studying Hunger*, 28.

42. *Studying Hunger*, 7.

43. Mayer, *Memory*, 188.

44. Mayer, *Studying Hunger*, 8, 32.

45. John Ashbery, *Collected Poems, 1956-1987*, ed. Mark Ford (New York: Library of America, 2008). The quotes can be found on these respective pages: "Summer" on p. 186, "These Lacustrine Cities" on p. 125, "Soonest Mended" on p. 184, and "Rural Objects" on p. 204.

46. Shoptaw, *On the Outside Looking Out*, 79.

47. All poems discussed in this Ashbery section, except for *Flow Chart*, can be found in *Collected Poems, 1956-1987*.

48. Ashbery, "The Impossible."

49. Peter Hulme and Tim Youngs, eds., *The Cambridge Companion to Travel Writing* (Cambridge: Cambridge University Press, 2006), 5.

50. Adam Phillips, *Missing Out: In Praise of the Unlived Life* (New York: FSG, 2013), 8.

51. Ashbery, "The Impossible."

52. Ann Keniston, *Ghostly Figures: Memory and Belatedness in Postwar American Poetry* (Iowa City: University of Iowa Press, 2015), 3.

53. Ben Hutchinson, *Lateness and Modern European Literature* (Oxford: Oxford University Press, 2016).

54. Edward Said, *On Late Style: Music and Literature Against the Grain* (New York: Pantheon Books, 2006), 14.

55. Ashbery, *Collected Poems, 1956-1987*, 135. All subsequent passages from "The Ecclesiast" can be found on pages 135-36.

56. Among linguists, the future tense is a debated topic. For the purposes of this chapter, I accept a broad rather than a narrow set of views as plausible. I accept both the modal and the tense functions of words like "will," while rejecting that a future tense has to be inflectional. Given the fictive scope of what occurs in a poem like "The Ecclesiast," it does not make sense to question whether there is epistemic unsettlement in reference to the "real" future when the objects of "will" or "shall" either do or do not take place. The typical conflict between what is believed to happen and what actually happens relies on the actual future, whereas in a poem, the writer is capable of suspending such a conflict, collapsing, or widening it depending on the time of the poem and its semantic content. See Philippe De Brabanter, Mikhail Kissine, and Saghie Sharifzadeh, eds., *Future Times, Future Tenses* (Oxford: Oxford University Press, 2014).

57. Maurice Blanchot, "Literature and the Right to Death," in *The Gaze of Orpheus and Other Literary Essays*, ed. P. Adams Sitney, trans. by Lydia Davis (Barrytown, NY: Station Hill Press, 1981), reprinted in *The Work of Fire*, trans. Charlotte Mandell (Stanford, CA: Stanford University Press, 1995), 327.

58. Georg Simmel, quoted and translated in Richard Swedberg and Wendelin Reich, "Georg Simmel's Aphorisms," *Theory, Culture & Society* 27, no. 1 (2010): 35.

59. Ashbery, "The Thief in Poetry," in *Collected Poems, 1956-1987*, 524.

60. Ashbery, *Flow Chart* (New York: Noonday, 1991), 201.

61. Ashbery, "John Ashbery," in *A Controversy of Poets: An Anthology of Contemporary American Poetry*, ed. Paris Leary and Robert Kelly (New York: Doubleday Anchor, 1965), 523-24.

62. In the contemporary poet Holly Melgard's work, the genre has even revised its historical revisions: Melgard has written a number of "Retrospective To Do" poems largely in the present tense.

Chapter Three

1. Hejinian not only takes Ovid's *Metamorphoses* as the model for the fifteen-book structure, but also uses forgetting as a way to enact the theme of change, conversion, and evolution. See my introduction for a description of Blanchot's phrase "forgetful memory."

2. Leslie Scalapino, *The Public World/Syntactically Impermanence* (Hanover, NH: Wesleyan University Press, 1999), 3.

3. Lyn Hejinian, interview by Rae Armantrout, in *Aerial 10*, ed. Rod Smith and Jen Hofer (Washington, DC.: Aerial/Edge Books, 2016), 36-37.

4. Hejinian, interview, 37.

5. Hilary Clark, "The Mnemonics of Autobiography: Lyn Hejinian's *My Life*," *Biography* 14, no. 4 (1991): 316.

6. Sianne Ngai, *Theory of the Gimmick: Aesthetic Judgment and Capitalist Form* (Cambridge, MA: Harvard University Press, 2020), 58.

7. Juliana Spahr, "Resignifying Autobiography: Lyn Hejinian's *My Life*," *American Literature* 68, no. 1 (March 1996): 144.

8. Henri Bergson, "Laughter" (1900), reprinted in *Comedy: "An Essay on Comedy" by George Meredith. "Laughter" by Henri Bergson*, ed. Wylie Sypher (Baltimore: Johns Hopkins University Press, 1980), 123.

9. Hejinian, in a letter to Kit Robinson from November 1, 1986, quoted in Robinson, "The Beginning of the Making of 'The Cell,'" in *Aerial 10*, ed. Smith and Hofer, 192.

172 **Notes to Pages 75-78**

10. Hejinian notes that "it was dizzying trying to think of the context for meaning, and therefore the context for knowledge [. . .] among people who are simultaneously Eastern and Western without resolution, without boundaries, at least not as I feel them," writing later, "to achieve a passage between Russian and American experiences, one negotiates vast fields of vertiginous shimmering. By that sixth day I felt enervated and motion sick from so much shimmering—and from absorbing so much disintegration." Lyn Hejinian, Michael Davidson, Ron Silliman, and Barrett Watten, *Leningrad: American Writers in the Soviet Union* (San Francisco: Mercury House, 1991), 47, 54.

11. Hejinian, letter to Kate Fagan, November 4, 2001, quoted in Fagan, "Strange Borders, Double Vision: *Oxota* as a Work of Trans-iteration," in *Aerial 10*, ed. Smith and Hofer, 227.

12. Hejinian, *Oxota: A Short Russian Novel* (1991; repr., Middletown, CT: Wesleyan University Press, 2019), 16.

13. *Oxota*, 95.

14. *Oxota*, 62.

15. *Oxota*, 7.

16. *Oxota*, 94.

17. *Oxota*, 201. In *Leningrad*, Hejinian and her coauthors write: "This book is not in any sense a single-voiced narrative of what a version of 'I' saw and did on our trip." They continue, "It should be somewhat unclear in reading this text just who is speaking." *Leningrad*, 26.

18. Marjorie Perloff, "Happy World," *Boston Review*, February 1, 2001, 21.

19. Hejinian, *The Language of Inquiry* (Berkeley: University of California Press, 2000), 119.

20. Hejinian, *A Border Comedy* (New York: Granary Books, 2001), 131.

21. Gertrude Stein, *Writings, 1932-1946*, ed. Catherine Stimpson and Harriet Chessman (New York: Library of America, 1998), 287.

22. Susanne Langer, *Feeling and Form* (New York: Charles Scribner, 1953), 334.

23. Rob Heilman, *The Ways of the World: Comedy and Society* (Seattle: University of Washington Press, 1978), 52.

24. *The Ways of the World*, 150.

25. Bergson, "Laughter," 169.

26. Lauren Berlant and Sianne Ngai, "Comedy Has Issues," *Critical Inquiry* 43 (Winter 2017): 235.

27. I use "they" here to refer to its plural use and not its singular form.

28. Hejinian, interview by Armantrout, 36.

29. "Lyn Hejinian," in *In the American Tree*, ed. Ron Silliman (Orono: University of Maine, 1986), 49.

30. Hejinian, *Writing Is an Aid to Memory* (Great Barrington, MA: The Figures, 1978), unpaginated. All subsequent quotes in this paragraph come from this text.

31. Hejinian, "Oblivion," in *The Cold of Poetry* (Los Angeles: Sun & Moon Press, 1994), 192.

32. "Oblivion," 185. In the new sections that constituted *My Life in the Nineties* (2003), forgetting also appears as a part of the memory project itself. "Who, I asked, was the nation's president the year Herman Melville wrote *Moby-Dick*. I don't remember, someone says, but she means she does not know, she feels no gap haunted by the rhythm of a name she can't quite say," Hejinian writes, as she suggests a difference

Notes to Pages 79–86 173

between the dynamic, rhythmic experience of temporality (forgetting's threshold) and the experience of non-experience. *My Life and My Life in the Nineties* (Middletown, CT: Wesleyan Press, 2013), 114. As recent as her book *Positions of the Sun*, she makes implicit forgetting's function within memory: "Memory's inability to assemble wholes is one of its greatest virtues, Ellie North Roth says to Albert Sing Roth." "From *Positions of the Sun*," PEN America, June 13, 2018, https://pen.org/from-positions-of-the-sun/.

33. Hejinian, "Oblivion," 191.

34. "Oblivion," 186–87.

35. Maurice Blanchot, *The Infinite Conversation* (1969), trans. Susan Hanson (Minneapolis: University Minnesota Press, 2003), 315.

36. Gerard Bruns, "A Poem of Laughter and Forgetting: Lyn Hejinian's *A Border Comedy*," in *Textual Practice* 23, no. 3 (2009): 405.

37. Hejinian, *A Border Comedy*, 151.

38. *A Border Comedy*, 27.

39. *A Border Comedy*, 35–36.

40. *A Border Comedy*, 140.

41. Langer, *Feeling and Form*, 331.

42. John Searle, "What Is a Speech Act?" in *Philosophy in America*, ed. Max Black (Ithaca, NY: Cornell University Press, 1965), 2, 3.

43. Stanley Cavell, *Must We Mean What We Say?*, 2nd ed. (Cambridge: Cambridge University Press, 2015), 175.

44. Sigmund Freud, *Jokes and Their Relation to the Unconscious* (1905), trans. James Strachey (New York: W. W. Norton, 1960), 8.

45. Bergson, "Laughter," 81.

46. "Laughter," 117.

47. Elsewhere in *A Border Comedy*, Hejinian writes, "Of course, sense have objects—everything provide evidence of this / The objects make themselves available and laugh / Suddenly you're one of them." *A Border Comedy*, 58.

48. *A Border Comedy*, 131.

49. *A Border Comedy*, 105.

50. Umberto Eco, "An *Ars Oblivionalis*? Forget It!" trans. Marilyn Migiel, *PMLA* 103, no. 3 (1988): 259.

51. Hejinian, *A Border Comedy*, 111–12.

52. Athene Seyler with Stephen Haggard, *The Craft of Comedy: The 21st Century Edition*, ed. Robert Barton (London: Routledge, 2013), 24.

53. The question of comedy and liberation is a site of debate. For Northrop Frye, the process of transgression leads to individual release and social reconciliation. Frye, "The Argument of Comedy" (1948), in *Northrop Frye's Writings on Shakespeare and the Renaissance*, ed. Troni Grande and Garry Sherbert (Toronto: University of Toronto Press, 2010), 3–13. Jean Paul Richter would agree: "Freedom produces jokes and jokes produce freedom. [. . .] Joking is merely playing with ideas" (quoted in Freud, *Jokes and Their Relation to the Unconscious*, 11). Yet, it could be argued that comedy merely reinforces the rules that it presupposes in order to temporarily transgress them. See Umberto Eco and New Historicist C. L. Barber for accounts of this position: Eco, *Carnival!*, edited by Thomas Sebeok (Berlin: Mouton, 1984); Barber, "The Saturnalian Pattern in Shakespeare's Comedy," *Sewanee Review* 59, no. 4 (1951): 593–611. For Hejinian, laughter is what she calls "a perfect manifestation of freedom," since there is at least temporary

174 Notes to Pages 86–94

liberation from one's identity and context (*A Border Comedy*, 102). Boundaries are necessary for Hejinian—as they are for Eco and Barber—but not in a pessimistic way. They are the site of encounter rather than limitation and can be displaced and reinstalled.

54. Hejinian, *A Border Comedy*, 18.

55. See Hejinian's essay "Barbarism" in *Language of Inquiry*.

56. *A Border Comedy*, 62.

57. *A Border Comedy*, 94.

58. Gotthold Ephraim Lessing, *Lessing's Prose Works*, ed. Edward Bell, trans. E. C. Beasley and Helen Zimmern (London: George Bell and Sons, 1890), 306.

59. Lessing, 306.

60. Jack Collom and Lyn Hejinian, *Situations, Sings* (New York: Adventures in Poetry, 2008), 30.

61. Hejinian, *Language of Inquiry*, 31.

62. *A Border Comedy*, 115.

63. *A Border Comedy*, 194.

64. *A Border Comedy*, 208–9.

65. Collom and Hejinian, *Situations, Sings*, 100.

66. Hejinian, *Language of Inquiry*, 13.

67. Peter Nicholls, "Of Being Ethical: Reflections on George Oppen," *Journal of American Studies* 31, no. 2 (1997): 168.

68. Louis Zukofsky, "Sincerity and Objectivism: With Special Reference to Charles Reznikoff," *Poetry* (February 1931): 280.

69. Hejinian, *Language of Inquiry*, 333.

70. George Eliot, *Adam Bede*, ed. Margaret Reynolds (New York: Penguin, 2008), 193.

71. *A Border Comedy*, 144.

72. Jack Collom, "A Conversation with Jack Collom," interview by Elizabeth Robinson, *OmniVerse* (January 13, 2013), http://omniverse.us/a-conversation-with-jack -collom/.

73. "A Conversation with Jack Collom."

74. "Interview with Jack Collom," by Jason Rawn, *Café Review* 15 (Summer 2004): 30.

75. Daniel Fischlin and Ajay Heble, eds., *The Other Side of Nowhere: Jazz, Improvisation, and Communities in Dialogue* (Middletown, CT: Wesleyan University Press, 2004), 18.

76. Collom and Hejinian, *Situations, Sings*, 103.

77. In Hejinian's chapbook *Lola* (2005)—which is composed of various "chapters" that occur out of order and often begin again by rewriting their content—she writes: "It is much easier to be enthusiastic about what exists than about what doesn't." Like a callback, the idea itself reappears again and again throughout the poet's work, refusing to stay in the past. And yet, its reemergence depends on the reader and writer having lost sight of it before recognizing it in a new context. *Lola* (New York: Belladonna, 2005), 3.

78. Collom and Hejinian, *Situations, Sings*, 103.

79. Hannah Arendt, *The Human Condition* (Chicago: University Chicago Press, 1958), 50.

80. Collom and Hejinian, *Situations, Sings*, 100.

81. Bruce Andrews, *Paradise and Method* (Evanston, IL: Northwestern University Press, 1996), 186.

82. See Adam Phillips, *On Wanting to Change* (London: Picador, 2022).

Chapter Four

1. Ralph Waldo Emerson, "The Poet" (1844), in *The Complete Works of Ralph Waldo Emerson: Essays*, vol. 3 (Boston: Houghton Mifflin, 1903), 20.

2. John Hollander, "Originality," *Raritan* 2, no. 4 (Spring 1983): 27.

3. Gertrude Stein, "Why I Do Not Live in America" (1928), in *How Writing Is Written: Volume II of the Previously Uncollected Writings of Gertrude Stein*, ed. Robert Hass (Los Angeles: Black Sparrow Press, 1974), 51.

4. John Ashbery, "The Impossible," review of *Stanzas in Meditation* by Gertrude Stein, *Poetry* (July 1957): 251, available at https://www.writing.upenn.edu/~afilreis/88/stein-per-ashbery.html.

5. Laura Riding, "The New Barbarism, and Gertrude Stein," *transition 3* (June 3, 1927): 153–68, reprinted in *A Description of Acquaintance: The Letters of Laura Riding and Gertrude Stein, 1927–1930*, ed. Logan Esdale and Jane Malcolm (Albuquerque: University of New Mexico Press, 2023), 124–25. In their correspondences, Riding writes at one point to Stein: "dearest Gertrude I had a dream of you and the dream was gone and the feeling very easy, not remembering" (63).

6. Hollander, "Originality," 30, 35.

7. Paul de Man, *Blindness and Insight* (New York: Oxford University Press, 1971), 66. On the one hand, forgetting's ability to call attention to the presence of non-presence made it appealing to de Man as a way of thinking through modernism's figures of pure, spiritual negation: Baudelaire, Mallarmé, and Valéry. On the other hand, it defined modernity as a kind of portable condition, shaped by its negative relationship to tradition and precedence. Between the two, misremembering surfaced as a meta-device. It came to represent a new criticism, which blurred the line between an earlier, creative act of writing and a later, critical act of reading. In a new theory of reading and writing that did not depend on anteriority and posteriority—in other words, a theory that would not relegate critical texts to "secondary" material—forgetting came to suspend the fulfillment of a text's meaning, allowing for shared subjectivity and ongoing participation between an author and a critic. The critic's turn to Blanchot was not a coincidence, given the latter's interest in oblivion, most prominently in *L'Attente l'oubli* (1962) and *L' Entretien infini* (1969). De Man, whose own subterfuge had concealed his past collaborations with the Nazi regime, was particularly invested in forgetting as both the precondition for writing *and* evidence of the writer's self-deception, a sign that modernism failed to erase the past *and* a definition of modernism in terms of this failure.

8. De Man, 66.

9. Harold Bloom, *A Map of Misreading* (1975; repr., Oxford: Oxford University Press, 2003), 17.

10. T. S. Eliot, "Tradition and the Individual Talent," *The Egoist* 6, no. 4 (September 1919), reprinted in *The Sacred Wood* (New York: Alfred A. Knopf, 1921), 43.

11. Georges Braque, *Testimony Against Gertrude Stein* (The Hague: Servire Press, 1935), 13. For an expanded discussion, see also T. J. Clark's chapter "Cubism and Collectivity," in *Farewell to an Idea* (New Haven, CT: Yale University Press, 1999), where the stakes of individuality and impersonality extend to those of subjective life and objective reality. See also Rosalind Krauss's *The Originality of the Avant-Garde and Other Modernist Myths* (Cambridge, MA: MIT University Press, 1986).

12. See William Duff, *An Essay on Original Genius* (1767) for the linking between originality and genius.

176 Notes to Pages 98–104

13. Craig Dworkin, blurb for Robert Fitterman, *Rob the Plagiarist* (New York: Roof Books, 2009), https://www.roofbooks.com/rob-the-plagiarist.

14. As successors of New American poetry, my examples *are* also bound by their inheritance of certain countertraditions and certain theoretical concerns regarding intention, novelty, and identity. This is not to say that many of these countertraditions haven't since been codified by scholarship and institutions. They have. Thus, rather than seeing experimental poets as inheriting outsider positions, one should see them as inheriting the very paradoxes and problems that come with an outsider position that is always tempted or threatened by its reification as suddenly an "insider." What is inherited is not a stance but a set of debates.

15. Charles Bernstein, "I Don't Remember," in *Near/Miss* (Chicago: University of Chicago Press, 2018), 140.

16. Augustine, *The Confessions of Saint Augustine*, trans. Henry Chadwick (1991; repr., Oxford: Oxford University Press, 2008), 193.

17. Augustine, 195–96.

18. W. H. Auden, "Squares and Oblongs," in *Poets at Work*, ed. Rudolf Arnheim (New York: Harcourt, Brace, 1948), 174.

19. Ludwig Wittgenstein, *Philosophical Investigations* (1953), 4th ed., trans. by G. E. M. Anscombe, P. M. S. Hacker, and Joachin Schulte (Oxford: Wiley-Blackwell, 2009), 81.

20. Michel Foucault, "Nietzsche, Genealogy, History" (1971), in *Language, Counter-Memory, Practice*, trans. Donald F. Bouchard and Sherry Simon (Ithaca, NY: Cornell University Press, 1977), 140, 142.

21. See Benedict Anderson, "Memory and Forgetting," in *Imagined Communities* (London: Verso, 1991), 204.

22. Tom Weatherly, quoted in Rosanne Wasserman, "Weatherly's Words: A Tribute to Tom Weatherly," *Jacket2*, September 6, 2019, https://jacket2.org/article/weatherlys-words.

23. Alice Notley, *Doctor Williams' Heiresses* (Berkeley: Tuumba Press, 1980), 1.

24. Duncan is the one author in this chapter who was actually included in *The New American Poetry*.

25. Ed Dorn, *Ed Dorn Live: Lectures, Interviews, and Outtakes*, ed. Joseph Richey (Ann Arbor: University of Michigan Press, 2007), 89.

26. Robert Duncan, *A Poet's Mind: Collected Interviews with Robert Duncan, 1960–1985*, ed. Christopher Wagstaff (Berkeley: North Atlantic Books, 2012), 60.

27. Tyrone Williams, introduction to *Mary Wants to Be a Superwoman*, by Erica Lewis (Nashville: Third Man Books, 2017), 1. Tyrone also cites Ralph Ellison's famous distinction between a writer's unchosen "relatives"—bound by shared identities—and a writer's chosen "ancestors," marked by literary influence.

28. Kirsten (Kai) Ihns, blurb for Losarc Raal's *No Material* (New York: Black Sun Lit, 2023), back matter. Ihns here echoes Raal's own use of multiple identities, not only in the form of pseudonyms but also in his use of genealogical identification. Throughout *No Material* the poet creates a motif of sentences like "Goddamnit, I feel like Tristan Tzara," "Goddamnit, I feel like Wanda Coleman," "Goddamnit, I feel like Ronnie Burk (when he felt like Alejandra Pizarnik)," "Goddamnit, I feel like Sir Philip Sidney," and so on (Raal, 11, 17, 59, 61). Another contemporary example can be found in the contemporary poet Mohammed Zenia's sequence "The Rodrigo Lira of Sudanese Letters," where the poet suggests that he, Lira, and Paul Dunbar all write the same poem.

29. Paul Valéry, *Collected Works of Paul Valéry*, vol. 8, trans. James Lawler and M. Cowley (Princeton, NJ: Princeton University Press: 2015), 240–41.

30. Arthur Rimbaud, *A Season in Hell and Illuminations*, trans. and ed. Wyatt Mason (New York: Random House, 2005), 4.

31. Notley, *Doctor Williams' Heiresses*, 2.

32. Ron Padgett, afterword to *I Remember* by Joe Brainard (1970; repr., New York: Granary Books, 2001), 169.

33. Rochelle Owens, *I Am the Babe of Joseph Stalin's Daughter* (New York: Kulchur Foundation, 1972), 42, 48. See the poems "I Came from Judea" and "A Song for Passover."

34. Owens, 102.

35. Owens, 131, 133.

36. Ezra Pound, "Histrion," *Evening Standard & St. James Gazette*, October 25, 1908, reprinted in *Early Writings: Poems and Prose*, ed. Ira Nadel (New York: Penguin, 2005), 12.

37. John Dryden, preface to *Fables, Ancient and Modern* (London: Printed for Jacob Tonson at Gray's Inn Gate, 1700), unpaginated.

38. Alice Notley, *Coming After: Essays on Poetry* (Ann Arbor: University of Michigan Press, 2005), 5.

39. Robert Duncan, *The H.D. Book: The Collected Writings of Robert Duncan*, ed. Michael Boughn and Victor Coleman (Berkeley: University of California Press, 2011), 203.

40. Hilda Doolittle, "The Farmer's Bride," *The Egoist* 9, no. 3 (September 1916): 135.

41. Samuel Taylor Coleridge, quoted in Leslie Brisman, *Romantic Origins* (Ithaca, NY: Cornell University Press, 1978), 23. This kind of parallelism, of course, also appears in nonliterary usages: Marx famously lists a number of examples at the start of "The Eighteenth Brumaire of Louis Bonaparte" (1851).

42. Lisa Robertson, "Textures of Personhood: Lisa Robertson Interviewed," by Allison Grimaldi Donahue, *BOMB*, January 17, 2020, https://bombmagazine.org/articles /lisa-robertson/.

43. Jean-Paul Sartre, *Baudelaire*, trans. Martin Turnell (New York: New Directions, 1950), 143.

44. Lisa Robertson, *The Baudelaire Fractal* (Toronto: Coach House Books, 2020), 135.

45. In her book-length poem *Cinema of the Present* (2014), Robertson had already been playing with the twin notions of priorness and simultaneity, presenting a set of composed lines only to intersplice them with the same set of lines but rearranged in alphabetical order. There, each line could either contain a future memory of itself or be an identical duplicate of an earlier line. The reader would encounter all of the poetic material twice but in a way that did not map onto the "original" sequence of the author's thoughts.

46. Harryette Mullen, *Sleeping with the Dictionary* (Berkeley: University of California Press, 2002), 3.

47. Mullen, "An Interview with Harryette Mullen," by Elisabeth A. Frost, in *The Cracks Between What We Are and What We Are Supposed to Be* (Tuscaloosa: University of Alabama Press, 2012), 219.

48. Mullen, *Sleeping with the Dictionary*, 54.

49. See Samuel Beckett's final poem "What Is the Word" (1990), written after Beckett became aphasic.

178 Notes to Pages 112–118

50. See Laura Salisbury, "'What Is the Word': Beckett's Aphasic Modernism," *Journal of Beckett Studies* 17, nos. 1–2 (2009): 94.

51. Mullen, *Sleeping with the Dictionary*, 84.

52. Coleridge, *The Collected Works of Samuel Taylor Coleridge*, vol. 13, *Logic*, ed. James Robert de Jager Jackson (Princeton, NJ: Princeton University Press, 1981), 242. When Coleridge writes this, he is contrasting an etymological method of poetic composition with one based on visual images. For a clarification on the passage, see Nancy Struever's *Language and the History of Thought* (Martlesham, UK: Boydell & Brewer, 1995).

53. Ernest Fenollosa, "The Chinese Written Character as a Medium for Poetry," trans. Ezra Pound, in *The Chinese Written Character as a Medium for Poetry: A Critical Edition*, ed. Haun Saussy, Jonathan Stalling, and Lucas Klein (New York: Fordham University Press, 2008), 96.

54. Charles Olson, letter to Larry Eigner, dated June 20, 1956, quoted in *Collected Prose*, ed. Donald Allen and Benjamin Friedlander (Berkeley: University of California Press, 1997), 453.

55. Astrid Lorange, *How Reading Is Written: A Brief Index to Gertrude Stein* (Middletown, CT: Wesleyan University Press, 2014), 231.

56. Giles Goodland, "Long Poems about Everything: Dictionary as Subject and Model for Poem, 1974–2016," in *Poetry and the Dictionary*, ed. Andrew Blades and Piers Pennington (Liverpool: Liverpool University Press, 2020), 263.

57. Mullen, *Sleeping with the Dictionary*, 34.

58. Philip Sidney, "The Defence of Poesy" (1595), in *The Miscellaneous Works of Sir Philip Sidney, Knt*, ed. William Gray (London: William W. Gibbings, 1893), 97.

59. Goodland, "Long Poems about Everything," 268.

60. Mullen, "An Interview with Harryette Mullen," 222.

61. Hank Lazer, review of *Squeezed Light: Collected Poems, 1994–2005* by Lissa Wolsak, Rain Taxi (2010), https://raintaxi.com/squeezed-light-collected-poems-1994-2005/.

62. Colin Martindale, "History and Creativity," in *Encyclopedia of Creativity*, vol. 1, ed. Mark A. Runco and Steven R. Pritzer (San Diego: Academic Press, 1999), 827. The theories of Colin Martindale, from which I take this phrase, are rather interesting to consider given a rise in cognitive literary criticism. Martindale argues that artists move between rational concepts (used for problem solving) and irrational, free-associative images. Novelty works, he argues, by "regressing" from the former to the latter, with the caveat being that too much regression leads to hyper-diffusion (or what we might call chaos).

63. Charles Altieri, blurb for *Squeezed Light: Collected Poems, 1994–2005*, by Lissa Wolsak (Barrytown, NY: Station Hill Press, 2010), back cover.

64. Lissa Wolsak, "'Ardor is its undermost shaping': An Interview with Lissa Wolsak," by Kent Johnson, *VeRT Poetry Magazine*, no. 6 (Winter 2002), https://writing.upenn.edu/epc/mags/vert/Vert_issue_6/lwolsakinter.html.

65. Wolsak, *Squeezed Light*, 77.

66. Kent Johnson, quoted in Wolsak, "'Ardor is its undermost shaping.'"

67. David-Antoine Williams, *The Life of Words: Etymology and Modern Poetry* (Oxford: Oxford University Press, 2020), 114.

68. Wolsak, *Squeezed Light*, 12.

69. T. S. Eliot, *The Use of Poetry and the Use of Criticism* (Cambridge, MA: Harvard University Press, 1933; repr., London: Faber and Faber, 1964), 155.

70. Eliot, 155.

Notes to Pages 119–123   179

71. Wolsak, *Squeezed Light*, 13.

72. *Squeezed Light*, 24.

73. *Squeezed Light*, 56.

74. *Squeezed Light*, 23.

75. *Squeezed Light*, 161.

76. *Squeezed Light*, 80.

Chapter Five

1. A. R. Luria, *The Mind of a Mnemonist* (1968), trans. Lynn Solotaroff (Cambridge, MA: Harvard University Press, 1987), 16.

2. The oldest mention of the method of loci occurs in the *Rhetorica ad Herennium*, which was previously misattributed to Cicero. Cicero did, however, further popularize the notion in *De Oratore* with the story of Simonides.

3. Luria, *Mind of a Mnemonist*, 39.

4. Luria, 39.

5. Luria, 67.

6. Regardless of whether we take their disavowals of posterity at face value, notable exceptions include Marquis de Sade and Franz Kafka.

7. Craig Dworkin writes, "Our emphasis is on work that does not seek to express unique, coherent, or individual psychologies and that, moreover, refuses familiar strategies of authorial control in favor of automatism, reticence, obliquity, and modes of noninterference." Dworkin, "The Fate of Echo," in *Against Expression: An Anthology of Conceptual Writing*, ed. Craig Dworkin and Kenneth Goldsmith (Evanston, IL: Northwestern University Press, 2011), xliii–xliv. See also Timothy Morton, "Why Ambient Poetics? Outline for a Depthless Ecology," *Wordsworth Circle* 33, no. 1 (2002).

8. Leo Spitzer, "Milieu and Ambiance: An Essay in Historical Semantics," *Philosophy and Phenomenological Research* 3, no. 2 (1942): 169–218; Philip T. Kotler, "Atmospherics as a Marketing Tool," *Journal of Retailing* 49, no. 4 (1973–74): 50.

9. The full quote by Dworkin states, "With minimal intervention, the writers here are more likely to determine preestablished rules and parameters—to set up a system and step back as it runs its course." Dworkin, *Against Expression*, xliv. Adam Dickinson, "Pataphysics and Postmodern Ecocriticism: A Prospectus," in *The Oxford Handbook of Ecocriticism*, ed. Greg Garrard (Oxford: Oxford University Press, 2014), 137.

10. Paul Stephens, *Poetics of Information Overload* (Minneapolis: University of Minnesota Press, 2015), 163.

11. Jennifer Scappettone, "Versus Seamlessness: Architectonics of Pseudocomplicity in Tan Lin's Ambient Poetics," *boundary 2* 36, no. 3 (2009): 74.

12. For all three quotes here, see Tan Lin, "Ambient Stylistics," *Conjunctions* 35 (2000): 128, 131, 140.

13. Scappettone, "Versus Seamlessness," 64. General skepticism toward conceptual poetry notwithstanding (see Calvin Bedient, "Against Conceptualism: Defending the Poetry of Affect," *Boston Review*, July 24, 2013, http://bostonreview.net/poetry/against -conceptualism), writers affiliated with "experimental" poetry have also raised questions about ambient poetry: in *The noulipian Analects*, where Lin and others explore new media writing, editors Matias Viegener and Christine Wertheim wonder about the "qualities heralded in this writing," i.e., the downplaying of the authorial position and the "autonomy and self-sufficiency of *the system*"—asking what exactly is gained from

180 **Notes to Pages 123–124**

throwing subjectivity agency and who privileges from this. In the very same volume, Brian Kim Stefans remains skeptical of the feigned "egalitarianism" that "seems to be consistent with the hacker/libertarian ethos of internet culture, but which also takes its cue from John Cage and Robert Rauschenberg [. . . and] also derives from the fact that all types of sensible elements, such as sound, image, and text can be reduced to the same principle components of bytes." *The noulipian Analects*, ed. Christine Wertheim and Matias Viegener (Los Angeles: Les Figues Press, 2007), 149, 60. Elsewhere, Timothy Morton acknowledges that there are corrupted forms of ambience ("soothing panacea[s] for capitalist and technocratic alienation") as well as more utopian versions in which we are connected to our ecology. Morton, "Why Ambient Poetics?," 52.

14. J. J. Gibson, *The Senses Considered as Perceptual Systems* (Boston: Houghton Mifflin, 1966), 214, quoted in Elaine Scarry, "On Vivacity: The Difference Between Daydreaming and Imagining-Under-Authorial-Instruction," *Representations* 52 (Autumn 1995): 7.

15. Marcel Proust, *Remembrance of Things Past*, trans. C. K. Scott Moncrieff and Terence Kilmartin (New York: Vintage Books, 1982), 1:10, quoted in Scarry, 11.

16. Tierry Davila, "Duchamp with Mallarmé," *October* 171 (Winter 2020): 16.

17. Davila, 16.

18. Matisse, "Notes of a Painter," in *Matisse on Art*, ed. Jack Flam (New York: E. P. Dutton, 1978), 38.

19. Satie wrote: "We must bring about a music which is like furniture—a music, that is, which will be part of the noises of the environment, will take them into consideration. I think of it as melodious, softening the noise of the knives and forks, not dominating them, not imposing itself. It would fill up those heavy silences that sometimes fall between friends dining together. It would spare them the trouble of paying attention to their own banal remarks. And at the same time, it would neutralize the street noises which so indiscreetly enter into the play of conversation. To make such music would be to respond to a need." Satie, quoted in Alan Gillmore, *Erik Satie* (Woodbridge, CT: Twayne, 1988), 232.

Rollo Myers attributes this formulation of Satie's to Matisse: "The term 'musique d'ameublement,' which applies to many of the third period works, and of which [Satie's] 'Socrate' is the outstanding example, owes its origin to a statement made by the painter Matisse, who declared that he dreamed of an art without any distracting subject-matter, and which might be compared to an easy chair." Myers, "The Strange Case of Erik Satie," *Musical Times* 86, no. 1229 (July 1945): 203.

20. David Toop, *Ocean of Sound: Aether Talk, Ambient Sound and Imaginary Worlds* (London: Serpent's Tail, 1995), prologue.

21. Jerome McGann reads modernism according to William Morris's statement that "you can't have art without resistance in the material," an idea that is also echoed in Hegel's theory of art ("What resistance the material exerts here, e.g. a metal, when it is to be worked upon!"). McGann, *Black Riders: The Visible Language of Modernism* (Princeton, NJ: Princeton University Press, 1993), xiii; Georg Hegel, *Aesthetics: Lectures on Fine Art*, Vol. 1, trans. T. M. Knox (Oxford: Clarendon Press, 1975), 163. Clement Greenberg famously wrote, "The history of avant-garde painting is that of a progressive surrender to the resistance of its medium [. . .] sculpture, on its side, emphasizes the resistance of its material to the efforts of the artist to play it into shapes uncharacteristic of stone, metal, wood, etc." Contrast this sense of materiality to Niklas Luhmann's theory of me-

dium: "Medium itself is too diffuse to arouse attention [. . .] the uncoupled (or weakly coupled) elements of the medium can offer it no resistance." Greenberg, "Towards a Newer Laocoön" (1940), in *The Collected Essays and Criticism*, vol. 1, ed. John O'Brian (Chicago: University of Chicago Press, 1986), 23–38; Luhmann, "The Medium of the Art," *Thesis Eleven*, nos. 18/19 (1987): 103.

22. Edward Young writes in "Conjectures on Original Composition" (1759) that literary composition is "not only a noble amusement, but a sweet refuge [. . .] it gives us a respite, at least, from care; a pleasing pause of refreshing recollection." Young, "Conjectures on Original Composition" (1759), reprinted in *Critical Theory Since Plato*, 3rd ed., ed. Hazard Adams (Belmont, CA: Wadsworth, 2005), 347–57. Joseph Addison, in "Pleasures of the Imagination" (1712), argues that poetry differs from philosophy on the spectrum of rigor: the work of the imagination is a "gentle exercise" conducive to health rather than understanding, located somewhere between the work of thinking and idleness; it allows us to experience delight without inquiring into causes or circumstances of explanations. Addison, "Pleasures . . . ," in *Critical Theory Since Plato*, 307–13.

23. In the nineteenth century, boredom began to emerge at the front of social consciousness. According to Lars Svendsen, it "is not until the advent of Romanticism [. . .] that the demand arises for life to be interesting, with the general claim that the self must realize itself." Svendsen, *A Philosophy of Boredom* (London: Reaktion, 2005), 28. See Moira Roth's "The Aesthetic of Indifference" in *Artforum* 16, no. 3 (November 1977): 47–53, as well as Dick Higgins's "Boredom and Danger" and Ina Blom's "Boredom and Oblivion," both of which are available in *Boredom: Documents of Contemporary Art*, ed. Tom McDonough (London: Whitechapel and MIT Press, 2017). According to Higgins, boredom occurs when works fade into their environment and the environment infiltrates works, causing disappearance on multiple levels; only what has disappeared has the ability to be repeated, but there is no determining whether a work is opposed or derived from its context.

24. Gertrude Stein, *Everybody's Autobiography* (1937; repr., Cambridge: Exact Change, 1993), 101.

25. Richard Sieburth, "A Heap of Language: Robert Smithson and American Hieroglyphics," in *Robert Smithson*, ed. Eugene Tsai (Los Angeles: Museum of Contemporary Art, 2004), 219.

26. Harvey Eagleson, "Gertrude Stein: Method in Madness," *Sewanee Review* (April 1926): 171–72.

27. Sianne Ngai, "Stuplimity: Shock and Boredom in Twentieth-Century Aesthetics," *Postmodern Culture* 10, no. 2 (2000), https://muse.jhu.edu/pub/1/article/27722.

28. T. S. Eliot, "The Frontiers of Criticism" (1956), in *On Poets and Poetry* (repr., New York: FSG, 2009), 121.

29. Eliot, letter to Bonamy Dobrée, November 14, 1957, quoted in *The Poems of T. S. Eliot*, vol. 1 (London: Faber and Faber, 2015), 570.

30. Peter Ackroyd, *T.S. Eliot: A Life* (New York: Simon and Schuster, 1984), quoted in Elizabeth Gregory, *Quotation and Modern American Poetry: "Imaginary Gardens with Real Toads"* (Houston: Rice University Press, 1996), 40.

31. Gregory, *Quotation*, 40.

32. Eliot, "Tradition and the Individual Talent," *The Egoist* 6 (1919), quoted in Gregory, 40.

182 Notes to Pages 126–129

33. Richard Badenhausen, *T. S. Eliot and the Art of Collaboration* (Cambridge: Cambridge University Press, 2004), 107.

34. Tan Lin, "Disco as Operating System, Part One," *Criticism* 50, no. 1 (2008): 97.

35. Tan Lin, *Seven Controlled Vocabularies and Obituary 2004. The Joy of Cooking: Airport Novel Musical Poem Painting Film Photo Hallucination Landscape* (Middleton, CT: Wesleyan University Press, 2010), 26.

36. *Seven Controlled Vocabularies*, 32.

37. The quote comes from *Blipsoak01* (2003), where Lin also writes: "Beauty is over-appreciated; boredom is not. Like things that are blind, anyone who has every looked at a book [as opposed to read it] knows a page is just a literal repetition of what came before." *Blipsoak01* itself causes the reader's eye to wander across its spread while also scanning downward throughout a distracted kind of field. Lin, *Blipsoak01* (Berkeley: Atelos, 2003), 11.

38. Lin, "Disco as Operating System," 91.

39. As Lev Manovich puts it, "The new avant-garde is no longer concerned with seeing or representing the world in new ways but rather accessing and using in new ways previous accumulated media. In this respect new media is post-media or meta-media, as it uses old media as its primary material." Manovich, "Avant-Garde as Software" (1999), https://manovich.net/content/04-projects/027-avant-garde-as-software/24_article_1999.pdf, 15. Manovich successfully describes the continuities and changes between the early avant-garde and its successors. Some continuities include visual atomism (Seurat to digital pixels), montage, new typography, and new visualization (cubism and "New vision" photography to 3-D computer graphics), while the changes entail a focus on media to post- or meta-media. See also Manovich, "Remixability and Modularity" (2005), https://manovich.net/content/04-projects/046-remixability-and-modularity/43_article_2005.pdf.

40. Andy Warhol, *The Philosophy of Andy Warhol* (Orlando, FL: Harcourt, 1975), 199.

41. Jonathan Flatley, *Like Andy Warhol* (Chicago: University of Chicago Press, 2018), 67–68.

42. Gustavus Stadler, "'My Wife': The Tape Recorder and Warhol's Queer Ways of Listening," *Criticism* 56, no. 3 (2014): 440.

43. Sargent subsequently quotes these lines of poetry: "But little of the ambient poetry about us / Has yet been caught / Like the perfume of roses in attar / Or petals in a jar." Porter Sargent, "Our Poesy Is as a Gum," *Poet Lore* 42, no. 4 (1935): 333.

44. Flatley, *Like Andy Warhol*, 13.

45. Tan Lin, "Disco, Cybernetics, and the Migration of Warhol's *Shadows* into Computation," *Criticism* 56, no. 3 (2014): 489.

46. "Disco, Cybernetics, and the Migration," 490.

47. "Disco, Cybernetics, and the Migration," 487.

48. Flatley, *Like Andy Warhol*, 12.

49. Alan Davies, "Cereal," in *O One/An Anthology*, ed. Leslie Scalapino (Oakland: O Books, 1988), 134–37.

50. One of my favorite anecdotes recounts how, during his visit to Asia, Warhol was gifted a painting of a Chinese flower by a local artist and university department chair. To express his gratitude, Warhol subsequently took out a brushstroke pen and painted a dollar sign for the Chinese artist.

51. Paul Overy, "The Different Shades of Mao," *Times* (London), March 12, 1974, 7. Overy takes as his reference Rainer Crone's influential book *Andy Warhol* from 1970.

52. See Maurizio Lazzarato, "From Capital-Labour to Capital Life," trans. Valerie Fournier, Akseli Virtanen, and Jussi Vähämäki, *Ephemera* 4, no. 3 (2004): 188.

53. Lazzarato, 193, 204.

54. Maurizio Lazzarato, "Immaterial Labour" (1996), in *Radical Thought in Italy: A Potential Politics*, ed. Paolo Virno and Michael Hardt, trans. Maurizia Boscagli et al. (Minneapolis: University of Minnesota Press, 2006), 154.

55. Generally speaking, an attention economy also supplies an overabundance of information to a scarce pool of attention. The results are various: the subject may become impoverished after bearing the cost of constant attention-switching. The need to more efficiently select information can replace the need to remember it. The rise of an attention economy, which depends on attention's scarcity (hence its value), can also lead to an economy of *imitation*. According to Tiziana Terranova, "Paying attention to what others do on networked social platforms triggers potential responses of imitation by means of which network culture produces and reproduces itself." The triggered responses of imitation—a range of "acts such as reading and writing, watching and listening, copying and pasting, downloading and uploading, liking, sharing, following and bookmarking"—form an economy of attention that "is, then, also the economy of socialization of ideas, affects and percepts, and hence an economy of social production and cooperation." The more exposure an audience has to information, the more potential that audience has to replicate its attention-paying behaviors for others. Terranova, "Attention, Economy and the Brain," *Culture Machine* 13 (2012): 7–8, https://culturemachine.net/paying-attention/.

56. "An emotion is a pattern sampled," Lin writes, echoing Theodor Adorno's 1941 critique on popular music: "It induces relaxation because it is patterned and predigested." Lin, *Blipsoak01*, 62; Adorno, *Essays on Music* (Berkeley: University California Press, 2002), 458.

57. Kristen Gallagher, "The Authorship of Heath Ledger in the New Reading Environment: On Tan Lin's *Heath: Plagiarism/Outsource*," *Criticism* 51, no. 4 (2009): 701. Lin himself uses the phrase "text and image environment."

58. Lin, *Heath Course Pak*, n.p.

59. See Violet Spurlock, "Uses of Obviousness in *Seven Controlled Vocabularies*," in "Tan Lin" cluster, Post45 Contemporaries, August 23, 2024, https://post45.org/2024/08/uses-of-obviousness-in-seven-controlled-vocabularies/.

60. Tomas Kulka, *Kitsch and Art* (1994; repr., University Park: Pennsylvania State University Press, 1996), 37.

61. Clement Greenberg, "Avant-Garde and Kitsch," in *Art and Culture* (Boston: Beacon Press, 1961), 16.

62. Lin, "Disco as Operating System," 94.

63. More accurately, Lin describes Chan as "a kind of Asian American clown (who I like)." *Heath Course Pak*, n.p.

64. Tan Lin, "The Patio and the Index," Triple Canopy, 2011, https://www.canopycanopycanopy.com/contents/the_patio_and_the_index. All subsequent quotes from the essay have no pagination.

65. Tan Lin, *Insomnia and the Aunt* (Chicago: Kenning Editions, 2011), 10.

66. For more on archives and forgetting, see Geoffrey Bowker, *Memory Practices in the Sciences* (Cambridge, MA: MIT Press, 2005).

67. Anne Anlin Cheng, *Ornamentalism* (Chicago: University of Chicago Press, 2018), 21.

184   **Notes to Pages 143–150**

68. Mario Amaya, *Pop as Art: A Survey of the New Super Realism* (London: Studio Vista, 1965), 20. Lin cites Duchamp's work as something that embodies this recycling of things' identities. Another modernist example might be Picasso's *Bull's Head* (1942), which also works as a bicycle part.

69. Cheng, *Ornamentalism*, 3.

70. Mary Doane, "Information, Crisis, Catastrophe," in *New Media, Old Media: A History and Theory Reader*, ed. Wendy Chun and Thomas Keenan (New York: Routledge, 2006), 255. Fredric Jameson also states, "[M]emory seems to play no role in television." Jameson, *Postmodernism, or, The Cultural Logic of Late Capitalism* (1991; repr., Durham: Duke University Press, 2003), 70.

71. Doane, 254.

72. Lin, *Insomnia*, 11.

73. *Insomnia*, 21. Lin echoes here Eliot's famous claim, "Poetry is not a turning loose of emotion, but an escape from emotion; it is not the expression of personality, but an escape from personality. But, of course, only those who have personality and emotions know what it means to want to escape from these things." Eliot, "Tradition and the Individual Talent," 33.

74. As far as I know, the first discussion of Lin's generic "auntie" appears in Irene Kim's "On Ambience, Tan Lin, and American Minimalisms," *Post45*, April 27, 2023, https://post45.org/2023/04/on-ambience-tan-lin-and-american-minimalism/.

75. W. E. B. Du Bois, *The Souls of Black Folk* (1903; repr., New York: W. W. Norton, 1999), 11.

76. Lin, *Insomnia*, 45.

77. *Insomnia*, 39, 42.

Coda

1. Denise Levertov, "The Secret," in *Poems, 1960–1967* (New York: New Directions, 1983), 93.

2. T. J. Clark, *The Sight of Death* (New Haven, CT: Yale University Press, 2006), 8.

3. Clark, 118.

4. Stephen Jonas, *Arcana: A Stephen Jonas Reader* (San Francisco: City Lights, 2019), 137.

5. Richard Howard, *Alone with America: Essays on the Art of Poetry in the United States Since 1950* (New York: Atheneum, 1980), 88.

6. W. H. Auden, *The Dyer's Hand and Other Essays* (London: Faber and Faber, 1963), 305.

7. Tan Lin, *Seven Controlled Vocabularies and Obituary 2004. The Joy of Cooking: Airport Novel Musical Poem Painting Film Photo Hallucination Landscape* (Middleton, CT: Wesleyan University Press, 2010), 24.

8. John Keats, "Letter to Benjamin Bailey" (October 8, 1817), in *The Complete Works of John Keats*, vol. 4: *Letters 1814 to January 1819*, ed. H. Buxton Forman (Glasgow: Gowars & Gray, 1901), 38.

References

Ackroyd, Peter. *T.S. Eliot: A Life*. New York: Simon and Schuster, 1984.

Addison, Joseph. "Pleasures of the Imagination." 1712. Reprint in *Critical Theory Since Plato*. 3rd ed., edited by Hazard Adams, 307–13. Belmont, CA: Wadsworth, 2005.

Adorno, Theodor. *Essays on Music*. Berkeley: University of California Press, 2002.

Altieri, Charles. Blurb for *Squeezed Light* by Lissa Wolsak. Barrytown, NY: Station Hill Press, 2010.

Amaya, Mario. *Pop as Art: A Survey of the New Super Realism*. London: Studio Vista, 1965.

Anderson, Benedict. *Imagined Communities*. London: Verso, 1991.

Andrews, Bruce. *Paradise and Method*. Evanston, IL: Northwestern University Press, 1996.

Ankersmit, Frank R. "The Sublime Dissociation of the Past: Or How to Be(Come) What One Is No Longer." *History and Theory* 40, no. 3 (2001): 295–323.

Arendt, Hannah. *The Human Condition*. Chicago: University of Chicago Press, 1958.

Arendt, Hannah. *The Portable Hannah Arendt*. Edited by Peter Baehr. New York: Penguin, 2000.

Aristotle. *On Memory and Reminiscence*. Translated by David Bloch. Leiden: Brill, 2007.

Arnovick, Leslie K. "The Expanding Discourse of Promises in Present-Day English: A Case Study in Historical Pragmatics." *Folia Linguistica Historica* 15, nos. 1–2 (1994): 175–91.

Ashbery, John. *Collected Poems, 1956–1987*. Edited by Mark Ford. New York: Library of America, 2008.

Ashbery, John. *Flow Chart*. New York: Noonday, 1991.

Ashbery, John. "The Impossible." Review of *Stanzas in Meditation* by Gertrude Stein. *Poetry* (July 1957): 250–54. Available at https://www.writing.upenn.edu/~afilreis /88/stein-per-ashbery.html.

Ashton, Jennifer. *From Modernism to Postmodernism: American Poetry and Theory in the Twentieth Century*. Cambridge: Cambridge University Press, 2005.

Auden, W. H. *The Dyer's Hand and Other Essays*. London: Faber and Faber, 1963.

Auden, W. H. "Squares and Oblongs." In *Poets at Work*, edited by Rudolf Arnheim, 163–81. New York: Harcourt, Brace, 1948.

186 References

Augé, Marc. *Oblivion*. Translated by Marjolijn de Jager. Minneapolis: University of Minnesota Press, 2004.

Augustine. *The Confessions of Saint Augustine*. Translated by Henry Chadwick. 1991. Reprint, Oxford: Oxford University Press, 2008.

Badenhausen, Richard. *T. S. Eliot and the Art of Collaboration*. Cambridge: Cambridge University Press, 2004.

Barber, C. L. "The Saturnalian Pattern in Shakespeare's Comedy." *Sewanee Review* 59, no. 4 (1951): 593–611.

Beckett, Jane. "Dada and Surrealism." In *The Art Press*, edited by Trevor Fawcett and Clive Phillpot, 33–41. London: Art Book Company, 1976.

Bedient, Calvin. "Against Conceptualism: Defending the Poetry of Affect." *Boston Review*, July 24, 2013. http://bostonreview.net/poetry/against-conceptualism.

Belgrad, Daniel. *The Culture of Spontaneity: Improvisation and the Arts in Postwar America*. Chicago: University of Press, 1998.

Bell, Ian F. A. "The Real and the Ethereal: Modernist Energies in Eliot and Pound." In *From Energy to Information: Representation in Science and Technology, Art, and Literature*, edited by Bruce Clark and Linda D. Henderson. Stanford, CA: Stanford University Press, 2002.

Bergson, Henri. "Laughter." 1900. Translated 1911 by C. Brereton and F. Rothwell. Reprinted in *Comedy: "An Essay on Comedy" by George Meredith. "Laughter" by Henri Bergson*. Edited by Wylie Sypher. Baltimore: Johns Hopkins University Press, 1956.

Bergson, Henri. *Memory and Matter*. 1908. Translated by Nancy Margaret Paul and W. Scott Palmer. London: George Allen & Co., 1913.

Berlant, Lauren. *Cruel Optimism*. Durham, NC: Duke University Press, 2011.

Berlant, Lauren, and Sianne Ngai. "Comedy Has Issues." *Critical Inquiry* 43, no. 2 (Winter 2017).

Bernstein, Charles. "The Art of Immemorability." *Journal of Philosophy* 2, no. 6 (2006): 30–40.

Bernstein, Charles. "I Don't Remember." In *Near/Miss*. Chicago: University of Chicago Press, 2018. 140.

Berrigan, Ted. *The Collected Poems of Ted Berrigan*. Edited by Alice Notley, Edmund Berrigan, and Anselm Berrigan. Berkeley: University of California Press, 2007.

Berrigan, Ted. "Things to Do." Postcard to Pat Nolan. ca. 1970s. Reproduced in *The New Black Bart Poetry Society*. January 18, 2018. https://thenewblackbartpoetrysociety.wordpress.com/2018/01/18/bathroom-art-galleries/.

Bion, Wilfred. *Attention and Interpretation*. Lanham, MD: Rowman & Littlefield, 2004.

Bion, Wilfred. "Notes on Memory and Desire." 1967. Reprinted in *Melanie Klein Today: Developments in Theory and Practice*. Vol. 2, *Mainly Practice*, 17–21. Edited by Elizabeth Bott Spillius. New York: Routledge, 1988.

Blanchot, Maurice. *The Infinite Conversation*. 1969. Translated by Susan Hanson. Minneapolis: University of Minnesota Press, 1993.

Blanchot, Maurice. "Literature and the Right to Death." In *The Gaze of Orpheus and Other Literary Essays*. Edited by P. Adams Sitney. Translated by Lydia Davis. Barrytown, NY: Station Hill Press, 1981. Reprinted in *The Work of Fire*, translated by Charlotte Mandell, 300–344. Stanford, CA: Stanford University Press, 1995.

References 187

Blanchot, Maurice. *The Writing of Disaster*. Translated by Ann Smock. Lincoln: University of Nebraska Press, 1986.

Bloom, Harold, ed. *Bloom's Shakespeare Through the Ages: The Comedy of Errors*. Volume editor Janyce Marson. New York: Infobase Publishing, 2010.

Bloom, Harold. *A Map of Misreading*. 1975. Reprint, Oxford: Oxford University Press, 2003.

Boccioni, Umberto. "The Plastic Foundations of Futurist Sculpture and Painting." 1913. Reprinted in *Futurism: An Anthology*, edited by Christine Poggi, Lawrence Rainey, and Laura Wittman. New Haven, CT: Yale University Press, 2009.

Bolzoni, Lina. *The Gallery of Memory: Literary and Iconographic Models in the Age of the Printing Press*. Translated by Jeremy Parzen. Toronto: University of Toronto Press, 2001.

Booth, W. James. *Communities of Memory: On Witness, Identity, and Justice*. Ithaca, NY: Cornell University Press, 2006.

Bowker, Geoffrey. *Memory Practices in the Sciences*. Cambridge, MA: MIT Press, 2005.

Boym, Svetlana. *The Future of Nostalgia*. New York: Perseus Books, 2001.

Brainard, Joe. *I Remember*. New York: Angel Hair Books, 1970. Reprint, New York: Granary Books, 2001.

Brainard, Joe. "Things to Do Before I Move." In *Some Drawings of Some Notes to Myself*. New York: Siamese Banana Press, 1971.

Braque, Georges. *Testimony Against Gertrude Stein*. The Hague: Servire Press, 1935.

Bridgman, Richard. *Gertrude Stein in Pieces*. New York: Oxford University Press, 1970.

Brisman, Leslie. *Romantic Origins*. Ithaca, NY: Cornell University Press, 1978.

Bromberg, Philip. "Staying the Same While Changing Reflections on Clinical Judgment." *Psychoanalytic Dialogues* 8, no. 2 (1998): 225–36.

Bru, Sascha. "Avant-Garde Nows: Presentist Reconfigurations of Public Time." *Modernist Cultures* 8, no. 2 (2013): 272–87.

Bruns, Gerard. "A Poem of Laughter and Forgetting: Lyn Hejinian's *A Border Comedy*." *Textual Practice* 23, no. 3 (2009): 397–416.

Bryant, Rebecca. "Nostalgia and the Discovery of Loss." In *Anthropology and Nostalgia*, edited by Oliva Angé and David Berliner, 155–78. New York: Berghahn, 2014.

Burke, Edmund. *The Works of the Right Honourable*. Vol. 1. Boston: Wells and Lily, 1826.

Burliuk, D., Alexander Kruchenykh, V. Mayakovsky, and Victor Khlebnikov. "Slap in the Face of Public Taste." 1912. Reprinted in *Words in Revolution: Russian Futurist Manifestoes, 1912–1928*. Translated and edited by Anna Lawton and Herbert Eagle, 51. Washington, DC: New Academia Publishing, 2004.

Campbell, Sue. *Our Faithfulness to the Past: The Ethics and Politics of Memory*. Oxford: Oxford University Press, 2014.

Carlson, Gary. "References to Kinds in English." PhD diss., University of Massachusetts Amherst, 1977.

Carruthers, Mary. *The Book of Memory: A Study of Memory in Medieval Culture*. Cambridge: Cambridge University Press, 1990.

Carruthers, Mary. *The Craft of Thought*. Cambridge: Cambridge University Press, 1998.

Cavell, Stanley. *Must We Mean What We Say?* 2nd ed. Cambridge: Cambridge University Press, 2015.

Caws, Mary Ann, ed. *Manifesto: A Century of Isms*. Lincoln: University of Nebraska Press, 2000.

188 References

Cecire, Natalia. *Experimental: American Literature and the Aesthetics of Knowledge*. Baltimore: Johns Hopkins University Press, 2019.

Cheng, Anne Anlin. *Ornamentalism*. Chicago: University of Chicago Press, 2018.

Clark, Hilary. "The Mnemonics of Autobiography: Lyn Hejinian's *My Life*." *Biography* 14, no. 4 (1991): 315-35.

Clark, T. J. "Cubism and Collectivity." In *Farewell to an Idea*. New Haven, CT: Yale University Press, 1999.

Clark, T. J. *The Sight of Death*. New Haven, CT: Yale University Press, 2006.

Clune, Michael. "'Everything We Want': Frank O'Hara and the Aesthetics of Free Choice." *PMLA* 120, no. 1 (2005): 181-96.

Coleridge, Samuel Taylor. *The Collected Works of Samuel Taylor Coleridge*. Vol. 13, *Logic*, edited by James Robert de Jager Jackson. Princeton, NJ: Princeton University Press, 1981.

Collom, Jack. "A Conversation with Jack Collom." Interview by Elizabeth Robinson. *OmniVerse*, January 13, 2013. http://omniverse.us/a-conversation-with-jack -collom/.

Collom, Jack. "Interview with Jack Collom." By Jason Rawn. *Café Review* 15 (Summer 2004): 20-32.

Collom, Jack, and Lyn Hejinian. *Situations, Sings*. New York: Adventures in Poetry, 2008.

Connerton, Paul. "Seven Types of Forgetting." *Memory Studies* (2008): 59-71.

Corr, Bruno, F. T. Marinetti, and Emilio Settimelli. "The Futurist Synthetic Theatre." 1915. Reprinted in *Manifesto: A Century of Isms*, edited by Mary Ann Caws, 191. Lincoln: University of Nebraska Press, 2000.

Crystal, Jonathon D. "Prospective Memory." *Current Biology* 23, no. 17 (2013): 750-51.

Dames, Nicholas. *Amnesiac Selves*. Oxford: Oxford University Press, 2001.

Davies, Alan. "Cereal." *O One/An Anthology*, edited by Leslie Scalapino, 134-37. Oakland, CA: O Books, 1988.

Davila, Tierry. "Duchamp with Mallarmé." *October* 171 (Winter 2020): 3-26.

De Brabanter, Philippe. Mikhail Kissine, and Saghie Sharifzadeh, eds. *Future Times, Future Tenses*. Oxford: Oxford University Press, 2014.

Deleuze, Gilles. *Nietzsche and Philosophy*. New York: Columbia University Press, 1983.

De Man, Paul. *Blindness and Insight*. New York: Oxford University Press, 1971; 2nd ed. London: Routledge, 1983.

Derrida, Jacques. *Given Time: I. Counterfeit Money*. Translated by Peggy Kamuf. Chicago: University of Chicago Press, 1991.

Derrida, Jacques. *Spurs*. Translated by Barbara Harlow. Chicago: University of Chicago Press, 1978.

Dewey, John. *Human Nature and Conduct*. New York: Henry Holt, 1922.

Dickinson, Adam. "Pataphysics and Postmodern Ecocriticism: A Prospectus." In *The Oxford Handbook of Ecocriticism*, edited by Greg Garrard, 132-54. Oxford: Oxford University Press, 2014.

Diggory, Terence. *Encyclopedia of the New York School Poets*. New York: Facts on File, 2009.

Doane, Mary. "Information, Crisis, Catastrophe." In *New Media, Old Media: A History and Theory Reader*, edited by Wendy Chun and Thomas Keenan, 251-64. New York: Routledge, 2006.

References 189

Doolittle, Hilda. "The Farmer's Bride." *The Egoist* 9, no. 3 (September 1916): 135.

Dorn, Ed. *Ed Dorn Live: Lectures, Interviews, and Outtakes*. Edited by Joseph Richey. Ann Arbor: University of Michigan Press, 2007.

Dryden, John. Preface to *Fables, Ancient and Modern*. London: Printed for Jacob Tonson at Gray's Inn Gate, 1700.

Du Bois, W. E. B. *The Souls of Black Folk*. 1903. Reprint, New York: W. W. Norton, 1999.

Duchamp, Marcel. *Salt Seller: The Writings of Marcel Duchamp*. Edited by Michel Sanouillet and Elmer Peterson. New York: Oxford University Press, 1973.

Duff, William. *An Essay on Original Genius*. 1767.

Duhamel, Denise, Maureen Seaton, and David Trinidad. *Saints of Hysteria*. New York: Soft Skull Press, 2007.

Duncan, Robert. *The H.D. Book: The Collected Writings of Robert Duncan*. Edited by Michael Boughn and Victor Coleman. Berkeley: University of California Press, 2011.

Duncan, Robert. *A Poet's Mind: Collected Interviews with Robert Duncan, 1960–1985*. Edited by Christopher Wagstaff. Berkeley: North Atlantic Books, 2012.

Dworkin, Craig. Blurb for *Rob the Plagiarist* by Robert Fitterman. New York: Roof Books, 2009. https://www.roofbooks.com/rob-the-plagiarist.

Dworkin, Craig, and Kenneth Goldsmith, eds. *Against Expression: An Anthology of Conceptual Writing*. Evanston, IL: Northwestern University Press, 2011.

Dydo, Ulla, and William Rice. *Gertrude Stein: The Language That Rises, 1923–1934*. Evanston, IL: Northwestern University Press, 2003.

Eagleson, Harvey. "Gertrude Stein: Method in Madness." *Sewanee Review* (April 1926): 171–72.

Eco, Umberto. "An *Ars Oblivionalis*: Forget It!" Translated by Marilyn Migiel. *PMLA* 103, no. 3 (May 1988): 254–61.

Eco, Umberto. *Carnival!* Edited by Thomas Sebeok. Berlin: Mouton, 1984.

Eliot, George. *Adam Bede*. Edited by Margaret Reynolds. New York: Penguin, 2008.

Eliot, T. S. "The Frontiers of Criticism." 1956. In *On Poets and Poetry*, 113–34. Reprint, New York: FSG, 2009.

Eliot, T. S. Letter to Bonamy Dobrée. November 14, 1957. In *The Poems of T.S. Eliot*. Vol. 1, 570. London: Faber and Faber, 2015.

Eliot, T. S. "Tradition and the Individual Talent." *The Egoist* 6, no. 4 (September 1919). Reprinted in *The Sacred Wood*, 42–53. New York: Alfred A. Knopf, 1921.

Eliot, T. S. *The Use of Poetry and the Use of Criticism*. Cambridge, MA: Harvard University Press, 1933. Reprint, London: Faber and Faber, 1964.

Emerson, Ralph Waldo. "The Poet." 1844. In *The Complete Works of Ralph Waldo Emerson: Essays*. Vol. 3, 1–42. Boston: Houghton Mifflin, 1903.

Emerson, Ralph Waldo. "Self-Reliance." 1841. In *Emerson: Essays and Lectures*, 257–82. New York: Library of America, 1983.

Fagan, Kate. "Strange Borders, Double Vision: *Oxota* as a Work of Trans-iteration." In *Aerial 10*, edited by Rod Smith and Jen Hofer, 223–47. Washington, DC: Aerial/ Edge Books, 2016.

Fagin, Larry. *The List Poem: A Guide to Teaching and Writing Catalog Verse*. New York: Teachers & Writers Collaborative, 2000.

Fenollosa, Ernest. "The Chinese Written Character as a Medium for Poetry." Translated by Ezra Pound. In *The Chinese Written Character as a Medium for Poetry: A*

190 **References**

Critical Edition, edited by Haun Saussy, Jonathan Stalling, and Lucas Klein, 75–104. New York: Fordham University Press, 2008.

Fischlin, Daniel, and Ajay Heble, eds. *The Other Side of Nowhere: Jazz, Improvisation, and Communities in Dialogue*. Middletown, CT: Wesleyan University Press, 2004.

Fitterman, Robert, and Vanessa Place. *Notes on Conceptualisms*. Brooklyn: Ugly Duckling Presse, 2013.

Flatley, Jonathan. *Like Andy Warhol*. Chicago: University of Chicago Press, 2018.

Foucault, Michel. "Nietzsche, Genealogy, History." 1971. In *Language, Counter-Memory, Practice*. Translated by Donald F. Bouchard and Sherry Simon, 139–43. Ithaca, NY: Cornell University Press, 1977.

Franklin, Benjamin. *The Autobiography of Benjamin Franklin*. Boston: Houghton Mifflin, 1906.

Freeman, Elizabeth. "Hopeless Cases: Queer Chronicities and Gertrude Stein's 'Melanctha.'" *Journal of Homosexuality* 63, no. 3 (2016): 329–48.

Freud, Sigmund. "Fragment of an Analysis of a Case of Hysteria." 1905 (1901). In *The Standard Edition of the Complete Psychological Works of Sigmund Freud*. Vol. 7, 7–124. Translated by James Strachey. London: Hogarth Press, 1953.

Freud, Sigmund. *Jokes and Their Relation to the Unconscious*. 1905. Translated by James Strachey. New York: W. W. Norton, 1960.

Frye, Northrop. "The Argument of Comedy." 1948. In *Northrop Frye's Writings on Shakespeare and the Renaissance*. Edited by Troni Grande and Garry Sherbert, 3–13. Toronto: University of Toronto Press, 2010.

Gallagher, Kristen. "The Authorship of Heath Ledger in the New Reading Environment: On Tan Lin's *Heath: Plagiarism/Outsource*," *Criticism* 51, no. 4 (2009): 701–9.

Gillmore, Alan. *Erik Satie*. Woodbridge, CT: Twayne, 1988.

Gilmour, Robin. *The Victorian Period: The Intellectual and Cultural Context of English Literature, 1830–1890*. London: Longman, 1993.

Golding, Alan. "Faking It New." *Modernism/modernity* 16, no. 3 (2009): 474–77.

Goldsmith, John, and Erich Woisetschlaeger. "The Logic of the English Progressive." *Linguistic Inquiry* 13, no. 1 (1982): 79–89.

Goodland, Giles. "Long Poems about Everything: Dictionary as Subject and Model for Poem, 1974–2016." In *Poetry and the Dictionary*, edited by Andrew Blades and Piers Pennington, 257–80. Liverpool: Liverpool University Press, 2020.

Greenberg, Clement. *Art and Culture*. Boston: Beacon Press, 1961.

Greenberg, Clement. "Towards a Newer Laocoön." 1940. In *The Collected Essays and Criticism*. Vol. 1, 23–38, edited by John O'Brian. Chicago: University of Chicago Press, 1986.

Gregory, Elizabeth. *Quotation and Modern American Poetry: "Imaginary Gardens with Real Toads."* Houston: Rice University Press, 1996.

Grossman, Allen, and Mark Halliday. *The Sighted Singer: Two Works on Poetry for Readers and Writers*. Baltimore: Johns Hopkins University Press, 1992.

Halbwachs, Maurice. *Collective Memory*. 1950. Edited and translated by Lewis A. Coser. Chicago: University of Chicago Press, 1992.

Halprin, Lawrence. "The RSVP Cycles." 1969. Reprinted in *Theory in Landscape Architecture: A Reader*, edited by Simon Swaffield, 43–48. Philadelphia: University of Pennsylvania Press, 2002.

Hartog, François. *Regimes of Historicity: Presentism and Experiences of Time*. Translated by Saskia Brown. New York: Columbia University Press, 2003.

Hegel, Georg Wilhelm Friedrich. *Aesthetics: Lectures on Fine Art*. Vol. 1. Translated by T. M. Knox. Oxford: Clarendon Press, 1975.

Heilman, Rob. *The Ways of the World: Comedy and Society*. Seattle: University of Washington Press, 1978.

Hejinian, Lyn. *A Border Comedy*. New York: Granary Books, 2001.

Hejinian, Lyn. "Happily." *boundary 2* 26, no. 1 (1999): 137–39.

Hejinian, Lyn. "An Interview with Lyn Hejinian." By Rae Armantrout. In *Aerial 10*, edited by Rod Smith and Jen Hofer, 29–43. Washington, DC: Aerial/Edge Books, 2016.

Hejinian, Lyn. *The Language of Inquiry*. Berkeley: University of California Press, 2000.

Hejinian, Lyn. *Lola*. New York: Belladonna, 2005.

Hejinian, Lyn. "Lyn Hejinian." In *In the American Tree*, edited by Ron Silliman, 49–65. Orono: University of Maine Press, 1986.

Hejinian, Lyn. *My Life and My Life in the Nineties*. Middletown, CT: Wesleyan Press, 2013.

Hejinian, Lyn. "Oblivion." In *The Cold of Poetry*, 185–96. Los Angeles: Sun & Moon Press, 1994.

Hejinian, Lyn. *Oxota: A Short Russian Novel*. Berkeley: The Figures, 1991. Reprint, Middletown, CT: Wesleyan University Press, 2019.

Hejinian, Lyn. "From *Positions of the Sun*." PEN America. June 13, 2018. https://pen .org/from-positions-of-the-sun/.

Hollander, John. "Originality." *Raritan* 2, no. 4 (Spring 1983): 24–44.

Howard, Richard. *Alone with America: Essays on the Art of Poetry in the United States Since 1950*. New York: Atheneum, 1980.

Howard, Richard. "John Ashbery." In *John Ashbery*, edited by Harold Bloom, 17–49. New York: Chelsea House, 1985.

Hulme, Peter, and Tim Youngs, eds. *The Cambridge Companion to Travel Writing*. Cambridge University Press, 2006.

Hutchinson, Ben. *Lateness and Modern European Literature*. Oxford: Oxford University Press, 2016.

Ihns, Kristen (Kai). Blurb for *No Material* by Losarc Raal. New York: Black Sun Lit, 2023.

Ivic, Christopher, and Grant Williams, eds. *Forgetting in Early Modern English Literature and Culture: Lethe's Legacies*. London: Routledge, 2004.

James, William. *Pragmatism: A New Name for Some Old Ways of Thinking*. 1907. Reprint, New York: Cosimo, 2008.

James, William. *The Principles of Psychology*. New York: Henry Holt, 1890.

Jameson, Fredric. *Postmodernism, or, The Cultural Logic of Late Capitalism*. 1991. Reprint, Durham: Duke University Press, 2003.

Jonas, Stephen. *Arcana: A Stephen Jonas Reader*. San Francisco: City Lights, 2019.

Kant, Immanuel. *Critique of the Power of Judgment*. 1790. Translated by Paul Guyer and Eric Matthews. Edited by Paul Guyer. Cambridge: Cambridge University Press, 2000.

Keats, John. "Letter to Benjamin Bailey." October 8, 1817. In *The Complete Works of John Keats*. Vol. 4, *Letters 1814 to January 1819*, pp. 37–39. Edited by H. Buxton Forman. Glasgow: Gowars & Gray, 1901.

Kebede, Messay. "Action and Forgetting: Bergson's Theory of Memory." *Philosophy Today* 60, no. 2 (Spring 2016): 347–70.

192 References

Keniston, Ann. *Ghostly Figures: Memory and Belatedness in Postwar American Poetry*. Iowa City: University of Iowa Press, 2015.

Khatab, Rhonda. "Timelessness and Negativity in *Awaiting Oblivion*: Hegel and Blanchot in Dialogue." *text theory critique* 10 (2005): 83–101.

Kierkegaard, Søren. *Either/Or: Part I*. Translated and edited by Howard V. Hong and Edna H. Hong. Princeton, NJ: Princeton University Press, 1987.

Kim, Irene. "On Ambience, Tan Lin, and American Minimalisms." *Post45*, April 27, 2023. https://post45.org/2023/04/on-ambience-tan-lin-and-american -minimalism/. Kirsch, Sharon. *Gertrude Stein and the Reinvention of Rhetoric*. Tuscaloosa: University of Alabama Press, 2014.

Koch, Kenneth. *Wishes, Lies, and Dreams*. New York: Chelsea House, 1970. Reprint, New York: Harper Perennial, 1999.

Koselleck, Reinhart. *Futures Past: On the Semantics of Historical Time*. Translated by Keith Tribe. New York: Columbia University Press, 2004.

Kotler, Philip T. "Atmospherics as a Marketing Tool." *Journal of Retailing* 49, no. 4 (1973–74): 48–64.

Kotz, Liz. *Words to Be Looked At: Language in 1960s Art*. Cambridge, MA: MIT Press, 2007.

Krauss, Rosalind. *The Originality of the Avant-Garde and Other Modernist Myths*. Cambridge, MA: MIT University Press, 1986.

Krondorfer, Björn. "Is Forgetting Reprehensible? Holocaust Remembrance and the Task of Oblivion." *Journal of Religious Ethics* 36, no. 2 (2008): 233–67.

Kulka, Tomas. *Kitsch and Art*. 1994. Reprint, University Park: Pennsylvania State University Press, 1996.

Langer, Susanne. *Feeling and Form*. New York: Charles Scribner, 1953.

Lawton, Anna, and Herbert Eagle, eds. and trans. *Words in Revolution: Russian Futurist Manifestoes, 1912-1928*. Washington, DC: New Academia Publishing, 2004.

Lazer, Hank. Review of *Squeezed Light: Collected Poems, 1994-2005* by Lissa Wolsak. Rain Taxi. 2010. https://raintaxi.com/squeezed-light-collected-poems-1994 -2005/.

Lazzarato, Maurizio. "From Capital-Labour to Capital Life." Translated by Valerie Fournier, Akseli Virtanen, and Jussi Vähämäki. *Ephemera* 4, no. 3 (2004): 187–208.

Lazzarato, Maurizio. "Immaterial Labour." 1996. In *Radical Thought in Italy: A Potential Politics*. Edited by Paolo Virno and Michael Hardt. Translated by Maurizia Boscagli et al., 133–50. Minneapolis: University of Minnesota Press, 2006.

Leary, Paris, and Robert Kelly, eds. *A Controversy of Poets: An Anthology of Contemporary American Poetry*. New York: Doubleday Anchor, 1965.

Lefebvre, Henri. *Introduction to Modernity*. Translated by John Moore. London: Verso, 1995.

Lehman, David. *The Last Avant-Garde: The Making of the New York School of Poets*. New York: Anchor Books, 1999.

Lessing, Gotthold Ephraim. *Lessing's Prose Works*. Edited by Edward Bell. Translated by E. C. Beasley and Helen Zimmern. London: George Bell and Sons, 1890.

Levertov, Denise. "The Secret." In *Poems, 1960-1967*, 93. New York: New Directions, 1983.

Lewis, Erica. *Mary Wants to Be a Superwoman*. Nashville: Third Man Books, 2017.

Lin, Tan. "Ambient Stylistics." *Conjunctions* 35 (2000): 127–45.

Lin, Tan. *Blipsoak01*. Berkeley: Atelos, 2003.

Lin, Tan. "Disco as Operating System, Part One." *Criticism* 50, no. 1 (2008): 83–100.

Lin, Tan. "Disco, Cybernetics, and the Migration of Warhol's *Shadows* into Computation." *Criticism* 56, no. 3 (2014): 487–90.

Lin, Tan. *Insomnia and the Aunt*. Chicago: Kenning Editions, 2011.

Lin, Tan. "The Patio and the Index." Triple Canopy, 2011. https://www
.canopycanopycanopy.com/contents/the_patio_and_the_index.

Lin, Tan. *Seven Controlled Vocabularies and Obituary 2004. The Joy of Cooking: Airport Novel Musical Poem Painting Film Photo Hallucination Landscape*. Middleton, CT: Wesleyan University Press, 2010.

Lorange, Astrid. *How Reading Is Written: A Brief Index to Gertrude Stein*. Middletown, CT: Wesleyan University Press, 2014.

Luhmann, Niklas. "The Medium of the Art." *Thesis Eleven*, nos. 18/19 (1987): 101–13.

Luria, A. R. *The Mind of a Mnemonist*. 1968. Translated by Lynn Solotaroff. Cambridge, MA: Harvard University Press, 1987.

Mallarmé, Stéphane. *Selected Poetry and Prose*. New York: New Directions, 1982.

Manovich, Lev. "Avant-Garde as Software." 1999. https://manovich.net/content/04
-projects/027-avant-garde-as-software/24_article_1999.pdf.

Manovich, Lev. "Remixability and Modularity." 2005. https://manovich.net/content
/04-projects/046-remixability-and-modularity/43_article_2005.pdf.

Mapes-Frances, Alec. "Reading Machines: Ambient Writing and the Poetics of Atmospheric Media." Thesis. Brown University, 2017.

Martin, Ronald. *American Literature and the Destruction of Knowledge: Innovative Writing in the Age of Epistemology*. Durham, NC: Duke University Press, 1991.

Martindale, Colin. "History and Creativity." In *Encyclopedia of Creativity*. Vol. 1, 823–30. Edited by Mark A. Runco and Steven R. Pritzer. San Diego: Academic Press, 1999.

Matisse, Henri. *Matisse on Art*. Edited by Jack Flam. New York: E. P. Dutton, 1978.

Mayer, Bernadette. "From: A Lecture at the Naropa Institute, 1989." *O/two An Anthology: What is the inside, what is outside?*, edited by Leslie Scalapino, 89–97. Oakland: O Books, 1991.

Mayer, Bernadette. *Memory*. Plainfield, CA: North Atlantic Books, 1975.

Mayer, Bernadette. *Studying Hunger*. Berkeley: Big Sky, 1975.

McCallum, E. L. *Unmaking "The Making of Americans": Toward an Aesthetic Ontology*. Albany: State University of New York Press, 2018.

McDaniel, Mark A., and Gilles O. Einstein. *Prospective Memory: An Overview and Synthesis of an Emerging Field*. Los Angeles: Sage, 2007.

McDonough, Tom, ed. *Boredom: Documents of Contemporary Art*. London: Whitechapel and MIT Press, 2017.

McGann, Jerome. *Black Riders: The Visible Language of Modernism*. Princeton, NJ: Princeton University Press, 1993.

McLennan, Rachel. "'Like a Thief Returning to the Shelf': The Givens of Autobiography in Lyn Hejinian's *My Life*." *a/b: Auto/Biography Studies* 26, no. 2 (2011): 281–96.

Menand, Louis. *The Metaphysical Club*. New York: FSG, 2001.

Miller, Richard. "The Moral and Political Burdens of Memory." In *Friends and Other Strangers: Studies in Religion, Ethics, and Culture*, 228–73. New York: Columbia University Press, 2016.

194 **References**

Morgan, Benjamin. "Scale, Resonance, Presence." *Victorian Studies* 59, no. 1 (Autumn 2016): 109–12.

Morton, Timothy. "Why Ambient Poetics? Outline for a Depthless Ecology." *Wordsworth Circle* 33, no. 1 (2002): 52–56.

Moses, Omri. "Gertrude Stein's Lively Habits." *Twentieth-Century Literature* 55, no. 4 (2009): 445–84.

Mullen, Harryette. "An Interview with Harryette Mullen." By Elisabeth A. Frost. In *The Cracks Between What We Are and What We Are Supposed to Be*, 213–32. Tuscaloosa: University of Alabama Press, 2012.

Mullen, Harryette. *Sleeping with the Dictionary*. Berkeley: University of California Press, 2002.

Myers, Rollo. "The Strange Case of Erik Satie." *Musical Times* 86, no. 1229 (July 1945): 201–3.

Ngai, Sianne. "Stuplimity: Shock and Boredom in Twentieth-Century Aesthetics." *Postmodern Culture* 10, no. 2 (2000), https://muse.jhu.edu/pub/1/article/27722.

Ngai, Sianne. *Theory of the Gimmick: Aesthetic Judgment and Capitalist Form*. Cambridge, MA: Harvard University Press, 2020.

Nicholls, Peter. "Of Being Ethical: Reflections on George Oppen." *Journal of American Studies* 31, no. 2 (1997): 153–70.

Nickels, Joel. *Poetry of the Possible: Spontaneity, Modernism, and the Multitude*. Minneapolis: University of Minnesota Press, 2012.

Nietzsche, Friedrich. *The Birth of Tragedy and Other Writings*. Translated by Ronald Speirs. Edited by Raymond Geuss and Ronald Speirs. Cambridge: Cambridge University Press, 1999.

Nietzsche, Friedrich. *On the Genealogy of Morals*. 1887. Translated by Douglas Smith. Oxford: Oxford University Press, 1996.

Nietzsche, Friedrich. *On the Advantage and Disadvantage of History for Life*. 1874. Translated by Peter Preuss. Indianapolis: Hackett, 1980.

Nora, Pierre. *Realms of Memory*. Vols. 1–3. Translated by Arthur Goldhammer. Edited by Pierre Nora and Lawrence D. Kritzman. New York: Columbia University Press, 1996–98.

North, Michael. *What Is the Present?* Princeton, NJ: Princeton University Press, 2018.

North, Michael. "Where Memory Faileth: Forgetfulness and a Poem Including History." *Ezra Pound: The Legacy of Kulchur*, edited by Marcel Smith and William Andrew Ulmer, 145–65. Tuscaloosa: University of Alabama Press, 1988.

Notley, Alice. *Coming After: Essays on Poetry*. Ann Arbor: University of Michigan Press, 2005.

Notley, Alice. *Doctor Williams' Heiresses*. Berkeley: Tuumba Press, 1980.

Notley, Alice. *In the Pines*. New York: Penguin, 2007.

O'Hara, Frank. *The Collected Poems of Frank O'Hara*. Edited by Donald Allen. Berkeley: University of California Press, 1995.

Olson, Charles. *Collected Prose*. Edited by Donald Allen and Benjamin Friedlander. Berkeley: University of California Press, 1997.

Olson, Liesl M. "Gertrude Stein, William James, and Habit in the Shadow of War." *Twentieth-Century Literature* 49, no. 3 (Autumn 2003): 328–59.

Overy, Paul. "The Different Shades of Mao." *Times* (London), March 12, 1974, 7.

Owens, Rochelle. *I Am the Babe of Joseph Stalin's Daughter*. New York: Kulchur Foundation, 1972.

Padgett, Ron. Afterword to *I Remember* by Joe Brainard, 169-76. 1970. Reprint, New York: Granary Books, 2001.

Padgett, Ron. "Inaction of Shoes." *Collected Poems*, 625. Minneapolis: Coffee House Press, 2013.

Perec, Georges. *Species of Spaces and Other Pieces*. Edited and translated by John Sturrock. New York: Penguin, 1997.

Perelman, Bob. *The Marginalization of Poetry*. Princeton, NJ: Princeton University Press, 1996.

Perelman, Bob. *The Trouble with Genius*. Berkeley: University of California Press, 1994.

Perloff, Marjorie. "Happy World." *Boston Review*, February 1, 2001, 21-22.

Pessoa, Fernando. *The Book of Disquiet*. Translated by Margaret Jull Costa. Edited by Jerónimo Pizarro. 2017. Reprint, London: Serpent's Tail, 2018.

Phillips, Adam. *Missing Out: In Praise of the Unlived Life*. New York: FSG, 2013.

Phillips, Adam. *On Wanting to Change*. London: Picador, 2022.

Poggi, Christine, Lawrence Rainey, and Laura Wittman, eds. *Futurism: An Anthology*. New Haven: Yale University Press, 2009.

Pound, Ezra. *Guide to Kulchur*. London: Faber and Faber, 1938. Reprint, New York: New Directions, 1970.

Pound, Ezra. "Histrion." *Evening Standard & St. James Gazette*, October 25, 1908. Reprinted in *Early Writings: Poems and Prose*, 12. Edited by Ira Nadel. New York: Penguin, 2005.

Pound, Ezra. *Selected Prose, 1909-1965*. New York: New Directions, 1973.

Radvansky, Gabriel. *Human Memory*. 3rd ed. New York: Routledge, 2017.

Renan, Ernest. "What Is a Nation?" 1882. Reprinted in *Nation and Narration*. Edited by Homi Bhabha. Translated by Martin Thom, 8-22. London: Routledge, 1990.

Ricoeur, Paul. *Memory, History, Forgetting*. Trans. Kathleen Blamey and David Pellauer. Chicago: University of Chicago Press, 2004.

Ricoeur, Paul. *Oneself as Another*. Trans. Kathleen Blamey. Chicago: University of Chicago Press, 1992.

Riding, Laura. "The New Barbarism, and Gertrude Stein." *transition 3* (June 3, 1927): 153-68. Reprinted in *A Description of Acquaintance: The Letters of Laura Riding and Gertrude Stein, 1927-1930*. Edited by Logan Esdale and Jane Malcolm, 124-25. Albuquerque: University of New Mexico Press, 2023.

Rieff, David. *In Praise of Forgetting*. New Haven, CT: Yale University Press, 2016.

Rifkin, Libbie. "'Worrying about Making It': Ted Berrigan's Social Poetics." *Contemporary Literature* 38, no. 4 (1997): 640-72.

Rimbaud, Arthur. *A Season in Hell and Illuminations*. Translated and edited by Wyatt Mason. New York: Random House, 2005.

Robertson, Lisa. *The Baudelaire Fractal*. Toronto: Coach House Books, 2020.

Robertson, Lisa. "Textures of Personhood: Lisa Robertson Interviewed." Interview by Allison Grimaldi Donahue. *BOMB*. January 17, 2020. https://bombmagazine.org/articles/lisa-robertson/.

Robinson, Kit. "The Beginning of the Making of 'The Cell.'" In *Aerial 10*, edited by Rod Smith and Jen Hofer, 185-97. Washington, DC: Aerial/Edge Books, 2016.

Roth, Moira. "The Aesthetic of Indifference." *Artforum* 16, no. 3 (November 1977): 47-53.

Ruskin, John. *Modern Painters*. Vol. 3. London: Smith, Elder, & Co., 1872.

196 References

Russell, Nicolas. "Collective Memory Before and After Halbwachs." *French Review* 79, no. 4 (2006): 792–804.

Ryle, Gilbert. "Knowing How and Knowing That." *Proceedings of the Aristotelian Society* 46 (1945–46): 1–16.

Said, Edward. *On Late Style: Music and Literature Against the Grain*. New York: Pantheon Books, 2006.

Salisbury, Laura. "'What Is the Word': Beckett's Aphasic Modernism." *Journal of Beckett Studies* 17, nos. 1–2 (2009): 78–126.

Sargent, Porter. "Our Poesy Is as a Gum." *Poet Lore* 42, no. 4 (1935): 333.

Sartre, Jean-Paul. *Baudelaire*. Translated by Martin Turnell. New York: New Directions Press, 1950.

Scalapino, Leslie. *The Public World/Syntactically Impermanence*. Hanover, NH: Wesleyan University Press, 1999.

Scalapino, Leslie. "Thinking and Being/Conversion in the Language of Lyn Hejinian's *Happily* and *A Border Comedy*." In *Aerial 10*, edited by Rod Smith and Jen Hofer, 325–41. Washington, DC: Aerial/Edge Books, 2016.

Scappettone, Jennifer. "Versus Seamlessness: Architectonics of Pseudocomplicity in Tan Lin's Ambient Poetics." *boundary 2* 36, no. 3 (2009): 63–76.

Scarry, Elaine. "On Vivacity: The Difference Between Daydreaming and Imagining-Under-Authorial-Instruction," *Representations* 52 (Autumn 1995): 1–26.

Schmidt, Christopher. *The Poetics of Waste: Queer Excess in Stein, Ashbery, Schuyler, and Goldsmith*. New York: Palgrave Macmillan, 2014.

Schuyler, James. *Collected Poems*. New York: FSG, 1993.

Schuyler, James. "An Interview." By Mark Hillringhouse. *American Poetry Review* 14, no. 2 (1985): 5–12.

Schuyler, James. *Other Flowers: Uncollected Poems*. Edited by James Meetze and Simon Pettet. New York: FSG, 2010.

Searle, John. "What Is a Speech Act?" In *Philosophy in America*. Edited by Max Black. Ithaca, NY: Cornell University Press, 1965. 221–239.

Severini, Gino. "Plastic Analogies of Dynamism: Futurist Manifesto." 1913. Reprinted in *Futurism: An Anthology*. Edited by Christine Poggi, Lawrence Rainey, and Laura Wittman, 165. New Haven: Yale University Press, 2009.

Seyler, Athene, with Stephen Haggard. *The Craft of Comedy: The 21st Century Edition*. Edited by Robert Barton. London: Routledge, 2013.

Shoptaw, John. *On the Outside Looking Out: John Ashbery's Poetry*. Cambridge, MA: Harvard University Press, 1994.

Shoptaw, John. "Saving Appearances." Review of *April Galleons* by John Ashbery. *Tremblor* 7 (1998): 172–77.

Sidney, Philip. "The Defence of Poesy." 1595. Reprinted in *The Miscellaneous Works of Sir Philip Sidney, Knt*. Edited by William Gray, 59–124. London: William W. Gibbings, 1893.

Sieburth, Richard. "A Heap of Language: Robert Smithson and American Hieroglyphics." In *Robert Smithson*. Edited by Eugenie Tsai. Los Angeles: Museum of Contemporary Art, 2004.

Simmel, Georg. "[The concept of consolation]." Aphorism. Quoted and translated by Richard Swedberg and Wendelin Reich. "Georg Simmel's Aphorisms." *Theory, Culture & Society* 27, no. 1 (2010): 24–51.

Spahr, Juliana. "Resignifying Autobiography: Lyn Hejinian's *My Life.*" *American Literature* 68, no. 1 (1996): 139–59.

Spitzer, Leo. "Milieu and Ambiance: An Essay in Historical Semantics." *Philosophy and Phenomenological Research* 3, no. 2 (1942): 169–218.

Spurlock, Violet. "Uses of Obviousness in *Seven Controlled Vocabularies.*" "Tan Lin" cluster. Post45: Contemporaries. August 23, 2024. https://post45.org/2024/08/uses-of-obviousness-in-seven-controlled-vocabularies/.

Stadler, Gustavus. "'My Wife': The Tape Recorder and Warhol's Queer Ways of Listening." *Criticism* 56, no. 3 (2014): 425–56.

Stein, Gertrude. *Everybody's Autobiography.* New York: Random House, 1937. Reprint, Cambridge: Exact Change, 1993.

Stein, Gertrude. "Gertrude Stein Talking—A Transatlantic Interview." Interview by Robert Hass. *UCLAN Review.* 1962–64. Reprinted in *Gertrude Stein: A Primer for the Gradual Understanding of Gertrude Stein.* Edited by Robert Haas. Los Angeles: Black Sparrow Press, 1971.

Stein, Gertrude. *How Writing Is Written: Volume II of the Previously Uncollected Writings of Gertrude Stein.* Edited by Robert Hass. Los Angeles: Black Sparrow Press, 1974.

Stein, Gertrude. *The Making of Americans: Being a History of a Family's Progress.* 1925. Reprint, Normal, IL: Dalkey Archive Press, 1995.

Stein, Gertrude. "*The Making of Americans* (Selected Passages)." In *Selected Writings of Gertrude Stein.* Edited by Carl van Vechten, 321. New York: Vintage, 1990.

Stein, Gertrude. *Matisse Picasso and Gertrude Stein, with Two Shorter Stories.* Mineola, NY: Dover, 2000.

Stein, Gertrude. *Narration: Four Lectures by Gertrude Stein*, 1935. Reprint, Chicago: University of Chicago Press, 2010.

Stein, Gertrude. *Wars I Have Seen.* New York: Random House, 1945.

Stein, Gertrude. *Writings, 1903–1932.* Edited by Catherine Stimpson and Harriet Chessman. New York: Library of America, 1998.

Stein, Gertrude. *Writings, 1932–1946.* Edited by Catherine Stimpson and Harriet Chessman. New York: Library of America, 1998.

Steiner, Wendy. "The Steinian Portrait." In *Critical Essays on Gertrude Stein.* Edited by Michael Hoffman, 130–38. Boston: G. K. Hall, 1986.

Stephens, Paul. *Poetics of Information Overload.* Minneapolis: University of Minnesota Press, 2015.

Stewart, Susan. "The Last Man." *American Poetry Review* 17, no. 5 (1988): 9–16.

Struever, Nancy. *Language and the History of Thought.* Martlesham, UK: Boydell & Brewer, 1995.

Sullivan, Garrett. *Memory and Forgetting in English Renaissance Drama.* Cambridge: Cambridge University Press, 2005.

Summit, Jennifer, and Blakey Vermeule. *Action Versus Contemplation: Why an Ancient Debate Still Matters.* Chicago: University of Chicago Press, 2018.

Svendsen, Lars. *A Philosophy of Boredom.* London: Reaktion, 2005.

Sverjensky, Tatiana. "John Ashbery's Inoperative Poetics." *College Literature* 43, no. 2 (2016): 281–309.

Terdiman, Richard. *Present Past: Modernity and the Memory Crisis.* Ithaca, NY: Cornell University Press, 1993.

198 References

Terranova, Tiziana. "Attention, Economy and the Brain." *Culture Machine* 13 (2012): 1–19. https://culturemachine.net/paying-attention/.

Thoreau, Henry D. "Walking." 1862. In *The Essays of Henry D. Thoreau*. Edited by Lewis Hyde, 147–79. New York: FSG, 2002.

Toop, David. *Ocean of Sound: Aether Talk, Ambient Sound and Imaginary Worlds*. London: Serpent's Tail, 1995.

Valéry, Paul. *Collected Works of Paul Valéry*. Vol. 8. Translated by James Lawler and M. Cowley. Princeton, NJ: Princeton University Press, 2015.

Van Puymbroeck, Birgit. Introduction to "'Let Us Save China': Gertrude Stein and Politics," by Gertrude Stein. *PMLA* 132. no. 1 (2017): 198–205.

Vendler, Zeno. "Verbs and Times." *Philosophical Review* 66, no. 2 (April 1957): 143–60.

Vickery, Ann. *Leaving Lines of Gender: A Feminist Genealogy of Language Writing*. Lebanon, NH: University of New England Press, 2000.

Vincent, John Emil. "*April Galleons*: Forgetting, Evading, Holding Off." In *John Ashbery and You: His Later Books*, 26–46. Athens: University of Georgia Press, 2007.

Voris, Linda. *The Composition of Sense in Gertrude Stein's Landscape Writing*. Washington, DC: Palgrave Macmillan, 2016.

Warhol, Andy. *The Philosophy of Andy Warhol*. Orlando, FL: Harcourt, 1975.

Wasserman, Rosanne. "Weatherly's Words: A Tribute to Tom Weatherly." *Jacket2*, September 6, 2019. https://jacket2.org/article/weatherlys-words.

Watkin, William. "'Let's Make a List': James Schuyler's Taxonomic Autobiography." *Journal of American Studies* 36, no. 1 (2002): 43–68.

Wegner, Daniel, David Schneider, Samuel Carter, and Teri White. "Paradoxical Effects of Thought Suppression." *Journal of Personality and Social Psychology* 53, no. 1 (July 1987): 5–13.

Weinrich, Harald. *Lethe*. Ithaca, NY: Cornell University Press, 2004.

Wertheim, Christine, and Matias Viegener, eds. *The noulipian Analects*. Los Angeles: Les Figues Press, 2007.

Whitehead, Alfred North. "The British Association at Newcastle. Section A. Mathematical and Physical Science: The Organisation of Thought." *Nature* 98 (1916): 80–81.

Wilder, Thornton. Introduction to *Four in America* by Gertrude Stein. New Haven, CT: Yale University Press, 1947.

Williams, David-Antoine. *The Life of Words: Etymology and Modern Poetry*. Oxford: Oxford University Press, 2020.

Williams, Tyrone. Introduction to *Mary Wants to Be a Superwoman*, 1–5. By Erica Lewis. Nashville: Third Man Books, 2017.

Williams, Williams Carlos. *Kora in Hell*. In *Imaginations*. New York: New Directions, 1970.

Williams, Williams Carlos. *Paterson*. 1946–58. Reprint, New York: New Directions, 1995.

Winant, Johanna. "Explanation in Composition: Gertrude Stein and the Contingency of Inductive Reasoning." *Journal of Modern Literature* 39, no. 3 (2016): 95–113.

Wittgenstein, Ludwig. *Philosophical Investigations*. 1953, 4th ed. Translated by G. E. M. Anscombe, P. M. S. Hacker, and Joachin Schulte. Oxford: Wiley-Blackwell, 2009.

Wolsak, Lissa. "'Ardor is its undermost shaping': An Interview with Lissa Wolsak." By

Kent Johnson. *VeRT Poetry Magazine*, no. 6 (Winter 2002), https://writing.upenn.edu/epc/mags/vert/Vert_issue_6/lwolsakinter.html.

Wolsak, Lissa. *Squeezed Light: Collected Poems, 1994-2005*. Barrytown, NY: Station Hill Press, 2010.

Yates, Francis. *The Art of Memory*. London: Routledge, 1966.

Young, Edward. "Conjectures on Original Composition." 1759. Reprinted in *Critical Theory Since Plato*. 3rd ed. Edited by Hazard Adams, 347–57. Belmont, CA: Wadsworth, 2005.

Zukofsky, Louis. "Sincerity and Objectivism: With Special Reference to Charles Reznikoff." *Poetry* (February 1931).

Index

Ackroyd, Peter, 126
"Acquaintance with Description, An"
 (Stein), 30
action, 34–35, 53; active life of writing,
 40–42; activities and states, 36–37, 39;
 inaction, 49, 55–57, 62–63; vs. knowl-
 edge, 22–24; procrastination, 49, 64
Adam Bede (Eliot), 90
Addison, Joseph, 181n22
Adorno, Theodor, 183n56
Against Forgetting (Forché), 13
agency, 3, 74, 80, 85, 94
AIDS crisis, 169–70n28
Akhmatova, Anna, 13
Allen, Donald, 98
"All She Wrote" (Mullen), 111–12
Altieri, Charles, 116
ambience, 123; ambient forgettability,
 139; ambient forgetting, 126; ambient
 music, 122, 124–25; ambient poetry,
 122, 126–27, 179–80n13; ambient writing, 122; relaxation and forgettability, 124
Americana, 134
American pragmatists, 8; forgetting history, as American specialty, 11; habituation, 11
amnesia, 12, 95, 139; aphasia, 26; as catastrophic, 13; dreams, 85; forgetting,
 79–80, 88, 123; Freudian slips, 10; in
 political and public sphere, 15

anamnesis, 5–6
Anderson, Benedict, 13
Anderson, Margaret, 125
Ankersmit, Frank R., 161n54
aporia, 117–18
April Galleons (Ashbery), 169–70n28
Arendt, Hannah: public sphere, 92
Aristotle, 6, 44, 164n37; recollection, 26
Armantrout, Rae, 77
Arnovick, Leslie K., 48
Ashbery, John, 18, 47, 96, 104, 168n13;
 April Galleons, 169–70n28; *A Con-
 troversy of Poets*, 71; cultural late-
 ness, sense of, 65; "The Ecclesiast,"
 65–70; *Flow Chart*, 70–71; forgetting,
 60–61, 64–65, 68–70, 169–70n28;
 "The Impossible," 62; "The Instruction Manual," 61–64; intentionality,
 as omnipresent, 61; as "last man," 65;
 "Letters I Did or Did Not Get," 169–
 70n28; oblivion, desire for, 61, 64–65,
 74; otherness, 70; "Song of the Windshield Wipers," 169–70n28; Stein, influence on, 62, 64; "The Thief in Poetry," 70; to-do poems, 61–64, 68
Ashton, Jennifer, 25
Asian American: Asianness, as ambient effect, 135; assimilation, 128–29;
 J.Crew ads, 134–35; visibility, and difference, 134
assimilation, 19, 128–29, 135

202 **Index**

attention, 4, 8, 10, 17, 29–30, 33, 42, 59, 76, 82–84, 92, 113, 122, 132, 135–37, 142, 151; comedy, 88, 90; consciousness, 91; forgettability, 125; impatience, 78; lack of recall, 131; memory, 19, 25, 44, 129; realism, 90, 91; stream of consciousness, 11

attention economies, 130; economy of imitation, 183n55

Auden, W. H., 18, 102, 150; "Squares and Oblongs," 101; writing and thinking, 101

Augé, Marc: *Oblivion*, 4

Augustine, 110; *Confessions*, 102; forgetting and language, 100–101, 103; problem of forgetting, 100; trial and error, method of, 101; writing and thinking, 101

Autobiography (Franklin), 45

Autobiography of Alice B. Toklas, The (Stein), 161n2

autogenesis, 78, 104–5

avant-garde, 7, 131, 182n39

Bailey, Benjamin, 150

Barber, C. L., 173–74n53

Barthes, Roland, 130

Baudelaire, Charles, 108–10, 175n7

Baudelaire Fractal, The (Robertson), 108–9

Beckett, Samuel: "What Is the Word," 177n49

Bergson, Henri, 8–9, 12, 52, 74, 77; "Laughter," 83

"Bernard Fruchtman in Town & Country" (Owens), 106

Bernstein, Charles, 18, 24, 98, 111, 116; "I Don't Remember," 99–103

Berrigan, Ted, 47, 71, 169n23, 169–70n28; forgetting, 51–52; "Memorial Day" (with Waldman), 51; "Tambourine Life," 167–68n9; "10 Things I Do Everyday," 51, 169n21; "Things to Do in Anne's Room," 51, 57–58; "Things to Do in New York," 45, 51; "Things to Do in Providence," 45, 50–54; "Things to Do on Speed," 51; "Things to do

today" postcard, 45; to-do list poems, 50; "Wishes," 54

Bion, Wilfred, 9–10

Black Mountain School, 104

Blanchot, Maurice, 4, 67; "forgetful memory," 171n1; *The Infinite Conversation*, 79; oblivion, interest in, 175n7

BLAST (magazine), 23–24

Blipsoak01 (Lin), 182n37

Bloom, Harold, 97–98

Boccioni, Umberto, 7

Bonnefoy, Yves, 33

Book of Disquiet, The (Pessoa), 2

Booth, William James, 15; "moral imperative of memory-justice," 14

Border ballads, 74

Border Comedy, A (Hejinian), 74, 77, 79–80, 83–84, 88–89, 90–91, 173–74n53; as forgetful memory, 73, 87; forgetting, 86; Steinian quality of, 76

boredom, 124–26, 181n23, 182n37

Borges, Jorge Luis, 138

Brainard, Joe: *I Remember*, 59, 105; memory, discreteness of, 59–60; "Things to Do Before I Move," 45

Braque, Georges, 98

Brisman, Leslie: *Romantic Origins*, 105

Brokeback Mountain (film), 137

Browning, Robert, 107

Bru, Sascha: presentist regime, 24

Bruns, Gerard, 79–80

Bull's Head (Picasso), 184n68

Burckhardt, Jacob, 7

Burke, Edmund, 165n57

Byron, Lord, 150

Cage, John, 44–45, 167–68n9, 179–80n13

Campbell, Sue, 160n52; "good remembering," 16

capitalism, 123, 130; late capitalism, 76, 129

Carlson, Greg, 166n70

Carnegie, Dale, 47

Carruthers, Mary, 4–5

Cavell, Stanley, 82

Cecire, Natalia, 25

censorship, 12–13

Cezanne (Stein), 161n2
Chan, Jackie, 137, 183n63
Chaplin, Charlie, 75
Chaucer, Geoffrey, 107
Cheng, Anne, 135, 142
Christianity, 15
Cicero, 121, 158n14; *imitatio vitae*, 88; loci, 179n2
Cinema of the Present (Robertson), 177n44
civil rights, 16
Clark, T. J., 148
Clark, Tom, 59
Clune, Michael, 47
Cold of Poetry, The (Hejinian), 78
Cold War, 75
Coleridge, Samuel Taylor, 105, 108, 113, 178n52
collective identity, 13
Collom, Jack: "On Laughter" (with Hejinian), 91-93
comedy, 82-83, 85, 92; absent-mindedness, 87; art-making, 75; attention, 88, 90; autobiography, 74, 77, 93; boundedness, 76; denarrativization, 84; forgetting, 74, 84, 86, 88, 90, 93-94; as impersonal, criticism of, 93; improv, 91; in-group solidarity, 77; liberation, 173-74n53; objective spectators, 93; realism, link between, 89-91, 95; sociality, as core of, 76-77; tragedy, 76, 86; worldliness, reliance on, 77
Coming After (Notley), 107
Confessions (Augustine), 102
Connerton, Paul, 161n54
consumerism, 19; J.Crew ads, 132, 134-35, 140; shopping, 130, 139-41
Controversy of Poets, A (Ashbery), 71
Creeley, Robert, 149-50, 162n8

Davies, Alan, 128
Davila, Tierry, 123
Debussy, Claude, 124
"December" (Schuyler), forgetting, 55
Deleuze, Gilles, 158n17
de Man, Paul, 12, 23, 97-98, 175n7; forgetting, 105

Derrida, Jacques, 158n17
de Sade, Marquis, 179n6
Dewey, John, 11; habits, 159-60n39
Diary of Samuel Pepys, The (Pepys), 130, 138
Dickinson, Adam, 122
Diggory, Terence, 45-46, 167n6
"Doctor Williams' Heiress" (Notley), 104
Don Quixote (Cervantes), 138
Doolittle, Hilda (H.D.), 104, 107-8
Dorn, Ed, 104
Dostoyevsky, Fyodor, 10
Dragomoshchenko, Arkadii, 74-75
dreams, 2, 19, 49, 52, 71; amnesia, 85; daydream, 61-62; free association, 9
Dryden, John, 107
Du Bois, W. E. B.: double consciousness, 144-45
Duchamp, Marcel, 7, 123, 184n68
Duncan, Robert, 19, 104, 113, 176n24; *The H.D. Book*, 107
Dworkin, Craig, 122, 179n7, 179n9
Dydo, Ulla, 29

Eagleson, Harvey, 125
"Ecclesiast, The" (Ashbery): closure, as start of meaninglessness, 67; forgetting, 66, 68-70; futurity, 65-66, 68; oblivion, 65-66, 68
Eco, Umberto, 84, 164n51, 173-74n53; *ars oblivionalis*, 19-20; mnemotechnics, 164n51
Egoist, The (magazine), 107
"Eighteenth Brumaire of Louis Bonaparte, The" (Marx), 177n41
Eigner, Larry, 113
Either/Or (Kierkegaard), 2
Eliot, George, 91; *Adam Bede*, 90
Eliot, T. S., 98-99, 118, 130, 184n73; theory of impersonality, 127; "Tradition and the Individual Talent," 97; *The Waste Land*, 126
Ellison, Ralph, 176n27
Emerson, Ralph Waldo, 96, 98-99; poet, as namer, 82; "Self-Reliance," 11
epic poetry, 17-18
erasure, 43, 120, 131, 145; memory, 5

204 **Index**

Ethics of Memory, The (Margalit), 15
Everybody's Autobiography (Stein), 22, 27, 29, 34, 125, 161n2; "Indianapolis" passage, 113–14

Fagin, Larry, 46, 167n6; *The List Poem*, 168n11
Farmer's Bride, The (Mew), 107–8
fascism, 12–13
Fenollosa, Ernest, 113
figuration, 81
Fitterman, Robert: as "plagiarist extraordinaire," 98
flarf, 122
Flow Chart (Ashbery), 70–71
fluxus, 122
Forché, Carolyn: *Against Forgetting*, 13
forgetful memory, 4, 73, 77, 94; as habitual, 87; as phrase, 171n1; oblivion, 79; sleep, 85
forgetfulness: as ambient effect, 135; *lethargos*, 124; limits of memory, 32
"Forget Not Yet the Tried Intent" (Wyatt), 5
forgettability, 124, 126–28, 134, 140; of absent referent, 139; as aesthetic effect, 125, 130; ambient, 122, 130, 135; as Asian, 123, 135, 142, 144–45; attention, 125; familial love, effect of, 143; feedback loop, 141; as kind of mortality, 130
forgetting, 7, 18, 27, 32–36, 39–40, 45, 64, 69, 76–78, 84, 86, 106, 110, 115, 120, 122, 145, 147–48, 150, 172–73n32; absent-mindedness and forgiveness, kinship with, 5; acceptance, as form of, 55; accumulation of memory, 65, 73, 140–42; as active and positive, 19, 25, 37, 41–43; agency, 3, 66, 80; as aid to composition, 2, 73, 79; ambience, 123; ambient forgettability, 139; ambivalent nature of, 41; amnesia, 10, 79–80, 88, 123; avoidance of pain, 9; as collective 12; comedy, 86, 90, 93–94; comedy, natural expression in, 74; as compositional tool, 24, 26; continuity or interruption, form of, 95; creative

power of, 37; as creative principle, 1; as de-associating, 17; death, as form of, 70; disengagement and respite, 14–15; erasing, 29; etymology of, 4–5; everyday, 10; futurity, 54–56, 58, 68, 71–72; genealogy, 158n17; habituation, 11; as historical neglect, 169–70n28; illusory continuation, mode of, 65; individuality to sociality, 76–77; as individualized notion, 12; knowledge, twopronged approach to, 26; language of, 100–103; material traces, 2–3, 142; memory, 4, 6, 8–9, 11–13, 21, 26, 70, 81–82, 87, 158n15; misrecollection, 4; misremembering, 9; narrativization, 17; national identity, 14; as negative, 12; nomenclature, 111; not forgetting, 60–61; oppositional nature, 4–5; originality, 99, 108; of original meanings, 11; painful fate, as escape and relief from, 68; personal history, 51; presentism, 75; problem of, 100; as process, 3; as relational, 1–2; remembering, 16; remembrance, 51–52, 99; rereading, 150–51; signification, 19–20; social nature of, 92; as sociopolitical, 12; as temporary phase, 6; to-do poems, 52, 54; traumas, 13–14, 137, 146; as unifying structure, 151; utilizing of, 17, 22; violence and denial, as form of, 13; voluntariness and involuntariness, 2, 59, 66; writing as action, 22; writing as knowledge, 22; writing and self-deception, 105
Foucault, Michel, 103, 110, 130
Four Saints in Three Acts (Stein), 161n2
Freeman, Elizabeth, 26
French Symbolists, 24
Freud, Sigmund, 8, 12, 83, 92, 106, 110, 164n51; amnesia, as default state of childhood memory, 10; forgetting, an avoidance of pain, 9; infantile amnesia, 139; *Nachträglichkeit*, 137; narrative faculty, 9; *The Psychopathology of Everyday Life*, 10; "Screen Memories," 10
Frye, Northrop, 173–74n53

Index   205

Futurists, 7–8, 24, 97
futurity, 2–3, 19, 50, 54–55, 68, 168n13; as in-between space, 64

Genette, Gerard, 130
genius, 22, 25, 98, 129, 163n25; originality, 106
genocide, 12–13, 16
Geographical History of America, The (Stein), 24, 161n2
Gettysburg Address, 157n11
G.M.P. (Stein), 36
Goldsmith, John, 40
Goldsmith, Kenneth, 138
Gracq, Julien, 151
Green, J. R., 5
Greenberg, Clement, 180–81n21
Grossman, Allen, 13
Guide to Kulchur (Pound), 7

habituation, 11
Halbwachs, Maurice, 4, 14
Halliday, Mark, 13
Halprin, Lawrence, 44–45
Hamster's Nest, 136
Happily (Hejinian), 77; happiness, 75
Hartley, David, 164n51
Hartog, François, 24, 47
Hass, Robert, 167n80
H.D. Book, The (Duncan), 107
Heap of Language, A (Smithson), 125
Heath Course Pak (Lin), 130–31, 133–35, 138; Heath Ledger, news of, 136–37
Hegel, G. F. W.: theory of art, 180–81n21
Heidegger, Martin, 169n23
Heilman, Robert, 76
Hejinian, Lyn, 2–3, 18–19, 72, 90, 98–99, 111, 171n1, 172n10, 174n77; amnesia, 95; artistic collaboration, 91; *A Border Comedy*, 74, 77, 79–80, 83–84, 88–89, 90–91, 173–74n53; borders, obsession with, 74–75, 173–74n53; *The Cold of Poetry*, 78; comedic world, 77, 93; comedy, and art-making, 75; comic release, 87; forgetful memory, 73–74, 85, 87, 94; forgetting, 73–77, 78, 82, 84, 86, 92, 172–73n32; *Happily*, 77; happiness,

75; humor, 77; *The Language of Inquiry*, 89; laughter, and freedom, 173–74n53; *Leningrad*, 172n17; *Lola*, 174n77; mimetic nature, 83; *My Life in the Nineties*, 73, 75, 82, 172–73n32; negative rupture, 92; "Oblivion," 78–79; "On Laughter" (with Collom), 91–93; with others and to be othered, 76; *Oxota*, 75, 77, 87; poetics of presence, 91; *Positions of the Sun*, 79, 172–73n32; realism, as key to oeuvre, 88, 91; Steinian quality of, 76; *The Unfollowing*, 86; "Who Is Speaking?" 88; *Writing Is an Aid to Memory*, 77
Heller, Agnes, 74
Higgins, Dick, 181n23
Hillringhouse, Mark, 45
historicism, 7, 165n66
"Histrion" (Pound): as poetic incarnation, 106–7
Hollander, John, 97
Hours of the Blessed Virgin, 4
Howard, Richard, 149
Hutchinson, Ben, 65

I Am the Babe of Joseph Stalin's Daughter (Owens), 105
"I Don't Remember" (Bernstein): forgetting, language of, 102; forgetting and remembrance, 99; self-referentiality and paradox, 100–101; unoriginality, tension in, 100, 102
Ihns, Kirsten (Kai), 104, 176n28
"Impossible, The" (Ashbery), 62
"Inaction of Shoes" (Padgett), 57
inattention economy, 130
inauthenticity, 12, 83; and authenticity, 98, 110, 113, 135–36, 139
Infinite Conversation, The (Blanchot), 79
In the Pines (Notley), 169n23
Insomnia and the Aunt (Lin), 140–41, 143–45
"Instant Answer, An; or, A Hundred Prominent Men" (Stein), 29
"Instruction Manual, The" (Ashbery), 61; futurity, to-do and to-feel, 62–64; oblivion, 64; procrastination, 64

206 **Index**

intention, 47–48, 50–51, 58–59, 61, 70–71, 82, 90; intentional and deliberate forgetting, 9, 29, 43; poetics of not-doing, 43; realization, 57
I Remember (Brainard), 59, 105
Ivic, Christopher, 4, 158n15

James, William, 14, 110, 164n51; primary and secondary memory, 11–12
Jameson, Fredric, 184n70
J.Crew, 132, 134–35, 140
"Jinglejangle" (Mullen), 114; forgetting in, 115
Joe 82 Creation Poems, The (Owens), 105
Johnson, Kent, 117
Jonas, Stephen, 149
Judaism, 106

Kafka, Franz, 179n6
Kant, Immanuel, 86, 133
Katz, Bobbi, 168n11
Keats, John, 165n57; long poem, merits of, 150
Keniston, Ann, 65
kenning, 117–18
Kierkegaard, Søren: *Either/Or*, 2
Kim, Irene, 184n74
Kirsch, Sharon, 26, 29
kitsch, 130, 135
knowledge, 7, 33, 56, 150–51, 172n10; action, 24–25, 34–35, 41–42; accumulated, 162n11; as alternative to knowing, 29; based on inference, clarity, observation, and presence, 26, 32; common, 160n53; cultural, 115; direct and indirect, 164n37; forgetfulness, 32; of forgetting, 6, 102; of the future, 64, 66, 70; inert, 7; "knowledge destroyers," 23, 162n11; knowledge-types, 40; memory, kinship with, 24, 26–27, 31, 35; misremembrance, 101; nonhistorical, 165–66n66; objective, 27; as paradigmatic or revolutionary, 27; practical, 42–43; premonitory, 66; propositional, 42; remembering, 26; remembrance, 30; self-knowledge, 110; sociality, 88; virtue, as kind of, 5; writing as, 22, 43

Koch, Kenneth, 104; *Wishes, Lies, and Dreams*, 50
Kondo, Marie, 134
Kotler, Philip, 122
Kripke, Saul, 110–11
Krondorfer, Björn, 17

Langer, Susanne, 81
Language of Inquiry, The (Hejinian), 89
Language poets, 94, 99
Lara, Carlos, 104, 176n28
"Laughter" (Bergson), 83
Lavery, Grace, 90–91
Lazzarato, Maurizio, 129
learning, 25, 116; acquisition of, 26–27; as former knowledge of innate ideas, 5–6; memory, 26
Ledger, Heath, 136–37
Lefebvre, Henri, 162n11
Lehman, David, 45–46
Leningrad (Hejinian et al.), 172n17
Lessing, Gotthold Ephraim, 87
lethe, 5, 108
"Letters I Did or Did Not Get" (Ashbery), 169–70n28
Levertov, Denise: "The Secret," 147–48
Lewis, Erica, 104
LeWitt, Sol, 44–45
"Lifting Belly" (Stein), 80, 161n2
Lin, Maya, 139, 141–42
Lin, Tan, 2–3, 18–19, 98, 126–29, 132, 146, 179–80n13, 183nn56–57, 183n63, 184n68, 184nn73–74; ambient aesthetics, 123; ambient forgettability, 123; ambient work, 121–22; ambient writing, 130; amnesia, 123, 139; attention economy, 123; authenticity and assimilation, as dual notions of two sides of same coin, 135; *Blipsoak01*, 182n37; boredom, 182n37; borrowed memories, 143; Chinese American upbringing, 139–45; collapse of irony, 122; elders, love of, 139; erasure, 131, 145; "experimental" facet of, 128; forgetting, 122, 145–46; *Heath Course Pak*, 130–31, 133–38; indexical poems, 122; *Insomnia and the Aunt*, 140–41, 143–45; lateral shifts in attention, 150; memory,

141–43; "The Patio and the Index, Or 'The Anthropology of Forgetting in Everyday Life,'" 139, 141; planned obsolescence, fascination with, 122; race, as effect of signification, 135; radical disjuncture, 131; surface of things, 139

List Poem, The (Fagin), 168n11

Lola (Hejinian), 174n77

Long Gay Book, A (Stein), 28, 33, 36, 39–40; writing by explanation, 29

Lorange, Astrid, 114

Louis Vuitton (brand), 133–34

Loy, Mina, 117

Lozano, Lee, 44–45

Luhmann, Niklas: theory of medium, 180–81n21

Luria, A. R., 121–23

Making of Americans, The (Stein), 22, 125, 161nn2–3; modernity, giving voice to, 19

Mallarmé, Stéphane, 105, 123–25, 175n7

Manet, Édouard, 123–24

Manovich, Lev, 182n39

"Many Many Women" (Stein), 21, 36

Mao Zedong, 129

Margalit, Avishai: *The Ethics of Memory*, 15

Marinetti, Filippo Tommaso, 7–8, 99

Martin, Ronald, 162n11

Martindale, Colin, 178n62

Marx, Karl: "The Eighteenth Brumaire of Louis Bonaparte," 177n41

Marxism, 19

materiality, 123, 180–81n21

Matisse, Henri, 123–24, 126, 180n19

Matrix, The (Pritchard), 113

Mayer, Bernadette, 18, 59, 61; *Memory*, 59–60; *Studying Hunger*, 60

McCallum, E. L., 42

McGann, Jerome, 180–81n21

Mead, George Herbert, 11

Melgard, Holly: "Retrospective To Do" poems, 171n62

"Memorial Day" (Berrigan and Waldman), 51

memory, 8, 18, 20–21, 28, 32–33, 36, 40, 59, 67, 72, 116, 121, 130, 141–42; accumulation of, 65; aphasia, 111, 114; artificial, 160n53, 163n25; attention, 19, 25, 44, 129; borrowed, 143; categorizing of, 17; collective, 3, 160n53; collectivity, 14; community values, 13; creating of, 59–60; crisis of, 12; dictionary and encyclopedia, dual genres of, 114, 120; discreteness of, 59–60; "duty to remember," 14–16; episodic, 160n53; erasure, 5; ethics of, 15–16; etymology, as form of, 113; eyewitness, 15; folk, 160n53; forgetting, 4, 6, 8–9, 11–13, 21, 26, 65, 70–72, 82, 87, 158n15; gaps in, 12; great evils, 15; grief, 16; history, 165–66n66; humanity, belonging to, 14; institutional, 160n53; intergenerational debt, 15; justice, 14; knowledge, 27, 35; knowledge, kinship with, 24; learning, collaboration of, 26; morality of, 15; nomenclature, relationship to, 110–11; oblivion, 4, 78; perception, 164n37; poetry's recording abilities, 60; popular, as collective, 160n53; procedural, 13, 160n53; propositional, 13, 160n53; prospective, 44, 47–48, 50, 53, 56, 71, 169–70n28; prosthetic, 160n53; pure, 160n53; recollection, 29; recollective, 13; remembrance, 26, 158n15; retroactive, 44; rote, 163n25; semantic, 160n53; as social glue, 14; solidarity and survival, 14; spontaneous, 16; tape recorders, and bad memory, 127–28; television, 184n70; time and desire, contaminated by, 10; witnessing, 13

Memory (Mayer): memory, creating of, 59–60

Menand, Louis, 11

Meno (Plato), 5; Meno's paradox, 100

Metamorphosis (Ovid), 171n1

metaphor, 17, 33, 79, 86, 89, 165n57

Mew, Charlotte: *The Farmer's Bride*, 107–8

Miller, Richard, 13

Mills, Charles, 15

misreading, 10, 81, 106

misremembrance, 13, 17–18; as form of deconstructive play, 12; misrecollection, 10; misremembering, 106, 110,

208 Index

misremembrance (*continued*)
139, 175n7; poetic language, generating of, 20
Moby-Dick (Melville), 172–73n32
modernism, 8, 19, 21, 27, 42, 96, 105, 124, 126, 162n11, 165n66, 175n7, 180n21; paradox of, 98; writing as knowledge and action, 22–24
modernity, 19, 35; youthfulness of, 162n11
Montaigne, 93
"Morning of the Poem, The" (Schuyler): forgetting, 55; prospective memory, 56
Morris, William, 180–81n21
Morton, Timothy, 122, 179–80n13
Moses, Omri, 25–26
"Mouths and Wood" (Stein), 30
Moy, Afong, 142
Mullen, Harryette, 18–19, 98–99, 116–17; "All She Wrote," 111–12; *Everybody's Autobiography* (Stein), influence on, 113–14; forgetting and nomenclature, 111; "Jinglejangle," 114–15; reworking language, 113; "Zen Acorn," 112
Muther, W. S., 44
"Muy Bien" (O'Hara), 47
Muzak: "architecture music," 124
Myers, Rollo, 180n19
My Life (Hejinian), 73, 75, 82, 172–73n32

narrativization, 2, 17; denarrativization, 84–85; Stein and narrative, 25, 34–39, 62
New American poetry, 19, 98, 176n14
New York School, 2–3, 19, 44, 60, 104; prospective memory, 44; sociality of, 72; Stein's influence on, 59; to-do list poetry, 45, 47, 51, 56–57
Ngai, Sianne, 74, 125–26
Nicholls, Peter, 89–90
Nietzsche, Friedrich, 2, 6–7, 23, 48, 103, 158n17
No Material (Raal), 176n28
Nora, Pierre, 4, 16
nostalgia, 3, 63, 67
"Notes of a Painter" (Matisse), 124
Notley, Alice, 19, 105, 109, 169n21;

Coming After, 107; "Doctor Williams' Heiress," 104; *In the Pines*, 169n23
noulipian Analects, The (Viegener and Wertheim), 179–80n13

oblivion, 2, 5, 14, 61, 64–66, 68, 158n17, 175n7; absence of human presence, 3; comedy, 74; durée, 8; forgetful memory, 79; as kind of place, 3; memories, 4, 78; sleep, 85; time passing, 77; to-do list poems, 50; as willful and creative art, 6
Oblivion (Augé), 4
"Oblivion" (Hejinian), 78–79
Ogden, Thomas, 9
O'Hara, Frank, 47, 104, 107, 109, 168n13, 169–70n28; "I do this I do that" poems, 45
Olson, Charles, 113, 162n8
Olson, Liesl, 25–26
On the Advantage and Disadvantage of History for Life (Nietzsche), 6
"On Laughter" (Hejinian and Collom), 91–93; forgetting, 92
origin, 101, 103–4; etymological origin, 113–14, 117; and heritage, 105–7, 110–11, 139; human origin, 118; of memory, 4; original text and source material, 126, 130, 138; travel and return, 63
originality, 94, 96–98, 105, 107, 116; forgetting, 99, 108; as form of genealogy, 103–4; genius, synonymous with, 106
Ovid, *Metamorphosis*, 171n1
Owens, Rochelle: "Bernard Fruchtman in Town & Country," 106; *I Am the Babe of Joseph Stalin's Daughter*, 105; *The Joe 82 Creation Poems*, 105
Oxota (Hejinian), 75, 77, 87

Padgett, Ron, 59, 105; "Inaction of Shoes," 57
Paik, Nam June, 44–45
Paterson (Williams), 167n8
"Patio and the Index, The, Or 'The Anthropology of Forgetting in Everyday Life,'" (Lin), 139, 141
Peale, Norman Vincent, 47

Peirce, Charles Sanders: distinction, notion of, 28; habits, 160n40
Pen Chants (Wolsak), 117–18
Pepys, Samuel: *The Diary of Samuel Pepys*, 130, 138
Perec, Georges, 59
Perloff, Marjorie, 75
Pessoa, Fernando: *The Book of Disquiet*, 2
Phaedo (Plato), 5
Phillips, Adam, 50
Philosophical Investigations (Wittgenstein), 102
Philosophy of Andy Warhol, The (Warhol), 127
Picaba, Francis, 7
Picasso, Pablo, 34, 98; *Bull's Head*, 184n68
"Picnic Cantata, A" (Schuyler), 54–55
Pillow Book, The (Shonagon), 168n11
Plato: anamnesis, theory of, 5–6; *Meno*, 5, 100; *Phaedo*, 5; *The Republic*, 108
Poe, Edgar Allan, 109, 124–25
Poema Morale, 5
poetic forgetting, 1–2, 6, 17–19, 104
poetic incarnation, 106–7
"Poetry and Grammar" (Stein), 29, 41
Poetry Project, 169n22
Porter, Fairfield, 56
portraiture, 37, 161n2, 166n68; agency, 36
Positions of the Sun (Hejinian), 79, 172–73n32
Poulet, Georges, 109
Pound, Ezra, 8, 12–13, 23–24, 104, 113, 118, 126, 162n8; *Guide to Kulchur*, 7; "Histrion," 106–7
presence, 26, 119, 136, 162n11, 175n7; absence of, 3; affective, 33; aural, 28; happiness, link with, 75; newspapers, and false sense of, 35; of past, 28, 108; poetics of, 91; of present, 25, 28, 32–33; as term, 24; of thinking, 11
Pritchard, N. H.: *The Matrix*, 113
Project Gutenberg, 130–32
prosopopoeia, 81
Proust, Marcel, 123
Psychopathology of Everyday Life, The (Freud): misrecollection, 10

Raal, Losarc. *See* Lara, Carlos
Rauschenberg, Robert, 179–80n13
realism, 77, 88; comedy, link between, 89–91
recollection, 26, 34, 67; as kinetic reasoning, 6; strong justice, 15
Redford, Robert, 144–45
regressive forgetting, 116
remembering, 6, 28, 44; "duty to remember," 14–16; forgetting, 16; "good," 16; knowledge, 26; overdetermination, 164n44
remembrance, 4, 17, 35, 60, 140; false, 26; forgetting, 51–52, 99; knowing, 32–33; knowledge, 30; memory, 26, 158n15
Renan, Ernest, 14
repetition, 9, 20–22, 24–25, 39, 65, 87, 109, 128, 162n6, 165–66n66, 182n37; anxiety of, 105; comedy, 84; imitation, 83; monotony, 125; poetic forgetting, 2; subjecthood, 129
Republic, The (Plato), 108
Rhetorica ad Herennium, 179n2
Ribot, Théodule, 12
Richter, Jean Paul, 173–74n53
Ricoeur, Paul, 13, 15; memory, notion of, 70, 163n25
Riding, Laura, 96–97, 175n5
Rieff, David, 14, 16
Rifkin, Libbie, 47
Rimbaud, Arthur, 104–5
Robertson, Lisa, 109–10, 177n45; *The Baudelaire Fractal*, 108; *Cinema of the Present*, 177n44
Romanticism, 163n25, 181n23
Romantic Origins (Brisman), 105
Romeo and Juliet (Shakespeare), 5
Rosenberg, Harold, 162n8
Rothenberg, Jerome, 105
Rousseau, Jean-Jacques, 98
Ruskin, John, 165n57
Russell, Nicolas, 14
Russian formalism, 19

Said, Edward: late style, theory of, 65
Sargent, Porter, 127, 182n43

210 Index

Sartre, Jean-Paul, 109
Satie, Erik: "furniture music," 124, 180n19
Scappettone, Jennifer, 122
Scarry, Elaine, 123
Schmidt, Christopher, 168n13
Schuyler, James, 45, 71; "December," 55; "The Morning of the Poem," 55; "A Picnic Cantata," 54–55; prospective memory, 56; "Things to Do," 48–50; "Things to Do When You Get a Bad Review," 52, 168n20; to-do lists, 50; to-do poems, 167n6
"Screen Memories" (Freud), 10
Searle, John, 48, 81
"Secret, The" (Levertov), 147–48
self-help culture, 45, 47
"Self-Reliance" (Emerson), 11
Severini, Gino, 7
Shadows (Warhol), 128
Sidney, Sir Philip, 104, 115, 176n28
signification, 19–20; difference and similarity, 31; race, 135
Silliman, Ron, 19
sincerity, 48, 54, 56, 89–90
"Sincerity and Objectivism" (Zukofsky), 89
Situations, Sings (Hejinian and Collom), 91
Skinner, B. F., 161n2, 167n80
Smithson, Robert: *A Heap of Language*, 125
Snyder, Gary: "Things to Do" poems, 45, 167n6
sociality, 72, 76–77, 148
"Song of the Windshield Wipers" (Ashbery), 169–70n28
Spenser, Edmund, 107
Spitzer, Leo, 122
"Squares and Oblongs" (Auden), 101
Stadler, Gustavus, 127
Stanzas in Meditation (Stein), 27, 29–30, 34, 62; Stanza VI, 38
Stefans, Brian Kim, 179–80n13
Stein, Gertrude, 2–3, 11, 18–19, 44, 59, 62, 64, 98, 104, 113–14, 126–28, 175n5; "An Acquaintance with Description,"

30; activities and states, as kind of forgetting, 36–37; as ambient music's matriarch, 124–25; art of forgetting, as rooted in difference and distinction, 30–31; atelic actions, 25, 36, 62; *The Autobiography of Alice B. Toklas*, 161n2; automatic writing, denouncing of, 167n80; *Cezanne*, 161n2; as "comic writer," 75–76; continuous present, 37, 42–43; counting, method of, 29–30; deliberate forgetting, 29–30; direct observation, 164n37; erasure, use of, 43; *Everybody's Autobiography*, 22, 27, 29, 34, 113–14, 125, 161n2; everyday life, as activity, 35; everyday vocabulary of, 31; "false time," 35; forgetting, 24–25, 27, 33, 37, 39–40, 42–43; forgetting, and how to know, 34; forgetting, as ontological and epistemological issue, 24; forgetting, as topic and tool, 29; *Four Saints in Three Acts*, 161n2; generic pronouns, playing with, 29; genius, theory of, 22, 25; *The Geographical History of America*, 24, 161n2; "gist," 37, 150; *G.M.P.*, 36; immediacy, turn toward, 34; individual history, turn toward, 22; "An Instant Answer; or, A Hundred Prominent Men," 29; as international celebrity, 161n2; knowledge, 24–25, 29, 32–35, 41–43; knowledge, and memory, 27; knowledge, and remembering, 26; "Lifting Belly," 80, 161n2; *A Long Gay Book*, 28, 29, 33, 36, 39–40; *The Making of Americans*, 19, 22, 125, 161n2, 161–62n3; memory, 28, 32; memory, as alternative mode of knowing, 24; memory, belief in, 22; memory to attention, shift to, 25; memory and history, 165–66n66; metaphor, pivoting away from, 33; modernity, definition of, 35; modernity, giving voice to, 19; "Mouths and Wood," 30; newspaper writing, attack on, 35; New York School, influence on, 59; originality, redefining of, 96–97; poetics of action, as compatible with knowledge, 34; "Poetry and Grammar," 29, 41; presence of present, 25, 28, 32–33; remembering, 28, 31; remembrance, with observation of own thoughts, 41; repetition, use of, 21–22, 39, 125, 162n6, 165–66n66; sentences, as active process, 37–38; sentences, as adjustments of expected meaning, 32; sentences of, 40; *Stanzas in Meditation*, 27, 29–30, 34, 38, 62; subjective experience and objective experience, differentiation between, 27; temporal poetics, 25–26; *Tender Buttons*, 97, 161n2; *Three Lives*, 161n2; "two Steins," 161n2; on visual artists, 162n7; wars, as irrelevant, 34–35; *Wars I Have Seen*, 26, 161n2, 166–67n75; writing as action, 34, 39–43

Stephens, Paul, 122

Studying Hunger (Mayer), 60

subjecthood, 129

Surrealism: exquisite corpse, 73

Svendsen, Lars, 181n23

Sverjensky, Tatiana, 168n13

"Tambourine Life" (Berrigan), 167–68n9

Tender Buttons (Stein), 161n2

Tennyson, Alfred Lord, 165n57

"10 Things I Do Everyday" (Berrigan), 51, 169n21

Terranova, Tiziana, 183n55

"Thief in Poetry, The" (Ashbery), 70

"Things to Do" (Schuyler), 48–50

"Things to Do in Anne's Room" (Berrigan), 51, 57–58

"Things to Do Before I Move" (Brainard), 45

"Things to Do in New York" (Berrigan), 45, 51

"Things to Do in Providence" (Berrigan), 45, 50; forgetting and futurity, 54; forgetting and remembrance, 51–52; intentions, 51; prospective memory, 53

"Things to Do on Speed" (Berrigan), 51

"Things to Do When You Get a Bad Review" (Schuyler), 52, 168n20

Thoreau, Henry David, 11, 45

Three Lives (Stein), 161n2

to-do list poems, 45–49, 51, 53, 61–63, 68,

167n6; forgetting, 52, 54, 56–58; futurity, 54, 58; intentionality, 168n15; intentionality and realization, 57; oblivion, 50

Todorov, Tzvetan, 16, 160n52

to-feel poems, 47

Toop, David, 124

totalitarianism, 12–13

"Tradition and the Individual Talent" (T. S. Eliot), 97

Unfollowing, The (Hejinian), 86

Uniqlo, 134–35

United States, 96, 136, 142; American individualism, 134–35; "Ford America," of assembly-line production, 19; melting pot, myth of, 106; race problem, 16; turning away from one's past, 19

Valentino, 133

Valéry, Paul, 105, 162n8, 175n7

ventriloquism, 81, 83; laughter, 80

Vietnam War, 19, 136

virtue, 15; "doing good" on promises, 47–48, 54; epistemic, 25, 28; as kind of knowledge, 5

vita activa, 23

vita contemplativa, 23

Voris, Linda, 25

Vuong, Ocean, 133

Walden (Thoreau), 45

Waldman, Anne, 59, 169n22; "Memorial Day" (with Berrigan), 51

Warhol, Andy, 129, 135, 142–43, 182n50; ambience of, 128; *The Philosophy of Andy Warhol*, 127; *Shadows*, 128

Wars I Have Seen (Stein), 26, 161n2, 166–67n75

Waste Land, The (Eliot): as ambient poem, 126

Weatherly, Tom, 104

Wegner, Daniel: "white bear" cases, 10

Weiner, Bernard, 44

Weinrich, Harald, 10

Wesley, John, 5

"What Is the Word" (Beckett), 177n49

Index

Whitehead, Alfred North, 8
"Who Is Speaking?" (Hejinian), 88
Wilder, Thornton, 31
Williams, Grant, 4, 158n15
Williams, Tyrone, 104, 176n27
Williams, William Carlos, 23, 104, 162n8, 167n8
Winant, Johanna, 25, 27
"Wishes" (Berrigan), 54
Wishes, Lies, and Dreams (Koch), 50
Wittgenstein, Ludwig, 103, 111–12; *Philosophical Investigations*, 102
Woisetschlaeger, Erich, 40
Wolsak, Lissa, 19, 98–99; erasure poem, approximation of, 120; negative space, use of, 120; originality of, as model of regression, 116, 118–19; *Pen Chants*, 117–18

Wordsworth, William, 165n57
world-making, 129
World War I, 12
World War II, 12, 26
Writing Is an Aid to Memory (Hejinian), 77
Wyatt, Thomas: "Forget Not Yet the Tried Intent," 5

Yates, Francis, 4
Young, Edward, 181n22
Yuen Ren Chao, 142–43
Yugen (magazine), 105

"Zen Acorn" (Mullen), 112; *Everybody's Autobiography* (Stein), 113–14
Zukofsky, Louis, 89